SYLVIA CLAYTON

Edward

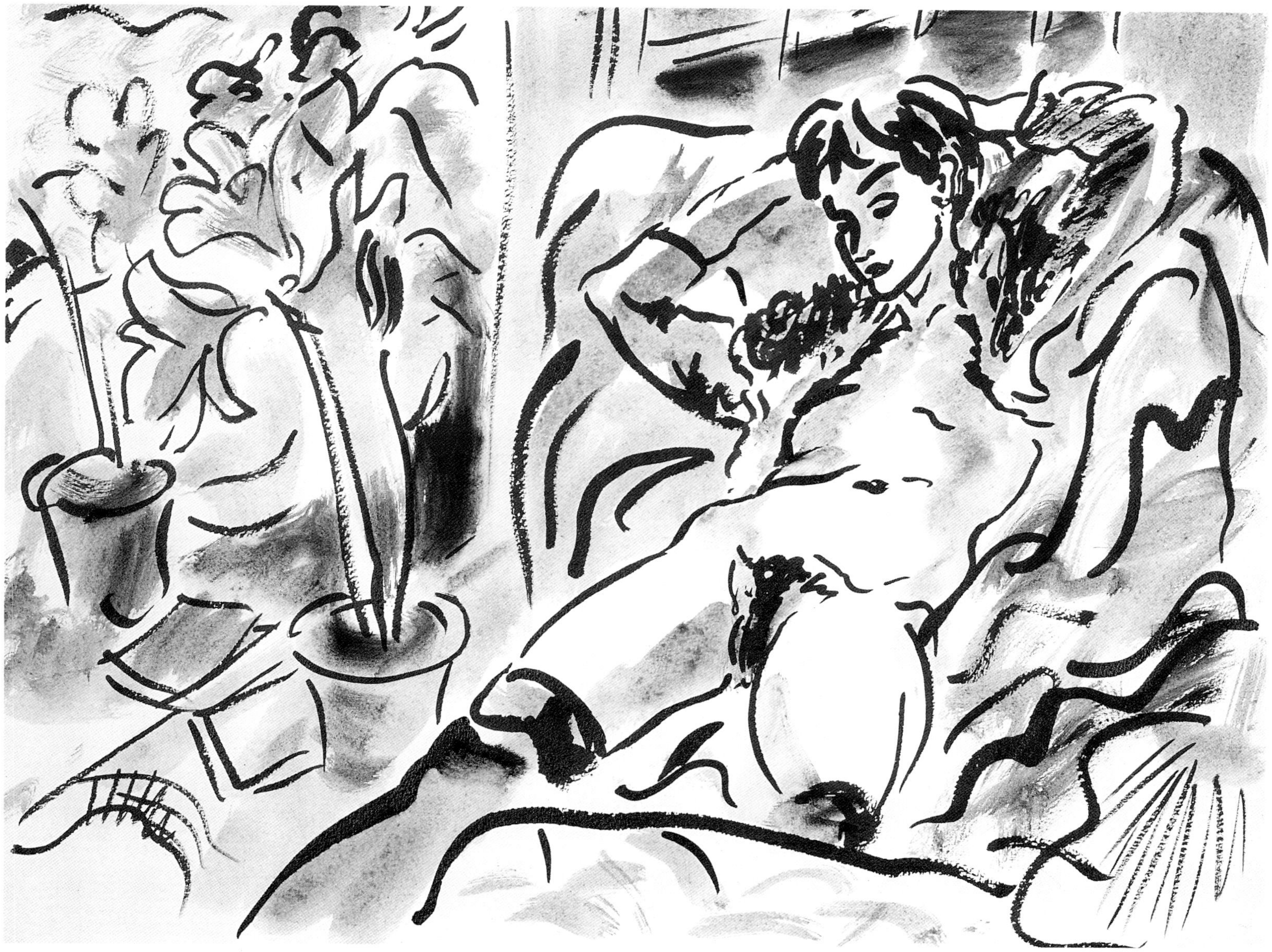

DAVID & CHARLES
Newton Abbot · London
in association with
THE CATTO GALLERY
London

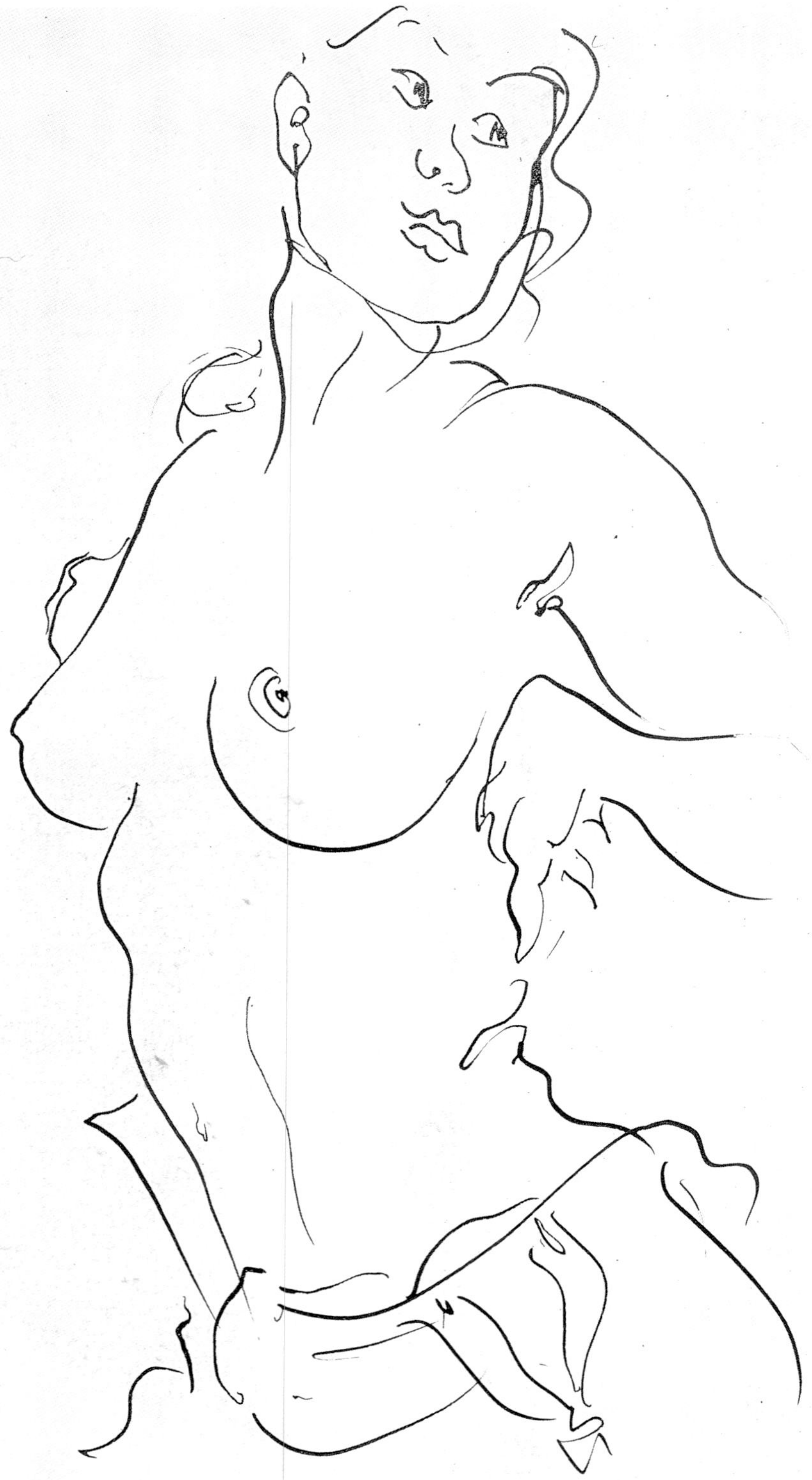

Above
Girl Standing (Head and Torso)
Pen and ink, 15½ × 12½ins, 1987

Previous page
Reclining Girl with Amaryllis
Ink and wash, 15 × 20 ins, 1988

What gives a work of art enduring value concerns the nature of its relationship to elements of experience which do not change, or rather which change at a very slow rate and may effectively be regarded as constants.
Peter Fuller, *Arts and Psychoanalysis*

It is the joy of life, cadenced and moderated by reason. The artist in those days had eyes to see, while those of today are blind; this is all the difference. The Greek women were beautiful, but their beauty lived above all in the minds of the sculptors who carved them.
Auguste Rodin on *Venus de Milo*

That fleeting instant so brief as to be almost timeless, when the spectator is at one with the work of art. He ceases to be his ordinary self, and the picture or building, or statue, or landscape or aesthetic actuality is no longer outside himself. The two become one entity.
Bernard Berenson, *Sketch for a Self-Portrait, 1949*

For Barbara and Nancy

Acknowledgements
Thanks go to Michael Gray for his help in photographing the paintings.

British Library Cataloguing in Publication Data
Clayton, Sylvia
Edward Piper.
I. Title
759.2

ISBN 0-7153-9913-6

Book designed by Michael Head
Typeset by Ace Filmsetting Ltd, Frome, Somerset
and printed in Singapore by CS Graphics Pte Ltd
for David & Charles plc
Brunel House Newton Abbot Devon

Contents

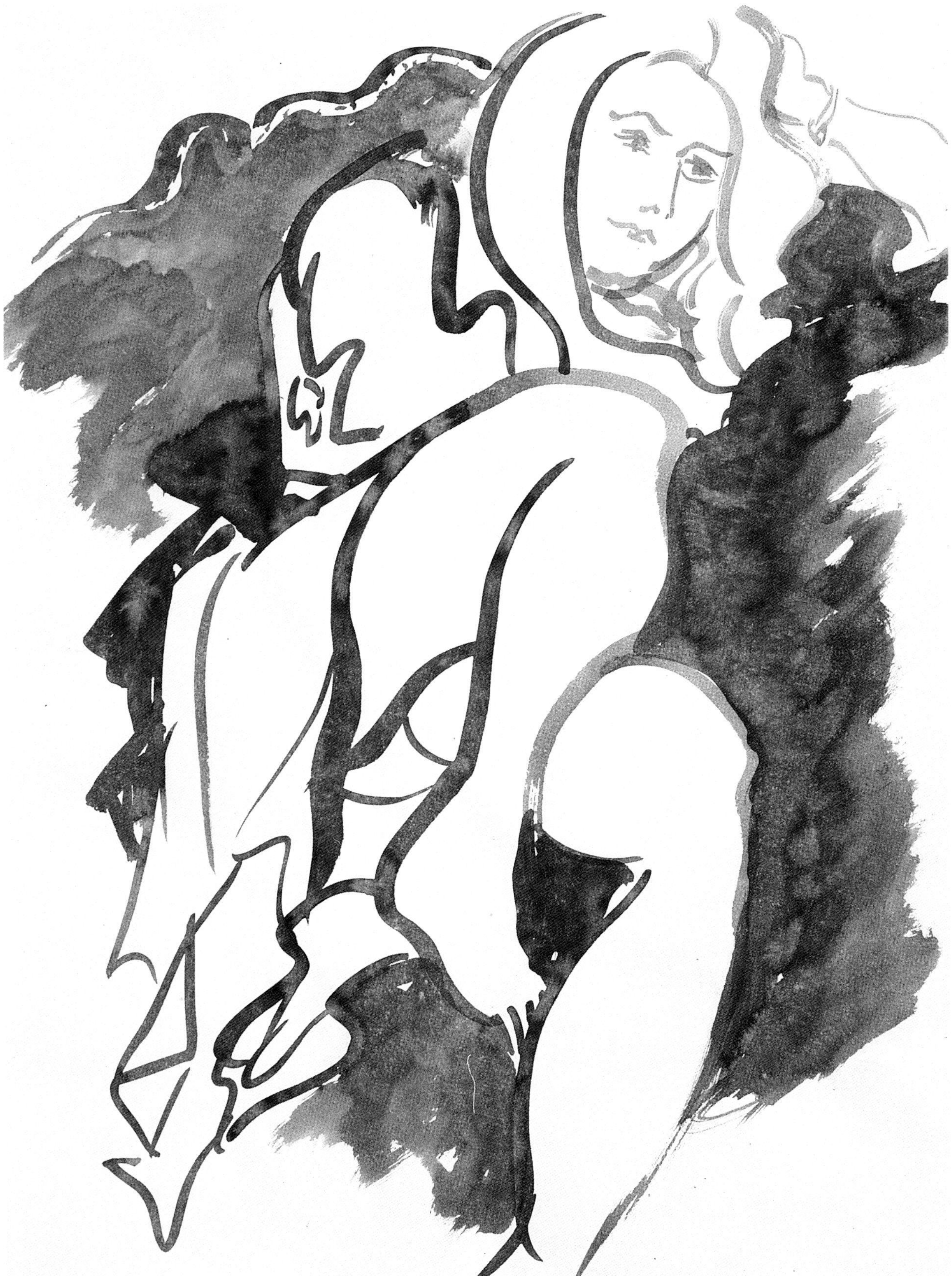

Seated Girl
Brush and ink, 23 × 16ins, 1975

Foreword

I first met Edward Piper on a warm sunny day at his home, a converted laundry of a large house in Somerset. Edward had invited me there to view his work for an exhibition I was due to hold at my gallery.

I was greeted first by his wife Prue, a highly intelligent and gentle lady who had helped to create what I could see immediately was a tightly knit family unit. She is also perhaps the greatest cook I have ever met. Being a scientist she understands exactly what happens when ingredients are put together and their effects on each other and on your palate.

Edward came rushing up to welcome me and I was completely captured by his warmth, excitement about life and overwhelming optimism. This last quality helped him, and certainly his friends, to come to terms more easily with his illness in the last few months before his death.

There is no doubt that Edward has achieved some measure of immortality with his paintings. The last six years have shown us a man who grew in confidence to produce wonderful relaxed nudes happily surrounded by large bunches of flowers, or intriguingly displayed in front of a mirror. His use of light and a stunning Mediterranean palette enhance the subject. Edward's landscapes are a joy of panoramic views taken from awe-inspiring positions. His use of lyrical brush strokes capture colour and light with such seeming ease.

Edward was working on this book when he died. I feel sure that he would have been so proud and happy with the result. It has been one of my greatest joys knowing Edward. I shall miss him.

GILLIAN CATTO

List of Colour Plates

Unique Signboard of an Artist

The wall of the gallery leading to the smaller of Edward Piper's two studios at Marston Bigot in rural Somerset, south-west England, displays a giant 12ft-wide screen with a frieze of a nude in twenty-nine marvellously differing poses. It is the unique signboard of an artist who was one of the finest contemporary painters of the nude.

Edward painted the kinetic frieze in one day in November 1981, observing the model while she sat, reclined, lounged, tried on a bangle, put up her hair, let it hang loose, and bent over athletically to peer through her legs in what so easily could have become an angular and ugly pose, but is actually full of grace. Her curves are emphasised by touches of pink wash.

Since Edward was drawing in Indian ink on a scroll of Japanese paper, thick-ribbed, pure white, he had no margin for error, and made none. The nudes of his last years, painted with a swift attack, sure economy of line and brilliant colour palette, have given us the *Edward Piper nude* with her intimations of Matisse, Derain, and Dufy, but still possessing her own entirely delightful and distinctive identity.

The nude has always been classically a subject for painters, but few can have responded with Edward Piper's passionate and obsessive love for the female figure. This obsession was literally lifelong, going back to his days at a correct English public school where he decorated his locker with collages of cheap and raunchy pin-ups cut from *Photoplay*, to his mature years as an artist when he was painting the nude with a sinewy economy of line and frank sensuality.

He gained confidence in his later years in his ability to place his nudes in provocative poses on the frontier between art and pornography, setting large exploding flowers in bold counterpoise to female genitalia. I was, of course, aware of Edward's ambition to communicate what he called his 'deep, inexplicable and fanatically obsessed feelings' about the female figure through his nude studies long before I agreed to collaborate with him in writing the text for an art book to accompany a major one-man show of his work at the Catto Gallery in Hampstead, London, in September 1991. But it was only when I came to the style and content of the art book he envisaged that I began to appreciate fully the intensity of his preoccupation with the female figure. When he asked me to work with him I told him that, although I had always loved paintings and made straight for the art galleries whenever I found myself in a new city, I was not an art historian. Edward replied that he was looking for a writer with a clear style and an intelligent understanding of art in a general way to help him achieve a text, which would, in effect, be a *validation* of his work as an artist and photographer expressed through his own words and concepts. His idea was for a voice-over to accompany a selection of his nudes, landscapes and photographic nudes in the landscape.

All his work provides ample evidence that he had emerged from the formidable shadow of his eminent father, John Piper (who was honoured by the Tate Gallery with a major retrospective in 1983). His mother, Myfanwy Piper, wrote libretti for three of Benjamin Britten's operas, and as founder and editor of an art review *Axis* dealing with abstract painting and sculpture, was at the centre of artistic controversy for years. His relationship with his brilliant parents, particularly his father, was complex, but soundly based on a mutual respect in a very English way.

I share the confidence Edward had, that his one-man show at the Catto Gallery in 1991 would show clearly that his work had developed with distinction and individuality. Edward's nudes, and his landscapes of English scenes such as the Dorset coast, the southern Mediterranean, and the country in which he was spiritually and artistically at home, France, are painted with freedom, exuberance and general *joie de vivre*, proclaiming triumphantly his essential belief that an artist concerned with what is joyous and beautiful and decorative is nonetheless serious.

While the nude retained his deepest and most constant affections, his sunlit *mouvementé* landscapes were painted with a growing authority and were increasingly recognised by the art public as carrying his individual signature. The breakthrough in landscape painting came in the early 1980s, relatively late in his career as a painter, through what can only be described as a most improbable subject – the combine harvester, 'those bloody great monsters' as he described them, attacking the harvest in Somerset fields in shimmering duststorms on high summer days.

He always regarded himself primarily as a painter, but, for all his modesty about his talents, he was far too good a photographer not to admit that he had had to resist a definite temptation, particularly in the years before his paintings became collectable, to concentrate on making a living from his superb studies of the nude; as it was, he had a marked influence on the artistic development of the nude in photography. Bob Lassam, until recently director of the Fox Talbot Museum at Lacock Abbey, near Chippenham in Wiltshire, is in no doubt that had Edward devoted himself to photography he would have made himself a name to stand alongside Cartier-Bresson, Fay Godwin and Bill Brandt. This judgment is underlined by the fact that when Edward Piper vintage prints go through the London art salerooms, they are fetching increasing prices from collectors.

When we began our collaboration, Edward justifiably considered himself a most fortunate man, contented in his family life and environment and happy in his chosen career. Over the previous six or seven years his paintings had begun to touch a responsive nerve not only with the British art public, but in Europe and America and more recently in Japan. He was enjoying the financial security this brought his family – his wife Prue and their sons Luke and Henry – and he celebrated his good fortune in a way which expressed eloquently, without words, his attitude to the consumer society: he bought the field at the bottom of their garden at Marston Bigot.

He and Prue had long wanted to buy this field and manage it as it had been managed in times past. Once bought, he then without delay, designed and supervised the building of a handsome, curvy one-acre lake, placed

Portrait of Reclining Girl. Brush and ink, 18 × 12½ins, 1979

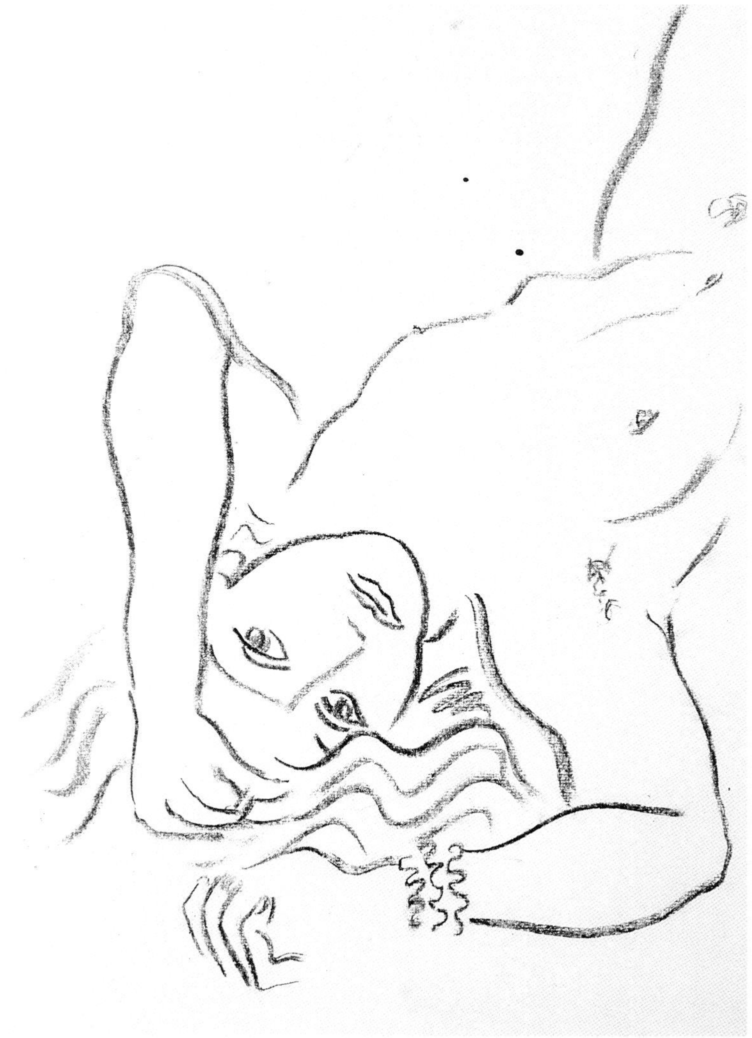

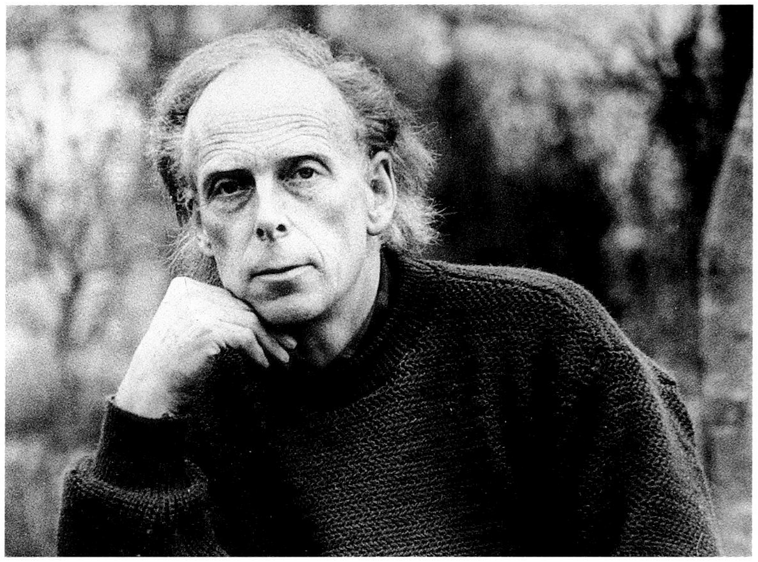

Edward Piper
(Copyright Valerie Cooper), 1988

with a painter's eye in perfect relationship to a Piperish parish church in the middle distance and leading the eye to the lovely sweep of the Wiltshire escarpment. He was not just painting landscapes, he was actually creating his own landscape to paint, he said, when he could no longer go charging up mountain roads in search of subjects. 'The lake is to be my modest version of Monet's gardens at Giverny for *my* water-lilies period', he said in mock serious comment – and one which was to assume such a tragic accent in so short a time in the future. I think it is fair to say that when he created his lake, Edward Piper had reached the point he must have dreamed of reaching when, in a boyish way, he announced at about the age of eight that he wanted to be a painter like his father.

We had decided that Edward's voice-over commentary would be assembled from a series of structured interviews, and had made an experimental tape recording. But his happiness was all too vulnerable. Edward phoned me at my home in a neighbouring Somerset village in January 1990, to tell me calmly and directly what his doctor had told him – that laboratory tests had confirmed he had cancer of the *bronchi*: 'It's a bloody nuisance, but they say the odds are rather in my favour, and that I can go ahead planning my one-man show – and may well be able to attend the private view myself,' he said.

He asked me to continue working with him on the text. Edward and Prue had already made their decision to continue to live as normally as possible in the circumstances, which they did with a courage that helped to make the tragedy bearable to Edward's family and friends over the remaining months of his life. For Edward, living a normal life could only mean continuing to paint so long as he had the strength to hold a brush. In March he told me he was going on a 'painting swing' through the mountainous interior of Andalucia to paint some Spanish hill villages he had seen on an earlier visit. His imagination had been caught by the way the simple Spanish houses of the farm workers and shepherds swarmed like bees ready to take flight.

'I think my one-man show at the Catto Gallery might benefit from a few recent landscapes,' he had said. I realise, looking back, that the passion with which he planned his trip was shadowed by a premonition of death. He was to spend a couple of days in Malaga, birthplace of Picasso, to paint one or two subjects he had marked down on earlier visits to the seaport. One such subject was an Edwardian fountain marooned on a traffic island off the Malagueno in a surround of palm trees, white finca and ochre-walled houses. From the moment he had seen the fountain two years earlier he had known that he would return one day to paint it, trying to catch on canvas the precise second the water bounced in the fountain's ornate basin.

He always liked to have a companion with him on his 'painting swings', in Scotland, Ireland, or Mediterranean islands such as Corsica, usually someone who was a Sunday painter so that in coaching them in their painting he could also clarify his own thoughts on the subject. His companion on the Malaga trip was Brian Thomas; 6ft 4in tall and with a heavyweight boxer's build, Brian must have made an impressive Commendatore in *Don Giovanni* when he was a principal bass singer at Glyndebourne. He is now managing director of a high quality printing firm in the homely, pleasant market town of Frome near Edward's studio in Marston Bigot; he had become first a patron, then the printer of Edward's work. Eventually he was a friend of Edward and his family, and it was Brian who had arranged for Edward to stay at the Thomas's holiday home in Mijas, near Malaga for the trip. Later, in describing the trip to me after Edward's death, Brian Thomas said:

> We drove down a road in a remote mountain area to look at a bridge with little carved parapets which Edward thought helped to bind the landscape into a unity. He was wearing black trousers, black plastic mac and a floppy black trilby, like Yehudi Menuhin used to favour; in Edward's case he wore it to hide the baldness resulting from his medical treatment.
>
> His face was terribly white, the landscape was white, the clay of the dried-up river bed was white, too, and suddenly you had Edward's tall, lean figure striding along the river bed looking like a figure in space.
>
> His treatment was sapping his strength and he fell over. I couldn't help recalling that he looked like the figure of Death from Bergman's *The Seventh Seal*, and then that image was swept away in Edward's gale of laughter at his fall.

Edward as usual drove fast and intrepidly round Malaga, Brian Thomas said, astonishing him once again with how easily his visual memory could absorb accurately such a remarkable amount of detail of street scenes while driving at speed. In one of the remoter rocky areas of Granada Edward drove so recklessly up tracks meant only for mountain goats to prospect a scene he fancied as a landscape subject that Brian felt he had to point out that *he* wanted to be able to sit down to a bottle of Spanish red wine and dinner later, whatever Edward's ambition. 'And all the time Edward painted like a man possessed,' he said, 'three or four landscapes in a day to take back to the villa for retouching.'

All this reminded me of Edward's childhood memories of sitting with his sister, Clarissa, in the back of John Piper's bull-nosed Morris when he drove up narrow Welsh roads to paint the slate quarries, for John Piper would also drive his car where most people would not have ventured to take a vehicle in search of angles from which to paint his landscapes.

I took a brief holiday myself in Granada, which partly overlapped Edward's painting trip. He had told me that the best place from which to view his fountain in Malaga was from below the walls of a Moorish castle high on a cliff overlooking the port. He had driven his car like a chariot up to the walls; I clambered up on foot, and found that Edward's description of the landscape was so vivid and accurate in detail that I could identify its vistas, the park lake below with its black swans, the crumbling walls of a villa clothed in purple bougainvillea, and the curve of the city's bullring in the distance with the gleam of the fountain's cascade of water through the palm trees.

I flew back to Somerset on the morning of Friday 11 May, and phoned Edward at his studio home – once the Victorian laundry which washed the Irish linen sheets from the country seat of the Earls of Cork and Orrery – half-a-mile away over the brow of Cheese Hill in the parish of Marston Bigot. Prue Piper answered the phone and said in her quiet voice, 'Edward died an hour ago.'

The image of *The Seventh Seal* presented by Edward in Granada had been prophetic. I remembered the winter evenings when, before the advent of TV video libraries, Edward had shown hired 16mm films to friends in the big studio at his home, Bunuel's *Viridiana*, and Cocteau's *Orphée* and *Beauty and the Beast*.

Edward Piper was 51, at the height of his creative life with a world of development before him when he died.

Characteristically on the morning of his death he had been talking of painting from a wheel chair, like Dufy and Renoir in their old age.

On a high desk in the big studio, where Victorian housemaids had once hung washing to dry, lay some of the paintings Edward had recently made of Venice. He had, while showing me his Venice paintings, recalled with warm affection a family trip to Venice in 1954 for the première of Benjamin Britten's opera, *The Turn of the Screw*, based on Henry James' book. His mother, Myfanwy, had written the libretto and John Piper had designed the stage sets.

Some nine months before he learned of his mortal illness, Edward had been given a commission by the Folio Society to prepare illustrations for a forthcoming edition of *The Aspern Papers* by Henry James. Joe Whitlock Blundell, of the Folio Society, who had briefed Edward on the commission, wrote in the autumn 1990 issue of the society's quarterly magazine for subscribers that Edward had 'leapt at the idea' of illustrating *The Aspern Papers*, for 'rather special reasons'. Joe Whitlock Blundell cited Edward's own account of these reasons in his appreciation of Edward in the quarterly magazine. Edward wrote:

> It has taken me a long time to realise myself as an artist, having lived somewhat in the shadow of my father. Since he has painted Venice so often I have felt shy of putting my own work up in comparison with his – now the time has come to lay the ghost.
>
> I haven't been to Venice myself since I was fourteen, when they were rehearsing *The Turn of the Screw* and my sister Clarissa and I made picnics for Ben Britten and Peter Pears and my parents which we ate in the courtyard at the back of the Fenice theatre.

Edward made a trip to Venice between bouts of chemotherapy for his illness, carefully following up the clues in Henry James' novel for the site of the mysterious palazzo featured in it. Joe Whitlock Blundell wrote in the quarterly magazine:

> By the time we came to print his lithographs for the book at the end of April 1990, the disease had taken its toll, and it was an act of real bravery for him to come to the printer and work on the plates. Even then he was not satisfied, and insisted on drawing additional plates for an extra printing.
>
> These transformed the illustrations, which were already hauntingly atmospheric, by giving them added strength and vigour. Sadly, he never saw the final results, dying on the very day they were being printed.
>
> I feel sure he knew by then they were very good indeed.

For Edward, the 'laying of the ghost' of his father's memorable and monumental paintings in Venice was an understatement of the drama inherent in his courageous effort, psychological and physical, to paint *his* Venice, in the light of the ravages of his illness.

On Edward's visit with his parents when he was fourteen, he and Clarissa had explored Venice and its neighbouring cities while John and Myfanwy were busy in the Fenice theatre. They went to Vicenza, where Edward was much intrigued by Palladio's three-dimensional scenery in the theatre; but most of all Edward soaked up the atmosphere of Venice, the shape of the Salute, the palazzos rotting at the water line. John had painted some of the palazzos dashingly in chalk and water-colour in 1959, and Edward found a deep inner satisfaction when he returned some thirty years later to make his own joyous and fluent versions of the Venice scenes.

I believe that when Edward came to paint Venice – 'with death no more than a handshake away', as he said to me – he did so without any sense of rivalry with his father, but only to prove to himself that landscapes of the city could be made with his own unmistakable signature of style. What I can surely say with confidence is that Edward's Venice was a city glittering with light and movement, full of changing reflections and varying angles, and that his paintings were a triumph, taking an honourable place in the long heritage of the paintings of Venice.

Making the Old Eve Respond

Completing the lithographs for the Folio Society's edition of *The Aspern Papers*, and finishing the retouching of his Venice paintings in the days before his death, meant that Edward fulfilled a promise he had made to himself: 'The one thing I will not do is leave a half-finished painting on the easel.' However, I was left with a question: could I go ahead with a text for the art book now that my principal source of information was silenced?

I knew from my initial research that there was no shortage of visual information. Edward was a great collector and had seemingly inexhaustible files of his work at Marston Bigot, his drawings and sketches, vintage prints and negatives, layouts of guide books, his glossy magazine photography. He had himself looked out a tattered copy of a 'girlie magazine' he had bought, when a young student at the Slade School of Art, from a barrow outside Charing Cross station so that, in the semibasement flat he occupied off Baker Street, he could copy diligently the pin-up poses of girls in high heels, suspenders, silk stockings and golden top hats.

I must say that at this point I was still finding it hard to understand how an artist as sensitive as Edward could find such cheap source material – 'girlie magazines', with features captioned 'The Pulsating Pick of Pulchritude' – refinable into information for his nudes. He told me how, as a young art student, he used to visit strip clubs in Soho 'to observe the absolutely devastating effects' of crude red and green spotlights on female flesh. Apparently he made no hesitation about producing a sketch book to record the movements of the strippers in action, unperturbed by the sniggers from the other spectators.

At this time Edward was fresh from a High Anglican public school, Lancing College. It was only later that I came to understand that he was always single-minded and zealous when pursuing some artistic objective; and he always retained underlying public school attitudes as an important substratum in his character.

From his earliest days as an art student Edward seldom let a day go by without practising his drawing, including making copies of the nudes of old and modern masters – Titian, Raphael, Botticelli, Klimt, Schiele, Renoir, Matisse, Dufy, Picasso – all apparently stored away in his archives. And alongside the copies (his 'rip-offs', as Edward called them) of famous nudes, including one by Cranach of *The Three Graces*, you find pin-ups of a series of sex icons including Marilyn Monroe, Madonna and Sharon Tate, victim of a notorious Hollywood murder in the 1960s.

They are joined by Edward's striking copies of explicit Japanese sex prints, from the period when he was experimenting with Japanese-style woodcuts, displaying a line as daring as Aubrey Beardsley but with none of Beardsley's desire for cruel mockery of his subjects. They are ranged with innumerable sketches of young couples in the sex act, drawn by Edward in his smaller studio at Marston Bigot. All of these things were part of his continuing, restless search for artistic understanding of the sensuality and eroticism of the female figure.

His hope, he said to me, was that his one-man show at the Catto Gallery would illustrate the fact that he had developed his nude studies to the point where he was communicating his esential belief that the female figure could, through its harmonious and voluptuous lines, express the most significant rhythms of human life, growth and procreation. He felt it was the urgent task of the artist to rescue the nude from the cruel, exploitative half-truth of *Playboy* and 'page 3' sensationalism and sexual imperialism.

My hesitancy about preparing a text on Edward's

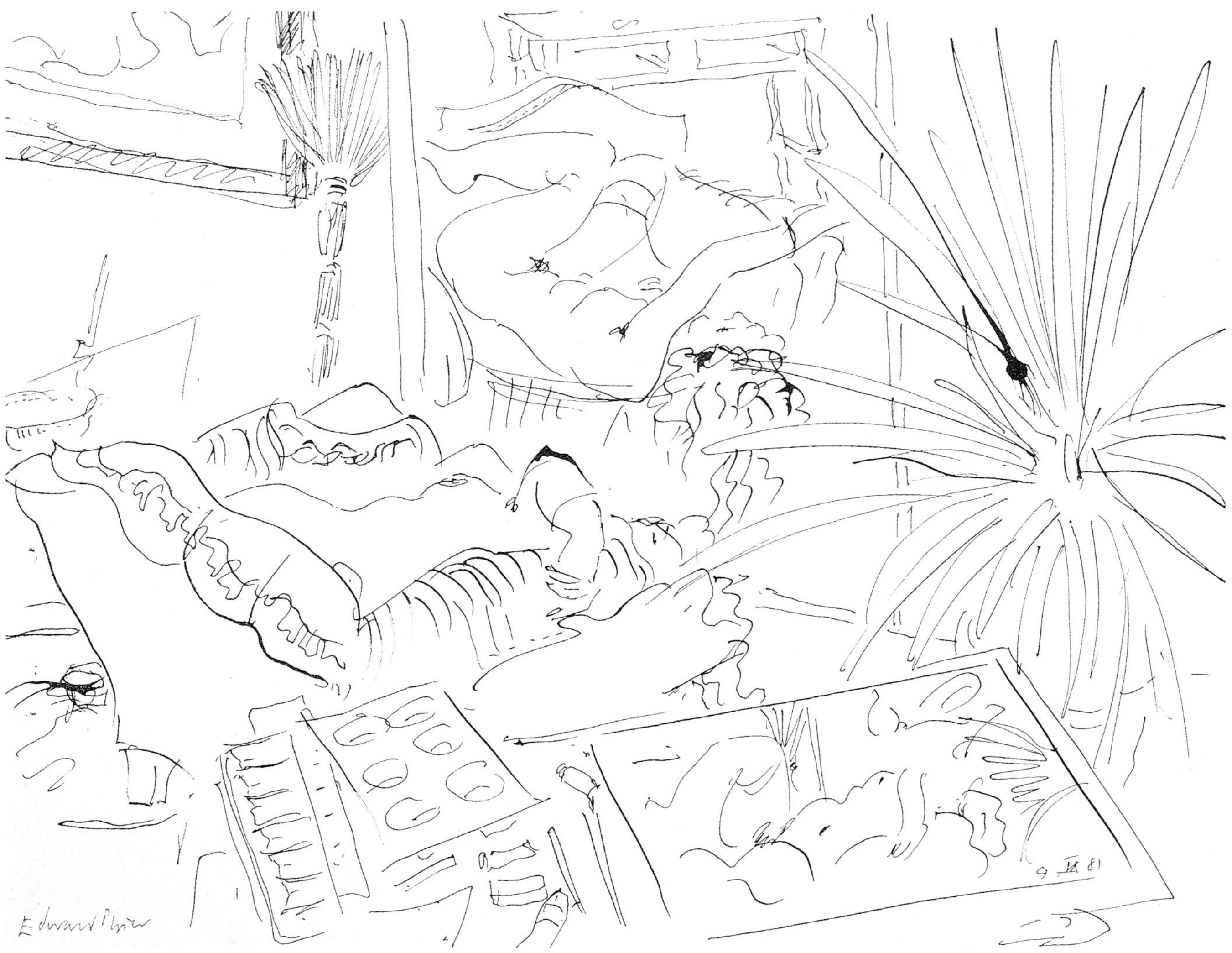

Artist and Model in the Studio
Pen and ink, 12 × 16ins, 1981

work for an art book had nothing to do with what Edward referred to as 'suburban moralistic attitudes' to his nude studies. He had worked seriously within a long and authentic artistic tradition. My difficulty was to decide whether or not I could find an approach which would come sufficiently near to his wish for a text validating his work in his own words within his concepts of what he was doing.

One of the major hazards was that Edward not only disliked theorising about art, but had made few written references to his aims and ambitions. He had impressed on me, in fact, that he distrusted the written word, believing that, apart from true poetry, anything one wrote could be twisted so its true and original meaning was unrecognisable. He stubbornly insisted in the face of argument that no words could be found to express in a sentence or two the experience and technical risks in art that could be found in one true line of painting.

He agreed with a painter he admired, Gustav Klimt, that if you wanted to know about him as a painter you had to study his paintings with care and find out through them what he was about and what he was trying to do. Still undecided, I turned to look not only at Edward's nudes and landscapes, but at his photographs, his landscapes with female figures; and these confirmed my impression that the information he had acquired of the female figure had given him the base for a series of inventive and innovative poses.

I studied again one of his most distinctive images, the vintage print of one of his long-legged, supple models. She was posed at eye-level among smooth stones on a Dorset seashore to create an aerial sculptural image, with the vulva subtly highlighted, looking somewhat surrealist, like a flying saucer, but without being in any way crude. I moved across to look again at a painting on the wall in his big studio, one from his pop-art period in the 1960s when, for once, the paintings which emanated from his studio found themselves in the fashionable mainstream of the day. This was an art which drew heavily on pin-up pictures, sleek motor-car advertising images, slogans and strobe lighting, one which helped sweep Britain away from the last vestiges of wartime austerity headlong into the hedonistic 1960s.

The painting I had returned to study was exhibited in the London Under-40 Exhibition at the Galeria Milano in Milan in 1966. It is a frieze depicting seven pin-up girls arranged with an easy rhythm reminiscent of Edward's enthusiasm for jazz, a long swinging string of beads asserting movement, with the legs and buttocks far more important than the faces. All the curves of the female body, especially the arch of the back and the sinuousness of the legs in high-heeled shoes, combine racily in clear lollipop colours to produce a painting both subtle and light-hearted.

The rooms and galleries, and even the kitchen at Marston Bigot, spacious with its large Aga and vermilion-painted plain pine table, teem with Edward's nudes: the nude with flesh painted a luscious lime-green, relaxing on a leopard-skin rug, gingery tuft of pubic hair an eye-catching motif, effortlessly recalling in imagination

After 'The Three Graces' by Cranach
Ink and acrylic on board, 14½ × 12ins, 1986

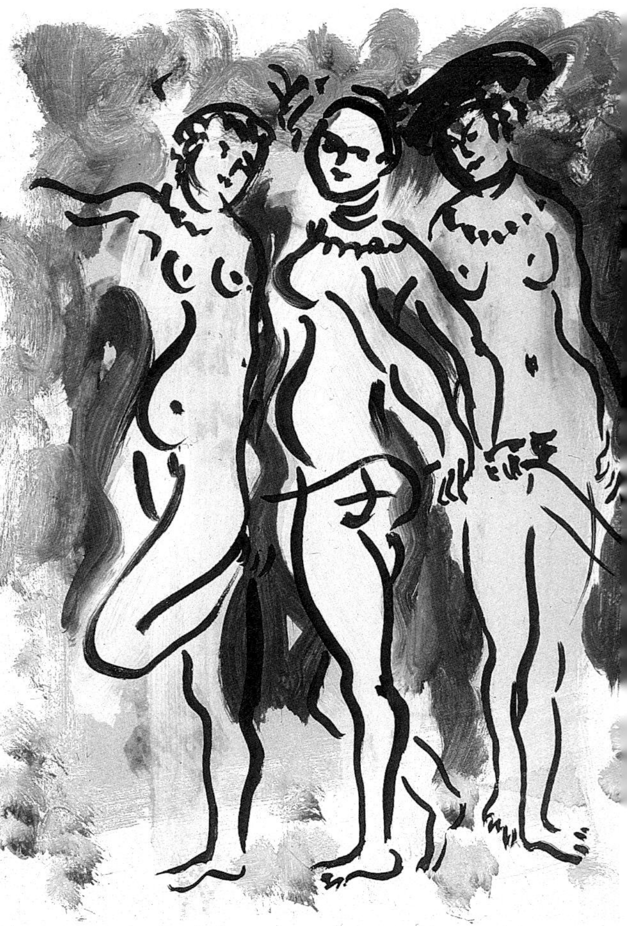

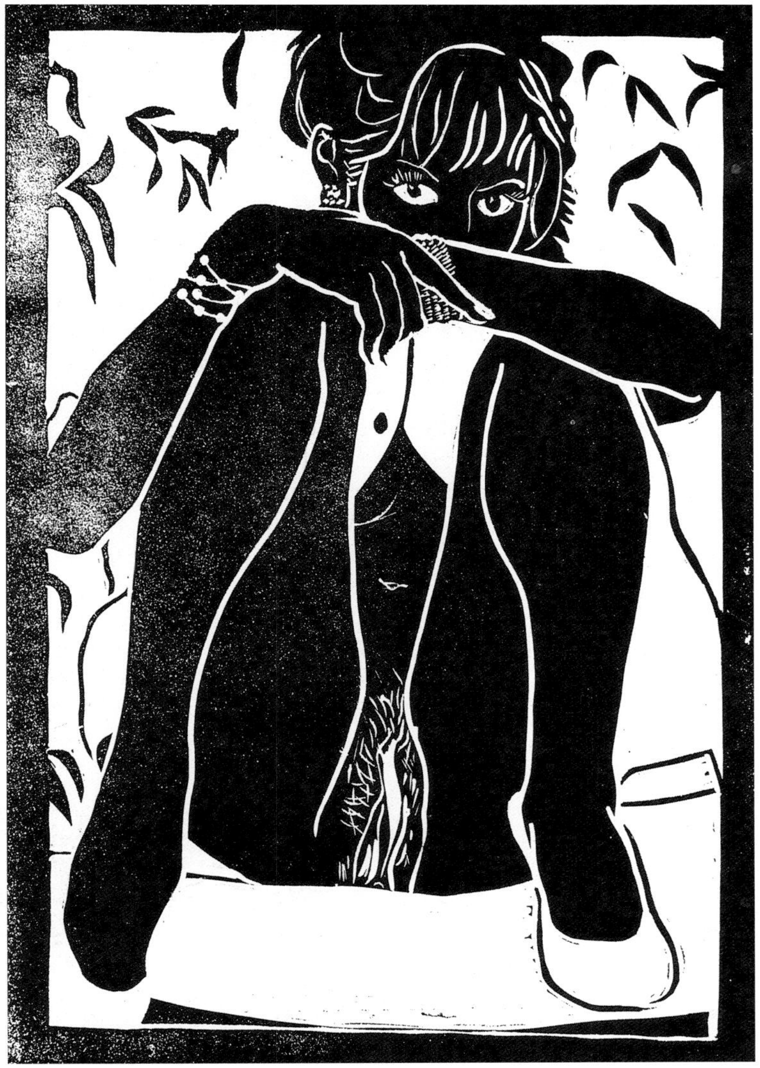

Under the Counter, Soho
Linocut, 14 × 10ins, 1964

an Elinor Glyn pose; arabesques of nudes; nudes existing between the pin-up and the odalisque, nudes reflected brilliantly in mirrors so that you see a female figure from several angles simultaneously.

Edward had always insisted that whatever we wrote in collaboration had to place his nudes where he believed they belonged as of right – at the heart of anything written about his work. Before his death he had actually already suggested two or three things I might do to prepare for later, more serious discussions on his obsessive concentration on the female form. The first was to make a descriptive inventory of the smaller studio he had built on the first floor of the old laundry, for his modelling sessions; and the second was to interview some of his female models.

'You will probably get more insights into the importance I attach to the artist/model studio relationship than from anything I might dream up in the big hypothesis,' he said, writing the word hypothesis with a gesture on the air.

I followed up his advice. Comments I had heard him make over the years of our friendship, concerning the care with which he built his studio relationships with his models, suggested something of the film director's approach. The small studio at the end of the first floor gallery seemed to confirm the impression: the modelling stage, the high-backed wicker chair, and above all what I labelled his 'basket of frivolity', filled with props for his models to dress up in and establish their femininity – silver dance shoes, Japanese silk kimono, lime-green fishnet tights, plastic bangles and opera masks.

Everything about the studio was intended to help towards the creation of a highly-charged atmosphere of sensuality and heightened sexual awareness, when Edward himself would take off his clothes to paint naked. He believed implicitly that all this was necessary to develop a technique for transferring more easily to paper the delicate eroticism he wished to depict, seen particularly in his finest nude studies of his later years.

At this point I was beginning to see – though it was not yet quite focused – an alternative format to Edward's voice-over for the art book text. I decided to try and resolve my doubts one way or the other through my reactions to the interviews Edward had suggested I hold with a representative group of his female models. Several had already approached me to say they would like to talk about their modelling with Edward.

The model with whom I first discussed Edward's studio relationship was his first and most enduring subject, his wife Prue, who initially posed for him when Edward was an unhappy student at the Slade School of Art. She, in fact, provided me with what was probably the most incisive view of Edward's attitude to his models when she said:

> Edward didn't judge women in the way we are often judged. Women knew he would admire and make much of their good points: 'Make the old Eve respond!' Probably most of his models responded to him intuitively too, through senses rather than mind, and to what was going on in his nude paintings.

The interviews with all the models yielded insights and information which were fresh and vivid, remarkably consistent, and dramatically unexpected, so much so that they not only gave me the confidence to press on with a text, but also influenced my choice of shape: a literary composite of monograph and personal memoir,

Nude 3. Oil on canvas, 30 × 48ins, 1963

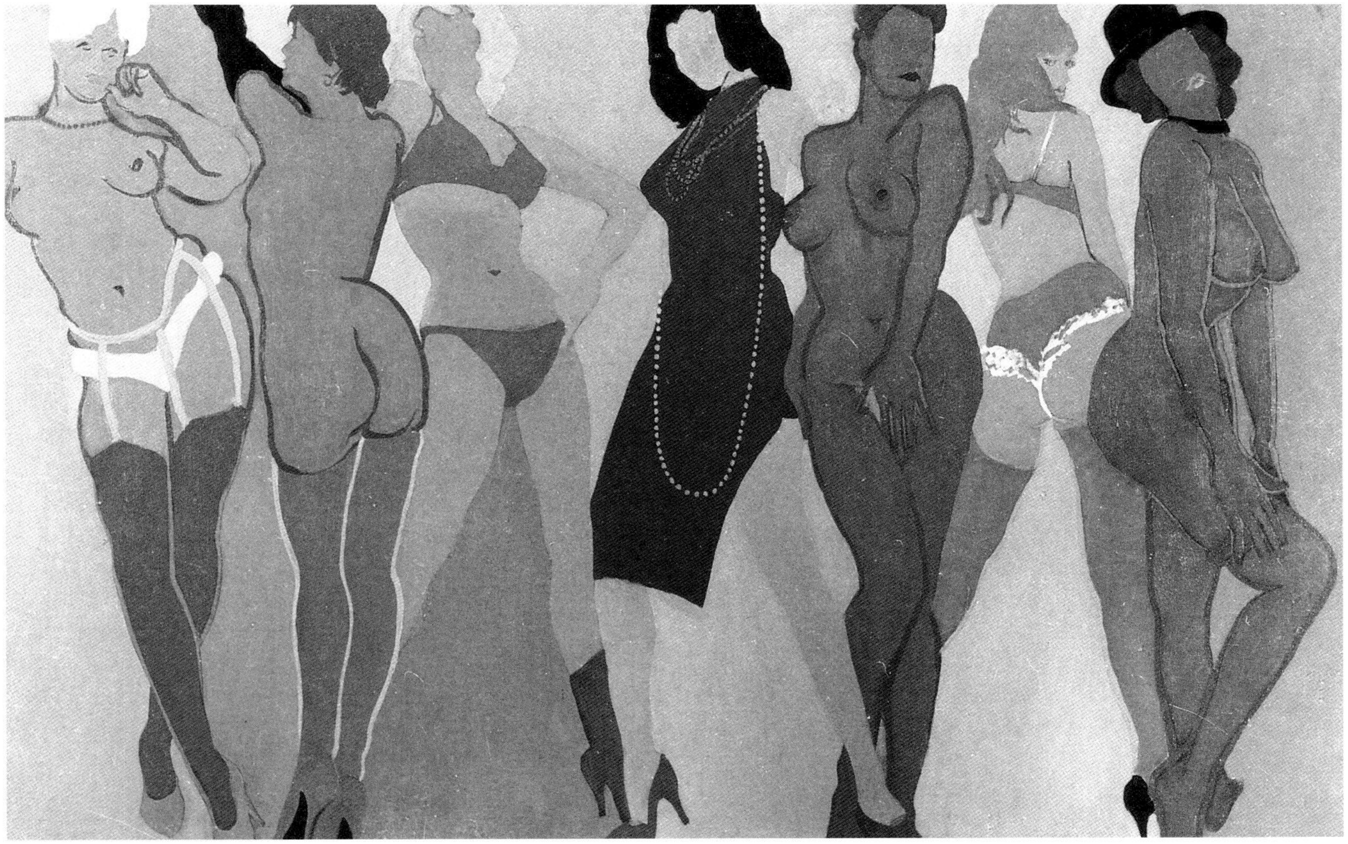

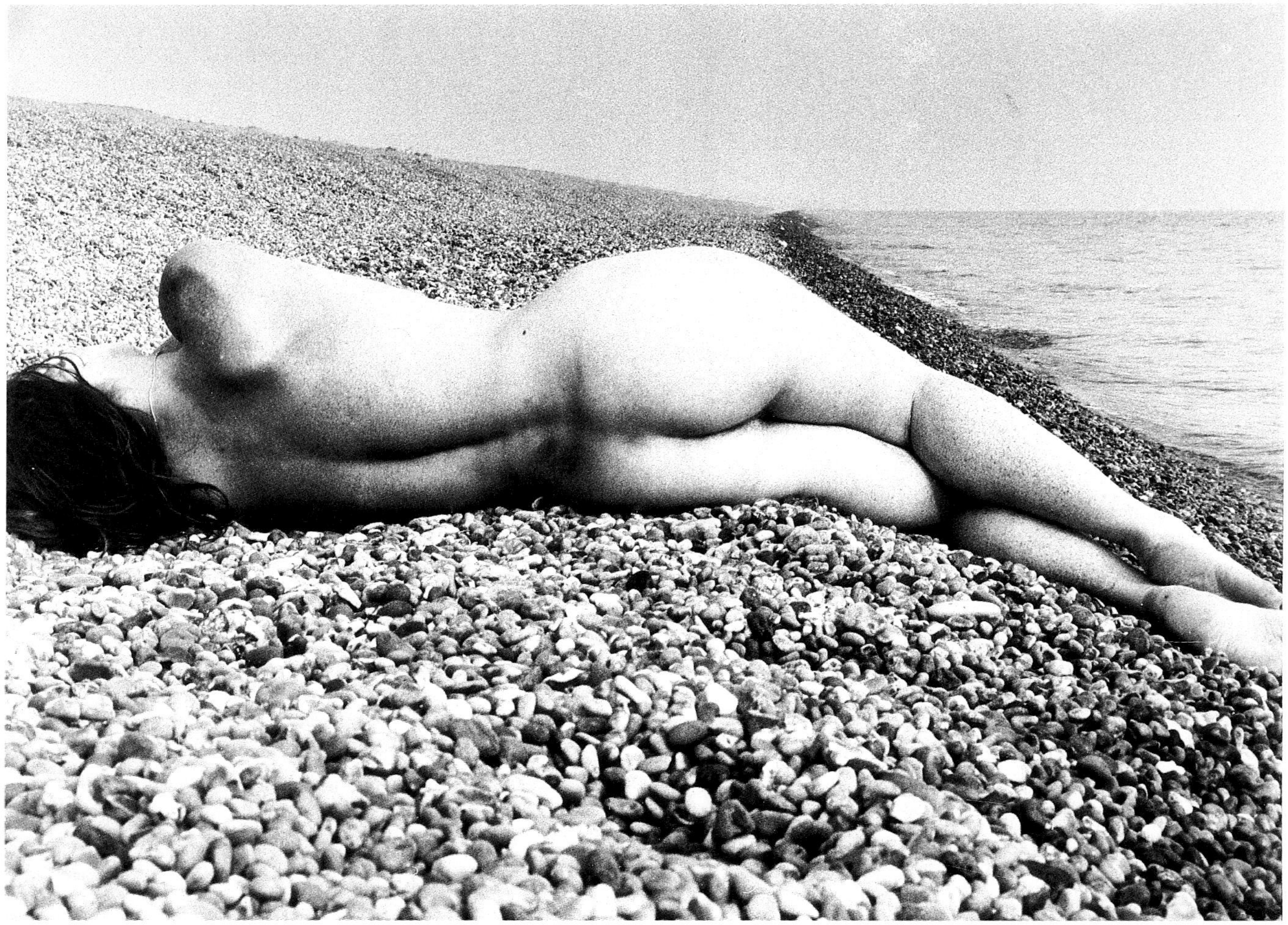

Girl on Chesil Bank, Dorset 1979

which would provide a context within which people might more clearly understand Edward's art and see him for the man he was.

Having made my decision, I walked the length of the big studio to look again at one particular painting, the one which had prompted the only question I ever asked which obviously fazed Edward, who otherwise answered questions spontaneously. The painting was a portrait of an ordinary working-class mother living in nearby Frome, made in the early 1980s. Edward came rather late in his career to portraiture, and this one, hanging to the right of the studio's large open fireplace, was (and not only in my view) the most completely realised portrait he ever painted.

If it reminds you of Matisse in technique, it also seems to me to make a poignant and original statement by Edward about the human condition, through the face of an ordinary young mother who has attained a hard-won peace after passing through an emotional storm. Edward had not given the portrait a title, in his belief that titles unduly conditioned responses to paintings. The young woman is called Christine and, although I didn't know it until some time later, had an Irish maiden name; yet I immediately saw the portrait in a Sean O'Casey context, a Dublin tenement face of the sorrows.

One of the pleasures of collaborating with Edward 'on tape' was the way in which he could, without preamble, produce an illuminating and exciting account of an experience that had impressed itself on his imagination. The account he gave me of the way in which he came to meet and paint Christine was so revealing of his attitudes to his art that the moment I taped it I realised I would have to reproduce it verbatim in anything I wrote about his work (see p.27).

And my question, which Christine's portrait inspired? It struck me that the portrait was the only one of his paintings I had seen which had a shadow of tragedy. Why had he apparently only painted what was joyous and beautiful in life? I asked him.

'I have to admit I hadn't thought about that until you just asked me', he replied after a pause. 'It's something we must "excavate" for a meaning later.'

He was jaded by the effects of his treatment for his illness. Fortunately – as there never was a 'later' for us he could not resist enlarging briefly on his answer there and then, thus providing a flash of insight into his artistic philosophy. He said:

> I really know that in my position today, with my doctor's opinion ringing in my ears, life isn't always really a good bargain. But the fact is that I never have, and don't think I ever will, see life as all tears. Most days I wake up and think 'Hello sun, hello flowers.' Is that a misquote from St Francis, or the Beatles? No, it's something Noddy and Big Ears used to say. The fact is that it would give me no pleasure to paint anything ugly, cruel or cold.
>
> I'm thinking of some of the artists I love most, Matisse, Dufy, van Gogh, and their paintings are full of the most wonderful things.
>
> (He hesitated, then continued:)
>
> In fact, you just name a 'gloom skull' among painters. Munch, perhaps. Then his pictures were still beautiful. Some happen to be on the dark side – painted rather from the inside of the head – but even his paintings can be full of sunsets, sea and flowers.
>
> The way I see life doesn't mean that I don't feel for the sufferings of concentration camps, the bomb, famine, dreadful individual misfortunes, everything oppressive and cruel in the world . . . I'm all for banning the bomb, I have always been 'green' and anxious about what we are doing to the planet for profits, all in a non-party political way . . . but yes, you can say that my answer to your question is that being the sort of artist I am, and the human being I like to think I am, I paint joy and beauty simply because I believe that we need every little bit of joy and beauty we can create to survive life's horrors . . . sorry, I must rest, but I will return to this later . . .

And that, so far as I ever discovered, was as near as Edward Piper ever came to articulating a *credo*. At the time we were standing alongside what I regard as one of Edward's most successful compositions, one so huge (5ft 4in by nearly 9ft) that it has never been publicly exhibited; a dozen female figures appear in striking red outline in pin-up poses, hands on knees, hands behind their heads, stretching, sitting, in panties and high-heeled shoes.

Placed centrally is the figure of Sharon Tate, one of the 1960s 'superfine pin-up beauties', whose symmetrical pop-icon face fascinated Edward for months. He painted her from publicity colour stills in a range of techniques, in pencil, ink, pastels, etchings, aquatint lithographs, oils, lino cuts and collages. In the painting she leans forward on her cupped hands, her head beautifully related to the buttocks of the adjacent figures. He painted the complicated outlines in scarlet, and then filled in all the background in cobalt blue, with most scrupulous care.

It was a technique in complete contrast to the free-flowing, fast-moving style he was later to adopt, yet there is a similarity of message. It is a serene, contented picture, which impresses its quality on the room. Sharon Tate's lips magnetise the attention of anyone walking into the studio and I cannot help wondering how many identify her and, like Edward, recognise her tragedy, a very modern tragedy.

Sharon Tate was a symbol of the swinging life-style of the 1960s. She was the wife of film director Roman Polanski when, eight months pregnant, she became the victim of the Charles Manson gang in a brutal murder which, briefly, stunned the world. She was transformed in 1990 from a symbol of life into the central figure of a 'horror musical' in an off-Broadway theatre in New York. And if this is a prefiguration of horror as one of the themes of the coming decade, we shall need all the joy and beauty we can find to make it bearable.

Candlelit Childhood

All his life Edward Piper was unusually sensitive to light; he noticed even the slightest variation of sun and shadow as if he had a built-in light meter. It may well have been this extreme sensitivity to changes in light which, combined with his remarkable visual memory, caused him to develop in the directions he did as a painter and photographer.

Among his earliest memories were the variations in light at his childhood home, Fawley Bottom Farmhouse, discreetly placed in a pleasant valley in the Chilterns; the candles on the polished dining-room table and the waxen yellowy glow of paraffin lamps with their lovely shapes, because for years after the Pipers moved in the farmhouse had no electricity.

John and Myfanwy Piper bought the former yeoman farmer's flint-and-brick farmhouse in 1935, and Edward was born there on 12 November 1938. His parents resolutely created the artistic and intellectual environment they wanted for the pursuit of their careers, John initially as an abstract artist, Myfanwy as a writer on art, and author of children's books and eventually of the libretti for Benjamin Britten operas.

Myfanwy Piper had sketched the type of house she wanted on the back of an envelope: a plain-fronted house with one central door opening on to a garden, which in turn led into an open field. It is an uncannily accurate description of Fawley Bottom Farmhouse. Edward may well therefore have inherited this characteristic of deciding what you wanted and then looking for it with unwavering zeal from his mother, London-born, but with Welsh ancestry.

His parents, Edward said, undoubtedly built the environment they needed to cultivate their professional ambitions – but they didn't place comfort high on their list of requirements. He sometimes recalled the pleasure he got listening to music on the old '78' speed records played on an old-fashioned wind-up gramophone with a horn, 'like the picture on the old record label, but without the fox-terrier', he said. When LPs became available, young Edward rigged up a Heath Robinson arrangement, powered by a generator running on a car battery, so they could play LPs by a log-fire.

Many of Edward's childhood memories were a mixture of music, light and shadow, John and Myfanwy and friends singing West End musical hit songs round the piano, with dancing shadows thrown by flickering candle-flames on the wall. He was, however, somewhat reticent about personal memories of Fawley Bottom. He had one all-embracing sentence about his early years: 'It was marvellous really, very consistent, unruffled and very happy.'

The Pipers – four children were born to John and Myfanwy – were clearly a warmly united family, so that Edward grew up within a solid, affectionate background, though one sensed there was a certain distance in their relationships.

During Edward's early years, his parents were at the centre of avant-garde art and passionate controversy. In World War II, which saw John Piper become 'a name' as a war artist and acquire royal patronage for his paintings, Fawley Bottom Farmhouse became if anything more of a home, at the centre of a sparkling, intricate web of aesthetic activity, with a constant flow of visitors from many areas of the arts.

What did Edward make of the activity going on around him?

'Oh, yes, I remember the buzzing activity,' he said, 'But to be honest, I remember it chiefly as a time when we Piper children inspired a great deal of 'For God's sake shut up, we are trying to think!' or '. . . to write!' with mother always on the phone to Ben Britten about the words for his opera.'

What effects did he think this highly-charged intellectual background had on his own development?, I asked him.

'I suppose it meant principally that I had somehow to find a way of defending my own space in the home as an individual, while the famous people visiting my parents didn't really impinge all that much. They were my parents' friends, and that was all they meant to me,' he said, making them appear to live on a separate plane from the Piper children.

The visitors included Kenneth Clark; Benjamin Britten and Peter Pears; the sculptor and artist Alexander Calder, who was a favourite visitor with the Piper children; John Betjeman and his wife Penelope – but when asked about his memories of them, Edward usually retreated behind the vague statement 'I really have a better memory for places than people.'

His memories often had a quality of innocence: Penelope Betjeman, a field marshal's daughter and first-class horsewoman, teaching the city-bred Myfanwy Piper to handle a pony and trap in the lanes around Fawley Bottom; perhaps a visit with Clarissa to Saltwood Castle, the home of Kenneth Clark (later Lord Clark) near the entrance to the Channel Tunnel on the English coast. Saltwood has an impressive art collection – Michelangelo, Degas, Gainsborough, Reynolds, Cézanne, and Renoir. 'I must have looked at the paintings,' Edward said, 'but what I remember most is that I got to play with some marvellous mechanical toys belonging to the Clark children.'

As a boy, Edward liked to be outdoors as much as possible. Visitors to Fawley Bottom remember him gathering kindling, chopping wood or repairing a wall, living the life of a healthy, energetic boy in country surroundings. He shared most of his early childhood with his sister, Clarissa, three years younger than he and from all accounts he seems to have taken his role as elder brother with unusual, though 'unbossy' seriousness; in due time he assumed this fraternal responsibility both for Suzannah, nine years his junior, and Sebastian, twelve years younger.

Myfanwy Piper, talking of Edward's childhood after his death, said: 'I think Edward was adult from an early age. When he was a weekly boarder at preparatory school and I met him from the bus at weekends, it was always with a feeling "Edward is home, everything is going to be all right." '

Clarissa provided me with an illustration of exactly what Myfanwy Piper meant, saying that as a child she was always afraid of the dark – but she recalled how Edward had comforted her one night with a comic strip he had sketched, of a man in a bowler hat on a bicycle doing comic things, like running into a lamp post. This aura of reassurance and security was something Edward carried through into adult life; you always felt safer when Edward was around.

Did his parents encourage him to paint?, I asked him once when we were setting up arrangements for a tape recording which would discuss the influences on his development as a painter.

> In no way that I can recall. Children are great accepters, and I was quite happy to be left in the care of Elsie, a girl from a nearby village who looked after

us while my parents got on with whatever work they had in hand.

Of course, I clearly recall being put in the back of JP's Morris with Clarissa, and driven to a spot where we sat and watched in the back while my father painted furiously, often through a rain-swept windscreen, wrapped up in his creative work. That may well have been the beginning of my education in topography, and I could usually see in the finished paintings what references my father had left out.

Yet as I say, we were never encouraged to paint, either to pass the time or to express ourselves. I know there are artist families where the children are pressed or coaxed into being little painters and end up at art college. I have never discussed it with my parents in any detail, but they probably felt that painting was not a safe path for us to follow. My father had some hard years financially when he was a struggling painter.

And I do know that John Piper never considered children's art to be relevant – and it isn't, really.

Myfanwy Piper said to me on the question of encouraging her children to paint, 'When a child who has any kind of creative ability, is brought up in a household where creative activity is going on all round him, he tends to follow suit. I remember watching Edward teach some of his friends how to use greasy chalk, having learned by watching his father; but I have to say it was a long time before John or I realised Edward was serious when he announced at about the age of eight that he was going to be a painter like his father.'

Public School Pin-up Collage

Edward's formal education was in the conventional pattern of middle-class professional parents. He went to a preparatory school as a weekly boarder, where although the atmosphere was pleasant, the classroom teaching missed the educational rigour which would have equipped him to pass the Common Entrance to Eton, for which his parents had entered him.

John and Myfanwy Piper were by this time close friends of Benjamin Britten and Peter Pears, through working together at Aldeburgh with the English National Opera group. Edward's parents had been shepherded into confirmation in the Church of England by Edward's godfather, John Betjeman; now, Britten and Pears influenced them in favour of Lancing College on the Sussex Downs as second choice for Edward's public school education.

I cannot presume to say anything about the choice of Lancing. Edward himself wasn't sure whether another choice of school would have made any difference to him, but he certainly looked back with some bitterness on his years at Lancing, 1951–6.

'My chief recollection is one of always being hungry. I could endure the system, if resentfully, because as a boy brought up in the country, I was quite used to enjoying my own company without in any way being a 'solitary' – and yet I never had any problems, either, about being part of a group.'

When the subject of his school days came up in conversation, Edward referred more than once to something Richard Ingrams, the journalist and former editor of *Private Eye* had said; Ingrams had collaborated with John Piper in making the art book *Piper's Places*, dealing with the scenes and locations of his English paintings. According to Richard Ingrams, 'the system at an English public school was so "Roman" that you had to conform completely, or rebel fiercely'.

However, Edward thought there might be a third way to survive the system intact as an individual. You could, he said, get to know its rules and ethos as well as, if not better than, its authors to enable you to manipulate it. 'It was years later that I came across in my reading *The Good Soldier Schweik*, who "worked" an authoritarian system so beautifully; then I realised I had found a character I could regard as my patron saint,' Edward said.

Perhaps Edward's legal heritage also helped him to 'work' systems. His paternal grandfather was a successful member of a prosperous firm of solicitors in the City of Westminster, and if his artistic impulse had not been so over-riding, John Piper might well have become a solicitor, and no doubt a successful one, too.

In his second year at Lancing, when he was fourteen, Edward won an argument with the headmaster, and this gave him the privilege – reserved under school rules for boys in the Vth and VIth forms – of cycling across the Downs to Brighton as an alternative to organised games days, which Edward loathed. 'I usually found myself stuck in goal,' he said.

He argued with 'the godlike figure' of the headmaster that in view of the fact that he intended to move eventually to art college, it would only be sensible to allow him to cycle to Brighton on games days to study its Regency architecture. He 'copper-bottomed' his case by offering to swim, say, thirty lengths of the school swimming baths as an alternative to team games.

He spent many agreeable half-days cycling round the conventional sights, often stopping to sketch the Regency terraces, the Pavilion, the roller-skating rink, and – pre-eminent in his memory – the cathedral-like proportions of the railway station, with trains gliding alongside platforms, full of day-trippers.

'I think you can actually see hints of the benefit I got from looking at Brighton scenes with the unjaded vision of a gauche schoolboy, in the photographs I shot for the Shell county guide series. Where the pictures do avoid the '*déjà vu*' of scenes photographed many times, it is down to my schoolboy vision,' he said at Marston Bigot, 'The Pavilion under snow was as magical as anything I have ever seen since.'

He used his cycling privilege to explore 'the other Brighton', as he called it, the seedy Edwardian Brighton of low cafés, painted prostitutes and the shabby-smart gilt and red plush interiors of pubs. As he said some thirty years later, it was an extension of his cutting out of pin-up figures from *Photoplay* to make collages to decorate his school locker, the beginning of his obsession with the female figure.

'There was nothing I enjoyed more than watching the tarts parading like alley cats in shady side streets,' he said, 'or lingering to admire posters of the half-naked film stars of 'X'-rated films, or even the glances I caught of barmaids through pub windows.'

It was, he added, many years before he realised this was the beginning of his habit of 'feeding his eyes', perpetually recording and storing up visual images on which he could draw in his art in the future. And it was certainly more use to him than idling his time away in goal or down at third man at cricket.

Did he think the masculine, 'girl-less' society of a public school had anything to do with his imaginative interest in the female figure? Yes, he said, it meant he had to subscribe by post to *Photoplay* for his source material.

'I think I can honestly say in answer to your question and what it implies, that I almost certainly had the usual hot, grubby-handed sexual curiosities of puberty; but I really believe my preoccupation with the female figure would have taken root in my artistic imagination wherever I had gone to school, co-ed or not. How it arose, or where it came from, is still something of a mystery to me but I wouldn't deny that public school segregation can work strangely on the sensual side of one's imagination.'

He was quite sure that what he called the 'Lancing formula' of Anglican ritual and adolescent sexuality in the enclosed society of a public school interacted to produce 'hot-house' schoolboy love affairs. He was never tempted to become involved personally, but didn't doubt the accuracy of the reporting and fiction inspired by schoolboy homoeroticism. He once said that in his own case it was possible that an intense, absorbing phase of religious experience in the VIth form was his way of sublimating his sensuality as an adolescent.

From what people have said who knew him as a teenager, Edward had the physical presence and that unobtrusive air of authority which should have led to his being made a prefect in the VIth form. The school authorities could have seen his *Photoplay* collages as a bit of bravado and accepted his dislike of team games as part of an artistic temperament. But to his disappointment he was not made a prefect, possibly because the authorities sensed his contempt for the system. His resentment at being passed over for a prefecture arose in large measure from the fact that it meant he was never given his own study at Lancing; and this was a real deprivation to Edward, who had the Pipers' love of privacy.

His father thought that as a schoolboy, Edward was more interested in science than the arts, perhaps through Edward's practicality with machinery, and this view seemed to be born out by his 'O' level results: his six 'O's in the Vth form included a distinction with a 98 per cent mark in physics. However, he quickly found himself 'bored and baffled' by abstract physics theory in the VIth form, and switched to English and History.

Edward always enjoyed the periods when he could escape from routine lessons to draw and paint in the crypt of the school church, storing his easel and brushes in an unused workman's hut on a school building site. Lancing had no particular artistic bent, but it did present Edward with his first artistic commission – designing a school Christmas card. He produced a beautifully detailed drawing of a Romanesque ivory box.

In his final year he was also given an assignment to paint a mural in the entrance to one of the Lancing school houses. His first shot was a scene of a derelict south coast beach, but this was thought to be too sombre – 'The only painting I ever did to be criticised on that ground,' he said. In its place he painted a terrace of Regency houses in Brighton in a lively, assured style, which inevitably owed a debt to his father's architectural style and palette.

The mural was prompted by the Lancing College master the Reverend Henry Thorold, one of the first people to recognise that Edward had inherited the Piper talent for art. As a young photographer after leaving the Slade School of Art, Edward worked with the Rev. Thorold as a photographer and designer of a series of publications edited by his former teacher. Thorold wrote to Prue Piper after Edward's death:

> I have always felt great affection and admiration for Edward, ever since he first came to Lancing. I tried to teach him Latin – his proses were always full of the most terrible mistakes, but always immaculately and beautifully written.
>
> He painted that wonderful mural of a Brighton street, just inside the front door of Gibbs House, which was and still is a great pleasure.

Several times in the years I knew him, Edward had mentioned the satisfaction the painting of the Lancing College mural had given him; and this may have been an intimation of a direction in art he would have liked to have taken further, if he had been given more years to live.

You Must Go Further, Piper

From Lancing, Edward went straight to the Bath Academy at Corsham, near Bath, run by an artistic couple who were friends of John and Myfanwy Piper. At the academy he was taught, along with other basic artistic disciplines, how to impart movement to figures in drawing; this was taught by Howard Hodgkin, whom he liked and got along with well. Once again, however, Edward did not fit into the matrix of the system, discovering, painfully, that his use of brilliant colour tones and linear style was at odds with the then fashionable style in favour at the academy, a style he was to encounter again later, at the Slade School of Art.

At the academy he was given the chance to work in spinning, weaving and rug-making, which made him appreciate for the first time that his ability to work practically and skilfully with his hands could actively help him to develop in fine art. He felt, looking back at Corsham, that this conviction arose from his experiments with mobiles – his 'fun sculptures' – fashioned out of decorative baking tins and cake moulds, and made to move with fans and heat from candles and reflectors or tiny clockwork engines taken from mechanical toys.

His mobiles derived from those he had observed at first hand in movement at Fawley Bottom Farmhouse, created by the sculptor Alexander Calder, who stayed for a time as house guest with John and Myfanwy Piper. The mobiles belong to the heady, optimistic late 1960s, when the kinetic art movement was at the height of its popularity. No ambitious business executive was without his mobile sculpture, a 'talking point' on his office desk. If this didn't actually authenticate the artistic values of kinetic art, it helped to make it a financial success for those involved.

Edward left Corsham in 1957 for the Slade School of Art; but this was another dispiriting period, without any encouragement for him to take the directions in painting he so fervently wished to take. He had four highly frustrating years, 1957 to 1961 – at the Slade, spent almost completely in a state of discouragement with, and defiance towards the Slade method of teaching and the general artistic ambience.

His period at the Slade had one compensation, the value of which to Edward cannot be measured. In 1959 he met a second-year student in biochemistry at University College, London: Prudence Mackillop, the seventh child of a seventh child. He was nineteen and she was a few months older at twenty. They were married three years later, and she became his helpmeet in every sense of that old-fashioned word.

Edward had one year as an art student on his own in London before he met Prue; in this time he plunged into metropolitan student life with all his enthusiasm and eagerness for new experiences. A fellow-student at the Slade was Ivor Uglow, who became a lifelong friend of Edward and was for some years an art teacher and director of a craft gallery in the West Country; he said the abrupt transition from public school to art college in the capital city went to Edward's head like champagne.

Remembering the Slade years, Ivor Uglow told me the days were spent in drinking China tea, always from French bowls, with Edward lying like Oblomov in bed by the hour listening to New Orleans jazz records, and occasionally leaping up like a salmon to play an old piano with a honky-tonk sound in Edward's semi-basement flat just off Baker Street.

When they went out in the evenings to do the student rounds of the *Orange Tree* pub on the corner of Euston Road and Gower Street, near the Slade, they drank half-pints of mild and bitter and smoked endless packets of Woodbines, frequently ending up in the *Hall of Mirrors*, a café in Soho run by an Italian family.

This student fun-year, as Edward always called it, lives for ever for Ivor Uglow in one small slapstick incident. He and Edward decided one evening, with the unquestioning finality achieved after 'a few ales', that the honky-tonk piano would sound better in the downstairs room of the flat. But in moving it, they got it wedged on the stairs and Edward had to clamber through a window to get help to rescue Ivor, who was pinned against the wall.

Edward himself observed to me, 'I found a metropolitan Arcadia with sex and drink always available, and it all had a startling effect on the raw public schoolboy that I was.' He enjoyed this student life, he said, so voraciously and exhaustively that towards the end of his first year at the Slade, shortly before he met Prudence Mackillop, he found he was beginning to experience the profound *ennui* which Chekov dramatises so accurately. Not the least of several conflicting traits in Edward's character was that, while his close personal relationships remained stable and 'on an even keel', he could 'use up experience' with a prodigious energy and appetite, and then move on.

Edward later thought that his teachers at the Slade

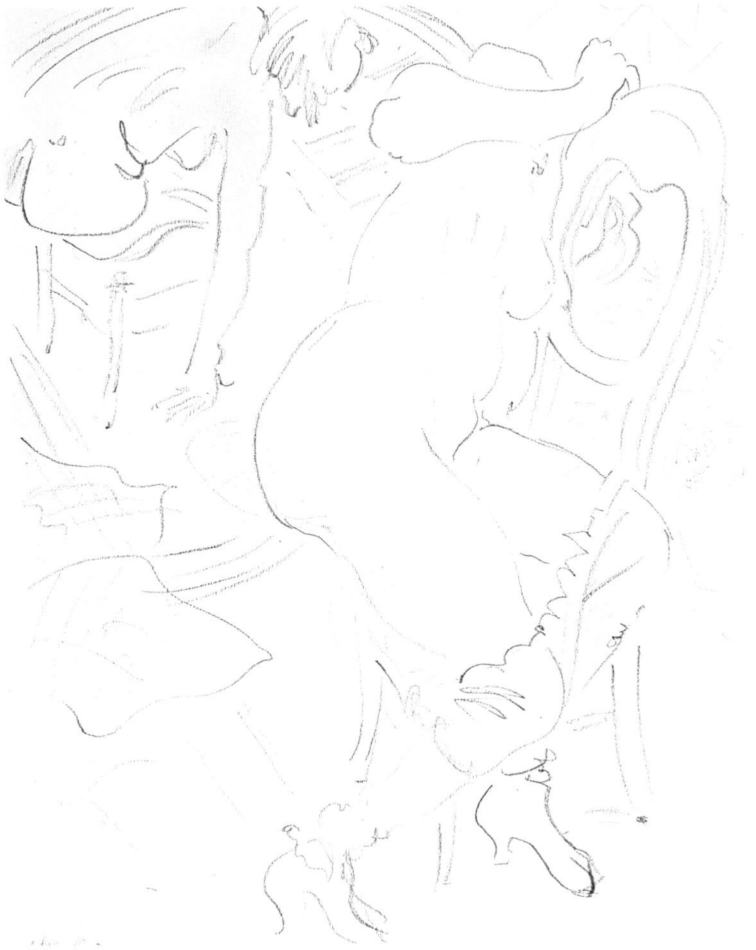

Seated Girl, Bending Over. Pencil, 20 × 15 ins, 1982

may well have sensed the *ennui* enveloping him, and have felt that it was affecting his studies adversely. He said:

> The Slade teachers were always saying that I didn't go deep enough in my drawing and painting. When they looked at my work they said 'Too shallow. You haven't worked hard enough at penetrating to the heart of the subject. Your picture lacks any interest.' I can recall now their battle cry, '*You must go further, Piper!*' I never really grasped – though I tried, God knows I tried! – where they expected me to find this 'further'; though strangely enough, I think I now sometimes find this 'further' they meant in my landscapes, but without ever finding a definition for it.

We were looking through some landscapes he painted in Menorca in the 1980s when he was beginning to discover the confidence to paint landscapes carrying his own definitive signature. He continued:

> You know, I actually believe now, thirty years on, that what the Slade called a weakness was in reality a strength. I dislike my work thoroughly when it seems laboured. I like it best when it is sweet and swift, without any signs of *graft*. The real graft that has actually gone into my better paintings is something I don't want to show through. And the fact that you don't want the graft to show, the sweat and pain that has gone into a work of art, is a concept many art teachers seem to find difficult to understand.

Ivor Uglow recalled watching Edward working at the Slade on a study of a yellowy Turner landscape, and said that all these years later he could still clearly see the resentment written in every angular line of Edward's hunched shoulders. He would have much preferred to have been copying a Derain, to discover its colour harmonies and line. Edward's preference for studying Derain rather than Turner had nothing to do with his appreciation of the paintings. He acknowledged Turner's genius, but the fact was that Derain was one of a group of French painters Edward felt were working in areas in which he wanted to work himself. But whichever way he turned at the Slade, he found no-one encouraged him to go down the road he wanted to follow – with the exception of a visiting teacher, Ceri Griffiths.

'Ceri Griffiths only visited the Slade occasionally,' Edward said, 'But I always felt when listening to him that here was an artist from whom I could really learn. At his best I believe Ceri Griffiths was as good as a painter I have always loved, Raoul Dufy, and I perhaps found Griffiths sympathetic because he was Celtic.'

In the time I knew him, Edward was seldom bitter or spiteful, but one could feel, even at a distance of many years, the anger and frustration he had felt against the Slade as a student. In a rare outburst of bitterness he said:

> At the time I was at the Slade there was a resistance in England to style and sophistication, and a liking for what they called 'the real', the 'kitchen sink' sort of stuff. I think it belonged to that side of the English character which believes there is some virtue in grubbing in the shit.
>
> I mean the Slade despised anybody who used bright colours, or left white spaces on the paper. They liked everything to be earth colours and charcoal, everything painted in a dark room with black floorboards. I didn't buy it then, I don't buy it now!

Edward was approaching his 21st birthday when the Slade teachers were haranguing him to 'go further' in his paintings, and every year he was beginning to look more disconcertingly like his father – tall, slim, spare, erect, with a high Gothic forehead and bright, darting eyes, energy in every movement. The handwriting of their autographs is as alike as a painting facsimile.

Why hadn't he turned to his father in the discouraging circumstances of the Slade? If John Piper had not actively discouraged him as a child to become an artist, he had certainly not discouraged him once he had seriously made up his mind to train as a painter. John Piper believed, as did Edward himself in his turn, that his children should choose and follow their own ways of life.

In one of the rare joint interviews John and Edward Piper gave to news journalists, for a *Good Housekeeping* article published in July 1987, Edward told Sally Brompton: 'For me it was perfectly normal to become an artist because of the environment I grew up in. In some ways I was almost deprived of rebellion.' (The 'almost' is intriguing, but I didn't see the feature before Edward died to ask him exactly what he meant.)

John Piper naturally used his contacts in the art world to help Edward plan his education as an artist. He arranged for Edward to attend the Bath Academy which had been founded by his friends, Clifford and Rosemary Ellis; he influenced him to apply for a place at the Slade where he had links with the governing body. I am not for an instant suggesting that Edward obtained his place at the Slade other than on merit, simply indicating that his father was in a position to have helped.

I asked Edward early in our work together why he hadn't consulted his father about his problems at the Slade.

'My father wouldn't have respected me if I had. He thought, as I do, that once your children as adults have made a decision they should live with it. The Slade was my own decision, like that of becoming a painter.' He then made a remark whose significance I didn't understand at the time, and didn't do so until later when we were discussing his zealous and unusual studies of the nude outside the Slade curriculum. 'Don't forget I had Prue on my side by this time and she was a revelation, inspiring me to go on painting in the face of the dispiriting attitude at the Slade.'

John and Edward, always fond of each other, enjoyed a working relationship based on mutual respect. For example, Edward co-operated quite amicably with his father in taking photographs and laying out Shell county guides when he left the Slade in 1961 and had to make his living. Later in Edward's career as an artist, he and his father shared in joint exhibitions of their work at the invitation of directors of art galleries and art festivals, notably at Bath and Aldeburgh in the early 1980s. Initially Edward acquired some publicity gloss from his father's name, but increasingly over the last six or seven years he found his own public for his nudes and landscapes.

Both John and Edward Piper had an exceptionally acute sense of personal privacy, and I suspect that both regarded their personal and professional dealings with each other as belonging strictly to their own private territory. My impression was, in fact, of a relationship that was very English – straighforward enough on the surface, but with enigmatic and unexplained twists. Ivor Uglow supported this view, saying:

> John Piper is one of the greatest living English artists, and I always had the idea that when Edward entered the Slade he began to realise more clearly than he had previously, that being John Piper's son was a double-edged legacy, one which could hinder as well as help him in his artistic development.
>
> I also have the suspicion that Edward usually asked himself, silently, what his father would have thought of a painting whenever he finished one. It is surely Edward's triumph that he became a fine painter, despite the difficulties of achieving individual recognition as the son of a brilliantly successful father in his own chosen profession.

In 1983, Edward had what he always regarded as one of the most exhilarating artistic experiences of his life: his visit to the marvellous exhibition marking the 30th anniversary of the death of Raoul Dufy (1877–1953) at the Hayward Gallery on London's South Bank. Edward drove back down the A303 to Marston Bigot at speed in a state of exaltation, and went straight to the old Somerset pub upright piano to play some of his favourite jazz, something he often did to work through a high tension mood.

He was, he said, still 'on a high' the next morning when he returned to his easel for his drawing practice – a daily route scrupulously upheld – to copy some Japanese woodcuts. The verve and vitality of Dufy were still dancing in his imagination when he sat down before the black iron wood-burning stove in the corner of the big studio of the Old Laundry to study the exhibition catalogue; and in Bryan Robertson's appreciation of Raoul Dufy, Edward for once found himself reading words which matched the splendour of an event. Robertson was a great admirer of the French master artist; he was also the director who made the Whitechapel Art Gallery in London's East End a centre of excellence. Edward revelled in his account of Dufy, an artist to whom he, Edward, readily acknowledged his personal debt; and let it also be said that he found a satisfying *Schadenfreude* in Robertson's acid criticism of Slade teaching in the late 1950s.

Bryan Robertson said the Slade at that time looked down on 'pure and bright colours as rather immoral'. The Degas/Sickert academic principles of the Euston Road school were firmly established among the teaching staff, and although lip service was paid to artists using a bright palette – and even to a token abstract artist – a low-keyed palette and diligent pursuit of figuration through tonality and slow life drawing were the order of the day at the Slade. And Edward particularly enjoyed – nearly a quarter of a century after his defiance at the Slade – the passage by Bryan Robertson which said:

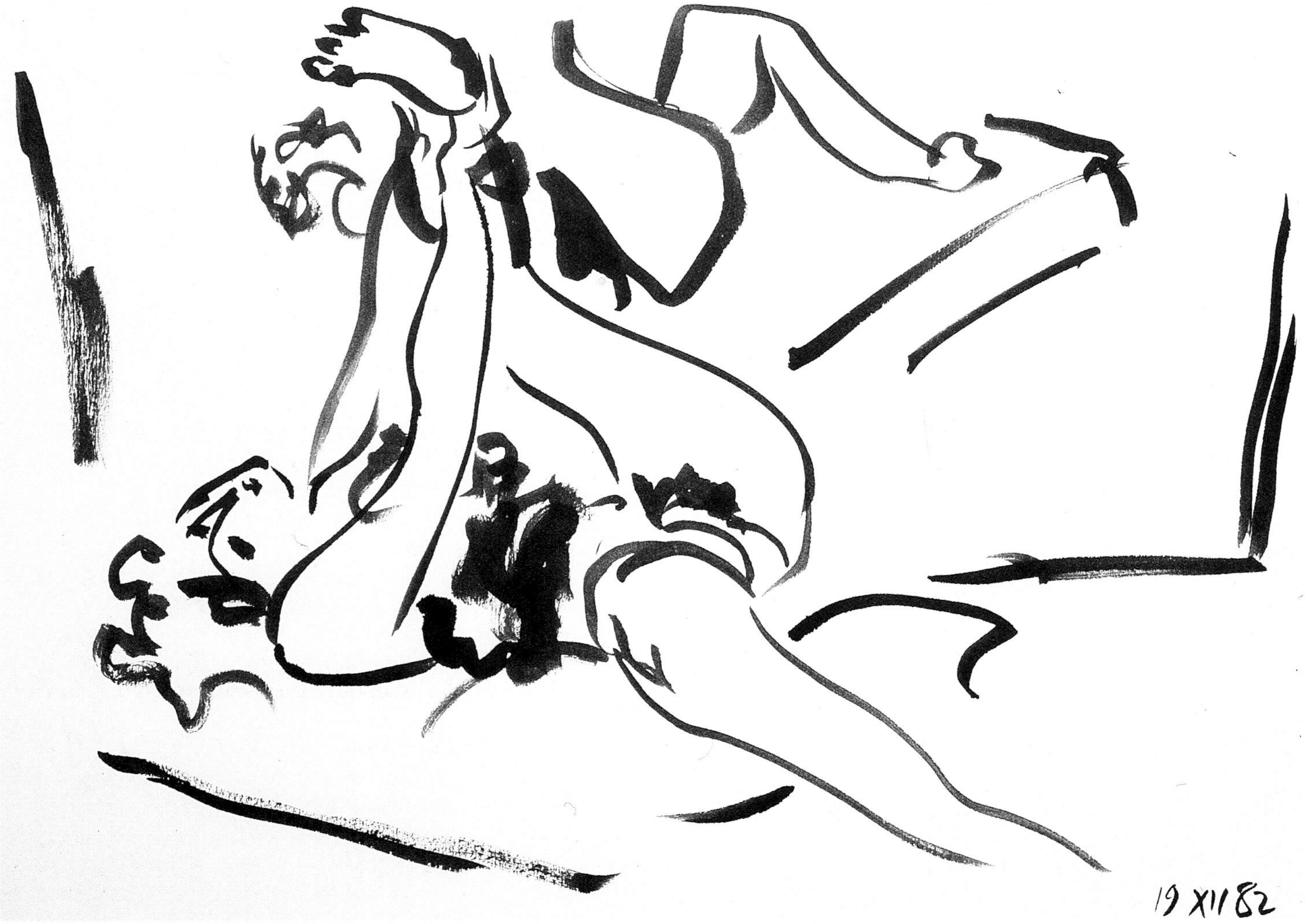

Girl Reclining by Mirror. Brush and ink, 12 × 16 *ins,* 1982

> As a young man it seemed to me that the English equated pure colour with frivolousness, immorality and irresponsibility. Tonality was the moral probity of art and the turgid and monochromatic followers at the Slade of David Bomberg, into whose expressionist principles at the Euston Road ideals seemed to flow, were a fairly dispiriting lot.

'I have always felt very sad that I never wrote to Bryan Robertson to say how much I loved his piece on Raoul Dufy,' Edward said to me a few weeks before his death. I am repairing that omission here in reporting Edward's appreciation.

The ethos at the Slade was completely alien to Edward's artistic instincts. But throughout his years there he resolutely pursued his fascination with the female figure, which he considered, deep within himself, would one day be the key to unlock what he wanted his art to say at the deepest levels of expression. In the interests of his private studies, which were quite outside the Slade curriculum, Edward used to go to a bookstall in Soho to buy such publications as *Folies de Paris et de Hollywood* for 15 shillings.

By now I was beginning to understand how Edward's imagination filtered and sifted visual information, even from such tawdry sources, to bend to his own purposes. In copying the pin-up figures, he moved towards an insight into the ways in which the female figure could survive the tawdry treatment of photographers catering

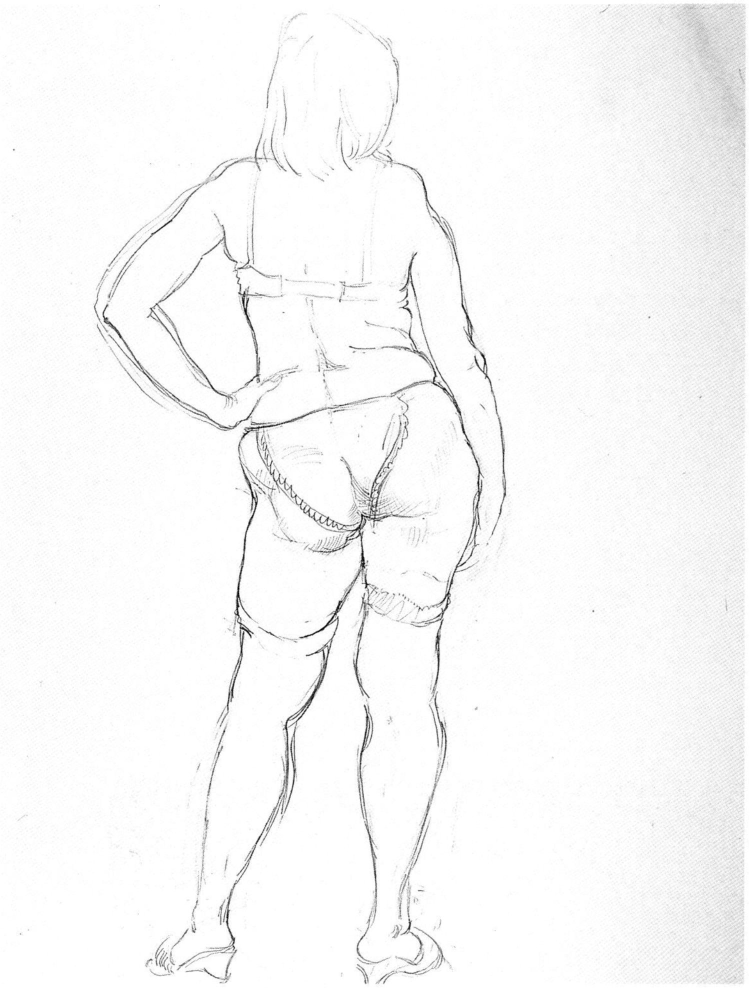

Girl in Frilly Underwear. Pencil, 30 × 22ins, 1959/60

for a public 'sense-shocked' by the crass visual bombardment of advertising, publicity and the mass media.

In his Baker Street flat Edward continued to copy, with an almost frenzied concentration, women in fishnet stockings, suspenders and elbow-length black gloves, women with small waists, big breasts and ample bottoms. To Ivor Uglow, he seemed to be ceaselessly driven by an inner dæmon to look as intensely as was humanly possible into the provocative and erotic movements of the female body.

At this stage Edward was using crayon and ink to draw, under the direct influence of Matisse's linear drawings – which, it should be pointed out, were not as widely appreciated by the British art public then as they are today.

Even a student life-style as demanding as that of metropolitan London could not use up all of Edward's phenomenal energy. He returned at the beginning of his second year with a renewed seriousness to his photography, combining it with his passionate interest in trains and railway stations. Apparently he began to spend hours with the timetable, planning unusual journeys round the capital to 'lost railway sites', and to scenes like the overgrown Crystal Palace High and Low Level Station, or to the remains he found of the Great Exhibition of Victorian times. Another of Edward's Slade contemporaries said to me that Edward was struggling with the temptation either to quit painting altogether, or find a technical college or polytechnic where he could study painting and photography – for even then, Edward was conscious of his inborn photographic skills.

Prudence Mackillop, his Favourite Model

Edward met Prudence Mackillop – always known as Prue – at the beginning of his second year at the Slade at a student party. She was starting her second year studying biochemistry at University College, London, a subject in which she eventually gained a PhD. They fell in love immediately and remained so for the rest of Edward's life.

Three years later they moved into a flat together in Fitzroy Street, over the premises of the well-known firm of skeleton repairers, Adam Rouilly, familiar to all London medical schools and students. Edward and Prue never forgot the pervasive sickly sweet smell which would emanate from the Rouilly premises when a fresh import of human bones from India was being sterilised to prepare skeletons for anatomy classes. One room in the flat they occupied was empty apart from a jungle of plants and a piano.

They were living here when they got married in the parish church. Though neither Prue nor Edward were Christians, it was a Church of England ceremony performed by the Reverend V. E. G. Kenna, one of Edward's godfathers, a retired naval chaplain and an authority on Cretan seals. The newly-weds lived, frugally but comfortably, on Prue's salary and Edward's allowance from his parents. They moved to their final flat in London in Camden Square when Edward was working for a printing firm, Balding & Mansell, and Prue was completing her postgraduate degree.

Prue's childhood and early life might not seem the ideal preparation for the role of wife to a struggling artist, but she adapted herself totally to that role; I have known few couples as happy in each other as Edward and Prue. Her father, a Highland Scot, was ambitious and intelligent, the seventh child of a soldier son of a gillie working on a Highland estate; he had escaped from his humble family origins through a scholarship to that centre of meritocracy, the Manchester Grammar School, and eventually became a member of the Government consular service. Prue was *his* seventh child.

The wandering early life Prue led with her family on the diplomatic circuit may well have been the reason for her fierce attachment to the studio home she and Edward eventually created in Somerset. The significant factor for Edward as an artist was that he had found his ideal model in his young wife. 'I was artistically besotted with Prue. She was a catalyst, a liberation for me,' he said later.

Literally hundreds of drawings he made of her, from the earliest days of their marraige, survive in the Marston Bigot archives. He drew her showing off the shape of her calf as she half-stood in high-heeled shoes on a kitchen chair. He sketched her wearing striped underwear from Frank's Pantie Bar in Shaftesbury Avenue, a shop specialising in lush lingerie. He modelled her in pink chalk on dark blue paper, and with a flesh-pink wash on white paper, standing her on the narrow mantelpiece of their Fitzroy Street flat so that he could have a better view of her legs, and he drew her reflected in a long mirror.

It was to Prue, he said, that he owed the artistic experience which gave him an unforgettable thrill of excitement, and confirmed his inner belief that he would one day paint nudes to compare in accomplishment with any being painted by his British or European contemporaries. He and Prue had taken a weekend in Paris to look at an exhibition of drawings of the late August Rodin. He said:

> I couldn't get over how beautiful the Rodin drawings were and on our return to London I immediately began to draw Prue and, suddenly, my hand went free, and I began to draw in a way I had never managed before in life classes. It was a breakthrough artistically at that moment for me, and a great promise for the future. The drawings were actually more like arabesques, and showed Prue sitting, leaning, always in high heels, but drawn with a line that if it was a little uncertain, was oh! so true and alive.

Prue became inseparable from Edward in people's memories of him at the Slade – indeed, from the moment they got together, everyone always thought of them as inextricably linked. Edward and Prue Piper.

Edward was keen on cars, and enjoyed nothing more wholeheartedly than driving Prue and his student friends round London at speed in his sunset grey Citroen Big 15, painted in a specialised paint which changed colour in differing lights, laughing aloud with pleasure at the way raindrops glowed purple in the rain against it. In some ways the Citroen Big 15 came to symbolise France for Edward. I sometimes had the fancy that the English part of Edward's character – the husband, father and friendly host at picnic parties at Marston Bigot – could belong nowhere else than in rural England. The artistic side of his personality, however, the side so passionately involved with the nude and latterly landscape, and so strongly influenced by the French painters he loved – Matisse, Renoir, Dufy, Derain, Monet and Ingres – could only be at ease in France.

Edward at this time also liked to borrow John Piper's Willys Jeep to drive to the coast, Prue sitting alongside him, flaxen hair blowing in the slip-stream, with friends in the back for impromptu picnics on a windswept beach or foreshore, sometimes as late as November. Edward, like most of the Pipers, did not just put up with Spartan conditions, but on occasions deliberately sought them.

All this student activity was extremely pleasant, but to his final day at the Slade Edward remained, he said, 'repressed and depressed'. He was retouching his Venice paintings in the big studio at Marston Bigot one day shortly before he died when he observed, quite out of the blue: 'I have come to believe that there is something I can only think of as "fantasy" which exists behind a figure or at the heart of a landscape view, which you cannot actually *see*, but which you must capture to make a painting worth looking at. It is possibly "the further" my teachers at the Slade were meaning when they said "Piper, you must go further".'

This undefined but real concept of 'the fantasy' in a painting was another topic which we promised ourselves we would revisit for the text for his voice-over commentary on his work; but there was never the time. In an essay on van Gogh, W. H. Auden says: 'Few painters read books and fewer can express in words what they are up to; Van Gogh is an exception.' To which Edward said 'Hear, hear'; though he did in fact read widely in art, so that one could sometimes find a clue to his thoughts through the literary references he made in discussion or conversation.

He once mentioned something Gertrude Stein had written on painting, which he thought had the ring of truth. I looked up the full quote, which goes thus: 'It is all so false, this idea that painters paint what they see, they use their eyes in order to paint what they *know*' (the emphasis is mine). The 'what they know' is perhaps what Edward meant when he referred to the 'fantasy' which can transform a painting from the ordinary to something animated and beautiful.

'A Good Creation, Unlike Anywhere Else'

With the arrival of their first child, Luke, in 1967, Edward and Prue decided it was about time to put down roots. They set about looking for a place they could make into a home and workshop, a place where a young photographer and graphics designer could make enough to keep his family, yet be left with enough time to pursue his ambitions of becoming a painter of nudes. They moved as systematically towards the choice of location as John and Myfanwy Piper had done some thirty-odd years earlier.

Edward's knowledge of the English counties was probably as thorough as that of any man in England, even before his travels and exploration of English towns, villages and countryside in pursuit of photographic subjects for the Shell county guides and in the course of journalistic assignments for glossy magazines. The couple ruled out the Home Counties as too urbanised and expensive. The Midlands? – too industrial; Lincoln? – no, they didn't like the way tax-loss farmers and agribusiness had bought so much property with the selfish intention of ensuring themselves exclusivity. Gloucestershire? – no, too 'horsey'; Devon and Cornwall? – too far from London for Edward's commercial sources of income. This left only Somerset or Wiltshire, with a slight bias by both Edward and Prue for the latter.

They and Luke were staying with friends at Corsham when they heard, late one evening, that an old Victorian laundry which had been converted into a house, was on the market. On impulse, they drove across Somerset that same night to look at it, their first view of it by the car headlights against a cloudy sky at midnight. It was a neglected building of simple design, its garden and surrounds knee-deep in a tangle of thistles, tall nettles and brambles.

But Edward and Prue were charmed by its location, its feeling of remoteness. To get to it, you turned off the Frome to Glastonbury main road, descended a fairly steep hill and soon turned right along a cart-track – and there was the house, standing secluded in a glade. They liked the sound of the stream which flowed powerfully

Euston Station. Etching, 7½ × 11ins, 1957

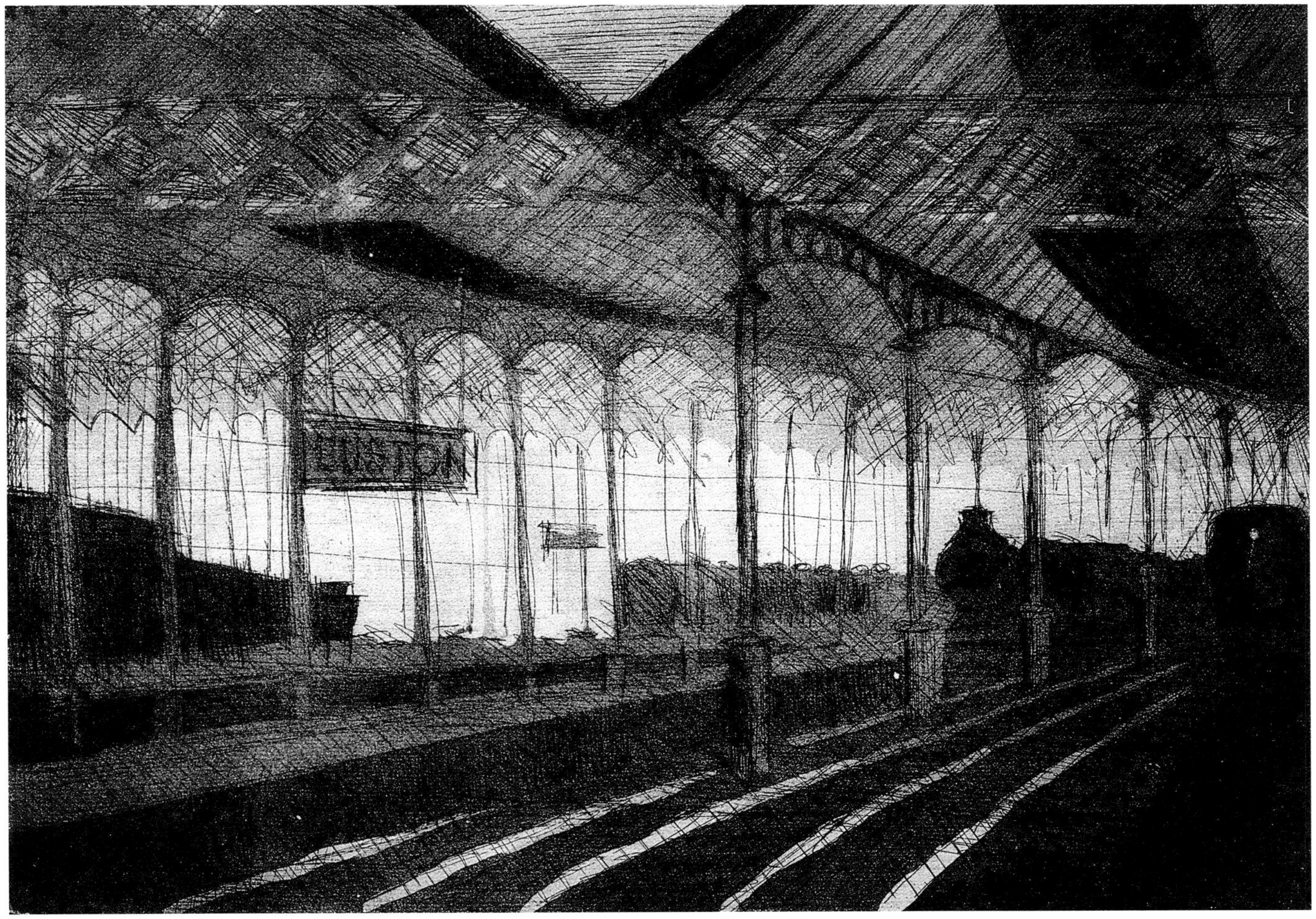

somewhere along a boundary of the neglected gardens. All they knew about the house, from the person who had told them about it, was that it had been built in 1869 in the mid-Victorian period to service the country seat and estate of the Boyle family, the Earls of Cork and Orrery.

The estate agents said the old laundry represented: 'a unique opportunity to buy a detached country property, 13 miles from Bath, 14 from Wells, and only two from the small working market town of Frome with its weekly cattle market, and a good rail service via Westbury to London. The property provides extensive views from its site on Cheese Hill across Marston Park and the surrounding countryside.' When Edward and Prue returned next morning to view it in daylight, they found the estate agent hadn't been exaggerating too much. You could look across fields which were probably much as Jonathan Swift had seen them when he had stayed at Marston House, family seat of the Boyle family, half a mile away. The couple were charmed by the splendid sweep of the Wiltshire escarpment, from the brow of the hill hiding the safari park of Longleat, past the historic site of a Carthusian monastery, Witham Friary, beyond a Piperish church in the middle distance – the parish church of Marston Bigot – out towards the great gardens of Stourhead with the folly, Alfred's Tower, in the far distance.

The house itself was rather forlorn, with cobwebbed windows, rusting hinges and crumbling boundary walls, having not been lived in for over three years. And Edward found the landscape round the house 'a bit tree-bare'; previous owners had chopped down trees in profligate fashion for firewood, and Dutch elm disease had accounted for others. However, the trees could be replaced; and Edward could see where he could place a small intimate studio with a superb view, while Prue could see how the gardens running down the hill and going to wilderness could be quickly reclaimed.

Both noticed the house had one rather strange but most welcome characteristic – that in the glade the sound of the traffic on the Frome–Glastonbury road was quite muted. They later discovered the old laundry had been built on the site of a large kennels for the pack of hounds with which the 9th Earl, Master of the Royal Buckhounds and Yeomanry ADC to Queen Victoria, had hunted the Quantocks. It was said that the glade had been chosen for the kennels because it provided some insulation against the sound of the baying of the hounds.

The kennels were demolished in 1869 to make way for the laundry; all that remained of them was one stretch of wall, beautifully weathered with red valerian growing out of it. Edward and Prue bought the old laundry at auction for £4,050 with money from an unexpected family legacy; this left them with about £200 in the bank to begin making the place habitable. They were, in fact, also given a quarter of an acre of a field, adjoining the house by the friendly neighbours – retired owners of a local bakery, who had once owned the old laundry – who felt the young Pipers had paid rather more than was warranted for the house.

The first thing Edward and Prue did was change the postal address from 'Old Laundry Cottage' to 'The Old Laundry, Marston Bigot', which describes the house with unusual felicity – Marston Bigot derives from the Old English *mersc-tun*, meaning a settlement in the marsh; and Bigot, meaning 'narrow-minded' in French, was the name of a clan of the Earl of Norfolk's family, the Earl Marshal of England who owned the land in the 12th century.

Edward drew the plans for turning the Old Laundry into a studio workshop and home. As is often the case with old houses, he and Prue made some unforeseen discoveries. On demolishing a gimcrack ceiling in the big downstairs room they found that it had the lofty roof typical of a Victorian laundry's drying-room, which meant it was easy for Edward to transform it into a spacious workroom and studio. They carried out most of the initial improvements to the house themselves, while at the same time beginning the creation of what became known to everybody as 'Prue's garden'; they spent days moving barrowloads of top soil, clearing weeds and big stones. Prue planted the long, sinuous hawthorn hedges.

The young Pipers had no conventional religious views. But they were 'green' before it became fashionable, and if they did pick up its political and social connotations, this was simply because these corresponded with their human values. Not surprisingly, they cultivated the garden and the orchards they planted, and the wilderness areas, completely organically and – once they owned it – they managed the large field adjoining the garden as it would have been before the advent of mechanised agriculture.

The design for the garden was largely dictated by the fall of the land, its natural features, and the impression made on it by previous occupants of the Old Laundry. Over the years they made a series of small gardens – micro-landscapes – which united to form one big garden landscape, serene and productive, naturally colourful and heavily scented with herbs. In the vegetable plots, herbs and wild flowers mixed with the large variety of vegetables, set off in what appeared to be random patches of big-petalled flowers and plants with large ornamental leaves – delphiniums, lilies, tall lupins, rudbeckias, giant scabious, peonies, acanthus and foxgloves – and, of course sunflowers, Mexican as well as the 'van Gogh' variety. For Prue grew these big splashy flowers because Edward liked to paint them in his nude studies.

Both Edward and Prue liked to see common weeds – dandelions, buttercups, ragged robin, comfrey and shaking grasses – growing in the garden, which had walls clothed in old-fashioned rambler roses, and tree stumps covered with honeysuckle. Two of the warmest images I carry with me of the Old Laundry are these: first, Edward unfolding to his full height to peer over an osier fence they had cut, peeping out from behind a black beekeeper's veil and protective clothing like a Martian; and Prue, with her shoulder-length flaxen hair, being followed by a gaggle of geese in one of the two orchards, with the apple trees in blossom.

You might have come across fat guinea fowl with their black, grey and white mosaic of feathers feeding with the flock of Dorset Horn sheep which the Pipers grazed for a friend; while the hen cotes sheltered Prue's Cuckoo Maran hens and the tall nettles by the stream hid the beehives. Eventually Prue's garden became, as they had always intended, a subject for Edward's brush, the highly popular *Garden at Marston Bigot* series.

One of the garden paintings I like best captures splendidly that brief period first thing in the morning when the first grey light of the English countryside is changing to the harsher chromatic light of morning. Almost all the garden paintings are in watercolour and pencil, where Edward used his 'reverse technique' of applying the colour first and the lines afterwards, to produce a particularly delicate quality, vivid and vibrant with light and movement.

His affection for Prue's garden shows through every touch of colour in the paintings; which may account for the fact that the art dealers handling Edward's paintings discovered a very ready sale for them. They were always pressing Edward to paint more, but he was not a man to paint to order – though no doubt had he lived, he would have returned often to Prue's garden as a subject.

For Edward, the Old Laundry was the centre of his close family life, a haven to which he could always return to savour in full the rhythm of the seasons, the pleasures of hospitality to friends while pursuing his artistic ambitions in what people usually thought of as an idyllic environment. It was Mark Girouard, the architectural historian and authority on the English country house for whom Edward frequently worked as a photographer, who described the Old Laundry with such complete accuracy when he said in his letter to Prue after Edward's death: 'The Old Laundry, it was such a good creation of yours and his, unlike anywhere else, but not at all self-conscious, and just really nice to be in.'

Piper Fireworks

Two features in the grounds of the Old Laundry exemplify in turn Edward's French sense of style, and his essentially English character. The French feature is a tall circular structure with an opening, a *gariott*, built by Edward using the dry-walling techniques typical of the original buildings used by French peasants and shepherds to stow their agricultural implements. The English feature is, of course, a croquet lawn.

You cannot move without coming across an example of Edward's practical skills, such as the fences for which he and Prue cut the osiers, walling, hedging. Nor were his skills confined to English rural crafts. When painting in northern Italy he admired some of the courtyards of the small villas in Siena. He sketched one, and on his return to Marston Bigot, used the sketch as a blueprint to build a Sienese courtyard of burnt yellow flat bricks, which Prue filled with large plant pots of tiger lilies, and pink and purple geraniums, and clematis. He added an aerial conservatory on the south side of the house in which Prue cultivated a fine Madresfield Court grape vine; he also built a rectangular pond in a corner of the ground floor conservatory which catches light reflections clearly and dramatically.

As he became increasingly financially secure through his growing following amongst the art public, he turned more seriously to his long-held ambition not only to *paint* landscapes, but actually to *create* his own personal landscape in the great field below the garden. He collected some heavy flattish stones, dug out during a road-widening scheme near Marston Bigot, to build a ha-ha, linking Prue's garden with the field. This time it was Prue who had an idea for the environment ahead of her husband. 'Can't we build a lake in the field?' she asked. 'Why not?' he replied, 'After all, it would cost no more than buying a new saloon car.'

They managed to buy the field, and building the lake seemed to be no sooner said, than accomplished. Edward studied from books the technicalities involved, and then drew a shape for the lake, with a small island in the centre to swim out to from the banks; he also staked out its curving shape so that a contractor could excavate its bed – later this would be filled with water from the underground springs situated on higher land.

Edward had the eye to have the lake dug out to varying levels so as to get the more subtle effects of light as it played across the water surface when ruffled by a breeze. He placed the lake – roughly one acre in size – in perfect relation to St Leonard's, the Anglican parish church of Marston Bigot where he now rests, and the great sweep of the escarpment. He and Prue together stocked it with roach, perch and carp, while Prue planted its edges and the surrounding field with wild flowers and grasses. She had collected the seeds herself, fox and cubs and yellow Welsh poppies from Pembrokeshire where the Piper families share a holiday cottage.

Edward took me to see the lake one morning.

'You know, we have planted plenty of white and yellow lilies round the edge. We are looking to the lake – as, in fact, we do with the garden – for a little bit of the magic of Monet's garden at Giverny. Water lilies and wild flowers in profusion here; great drifts of flowers in the garden,' he said. He then said with a rare flash of anger, one of the few I ever saw him display at the cruelty of his illness, 'I was happily making my own landscape so that I would have something to paint when I got too old to go charging up goat tracks in Spain looking for subjects.'

'Sorry!' he added quickly, 'Whatever else I have achieved with my lake, I have built a good stage for firework displays which you will be able to see from the garden and terrace of the Old Laundry.'

I think it must have been from one of the potters with whom Edward was friendly that I heard the following remark: 'Fireworks are instant, exuberant, exploding energy expressing itself in light and colour in the sky – somehow a natural extension of the character of Edward Piper.' And in truth Edward was an expert with fireworks, enjoying them in the way that some Old Masters like Rubens and the Italian court painters of the 16th century enjoyed them. He was also following directly in John Piper's footsteps.

John Piper was asked by Pains Fireworks to design a set-piece for the 1965 London Arts Festival, and he continued to act as artistic consultant to the firm for years, glad to find he could be paid for something he had done for so long for his family's pleasure at Fawley Bottom. Knowing Edward shared his love of fireworks, and out of respect for his practicality and ingenuity with mechanical things, too, it was logical for him to invite Edward to become a partner in the fireworks projects.

And when John considered he was too old to 'fire' displays for Pains, it was also natural for him to invite Edward to take over. For nine years Edward not only designed displays and fireworks, he did the graphics and layout for their annual sales catalogue and for publicity material. I asked John Deeker, the director of Pains Fireworks who worked closely first with John and then Edward, what he thought it was that an artist brought, which was special to fireworks. He replied that it was basically their ease and familiarity with patterns and colours; he also said:

> If you are an artist with a strong practical bent like Edward you quickly master an understanding of what fireworks can do in the way of making aerial patterns in the limited range of firework colours available – red, green, blue and white, and gold which is a mix of yellow and silver and a metallic white. Edward's jazz playing must also have given him an insight into how sounds can affect and change moods in musical firework displays. Primarily, the artist must have a real enthusiasm for fireworks, which Edward had in superabundance. And Edward instantly grasped the fact that the crux of any fireworks display is not the design of the fireworks, nor even the order in which you let them off; the important element is the actual timing of the individual components of a display. The entire psychology of a fireworks display is concerned with time, with building up an atmosphere of noise and visual spectacle, and generating excitement in a manner in which each spectator in the crowd becomes, briefly, a solitary individual, each enclosed in his own world in which time itself is suspended.

We were seated at the vermilion-painted table in the kitchen at the Old Laundry, almost underneath a round-faced eight-day clock which had once told the time in some provincial railway station. As a student, Edward had bought it at an auction of railway property. John Deeker caught my glance at the clock and added in emphasis, 'Time is everything. You know you have had a successful firework display when it seems to have lasted much longer, to the spectators, than it actually has in real time. You have created 'spectator time', as I hope you will experience yourself at the firework display here at the Old Laundry in a week or so.'

John Deeker was at the Old Laundry on the day I met

Reclining Girl. Pencil, 15 × 20ins, 1984

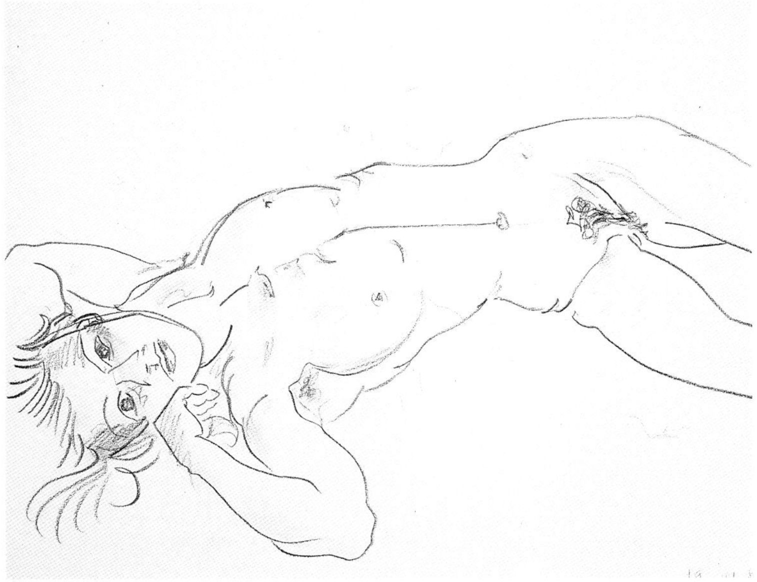

him, to liaise with Edward's sons, Luke and Henry, on the arrangements for this fireworks display which was to crown a big commemoration; this had been arranged so that Edward's friends, colleagues and neighbours would have the chance to take their leave of him with some formality. And indeed, at the commemoration on Saturday 9 June 1990, I was able to understand practically what John Deeker had explained so deftly.

In writing my notes on the discussion with John Deeker, it struck me that Edward would have had an instinctive reaction to fireworks, which transformed one into a solitary individual in the middle of the crowd. Several of his friends had said they occasionally saw him as rather a 'loner' in the Western film sense, and he did have a deep, courtly reserve into which he would sometimes withdraw, occasionally in anger, more often when he felt someone was touching on a subject he regarded as private. But a loner? I think Edward shared a trait one sometimes finds in the children of brilliantly accomplished parents. As Edward himself once said to me, such children have to create a space for themselves in which they can develop their individuality.

In his last few weeks Edward gave part of his remaining strength to designing, as artistic director, the annual firework display which would be the climax of the Fête Champêtre at Stourhead in July. He was hoping to supervise the firing over the three evenings himself, as he had in previous years, but as the ravages of illness weakened him further he decided to hand over to his chief assistant. The 1990 Fête had a Spanish theme, with visitors in fancy dress as bullfighters, itinerant Spanish friars, gypsies and Spanish ladies, all carrying large fans; there was even a bullfighter playing a pantomime bull.

Seated Girl, Back to Mirror
Pencil on grey Ingres paper, 13½ × 19½ins, 1985

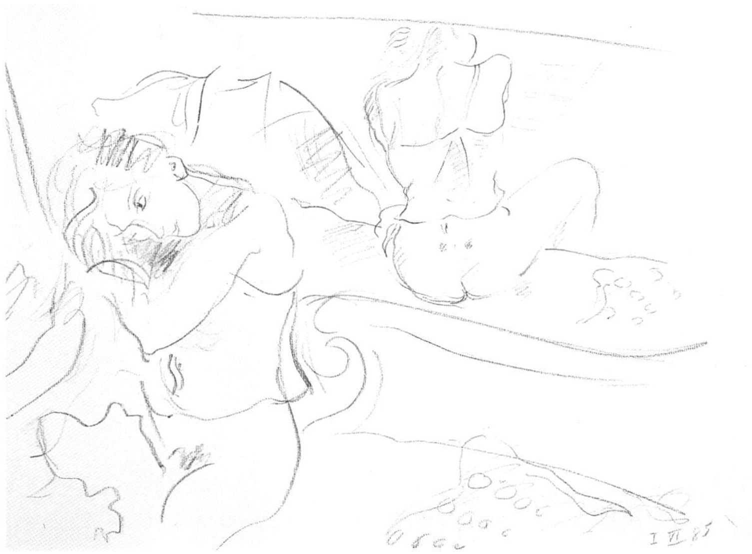

Edward was as much a perfectionist in fireworks as in other things, and I am sure it would have been in accordance with his wishes that the Stourhead display went off with precision and accuracy on all three evenings. The Spanish galleon sailed each evening, its silhouette outlined in glittering firework colours across the dark waters of the great Stourhead lake, illuminating the outline of the Greek temple folly on the hill which Edward had sometimes used as a backcloth for photographs of his nudes.

His assistant who helped to fire the display so efficiently was his younger son, Henry, by then twenty-one and a philosophy student at Sussex University.

Swan Song

In October 1990 the swanherd from the swannery at Abbotsbury on the Dorset coast came over to Marston Bigot to see if Edward's lake would provide a suitable home for two cygnets from the swannery. Every year the swannery finds homes for those cygnets which are unlikely to survive the winter in the exposed conditions in the estuary which houses the swannery, but which may do so in more sheltered lakes inland. Abbotsbury only let susceptible cygnets go after interviewing their prospective owners and ensuring they can provide a good environment for them.

The swanherd found Edward's lake an admirable home. Prue drove to Abbotsbury, to return with two white swan cygnets – and these were joined in November by an exotic black swan, presumably from another Somerset lake or river. The cygnets settled in, and the lake looks today as if it has been there forever, only waiting for Edward to paint the landscape in which he placed it.

The Basket of Frivolity

One way of approaching Edward's nudes is by looking through a large wicker basket in the small studio at the end of the gallery on the first floor of the Old Laundry: gold dancing shoes with impossibly high wedge heels made by Edward himself, flowered silk Japanese kimono, plastic bangles and lime-green fishnet tights.

It is a basket of frivolity.

The basket and its contents indicate the significance Edward attached to his relationship with his female models – the props were an essential element in 'the studio techniques' he used with his models, reminding one or two of them of a film director. In some ways his intention could be described as trying to make a 'star' of the model in a nude study. He aimed to persuade the model – whether a young mother from the market town of Frome, or an art student from Glastonbury earning a little cash to supplement a government educational grant, or an experienced professional model from Bath – to put aside her everyday persona.

The small studio, designed and furnished by Edward with care, unquestionably presents itself as an artist's workroom, but one with a touch of the boudoir. You would anticipate that any artist using it would create nudes as seductive as 'the superfine beauties' of Ingres' *Le Bain Turc*. On occasion, Edward liked to use Ingres' voluptuous line as a stimulus for his own drawing, just as an author may read a passage from a favourite book before settling down at the word processor.

Once you appreciated that everything in the cluttered studio was included deliberately, you could grasp something of the scrupulous psychology within which Edward co-operated with his models to create the tenderness and eroticism of his nudes. Take the three mirrors in the studio: Edward said he never tired of studying the shapes and curves of his models in these mirrors. They were ingeniously placed in relation to each other so that a model could see her figure in all three mirrors simultaneously and see her body from angles she had never seen it from before.

Few artists can have been as familiar and versed in classical nude poses as Edward – from the generous poses of Rubens; the frank, sometimes cruel ones of Schiele and those of his mentor Gustav Klimt, who focused gently on the erogenous zones; to those of Dufy which were affectionate and friendly.

Edward quite often asked his nudes to arrange themselves in angular variations of well-known poses, for example standing on tiptoe like a Degas ballet dancer, but with legs too slightly apart for comfort, or the body swivelled tautly to the window; all with the intention of making them acutely conscious of their body. What was surprising to the more experienced of his models was that in the finished nude study the pose appeared as one of grace and charm.

It wouldn't be right to say that Edward had a 'set piece' approach to his preparations for a modelling session, but he always knew exactly what he was doing in even the smallest detail. He would sometimes spend time walking round the garden while the model picked flowers, discussing his ideas for a nude. On other occasions he might take her into the big drying-room studio to listen to his jazz records, or would play jazz on his piano, or invite her to lunch and a glass of wine with Prue in the spacious kitchen of the Old Laundry.

On entering the studio a model would find that even

on summery days, Edward had lit a fire to make the studio as warm as a hot-house. While he mixed his paints or prepared the paper on his easel, he would encourage her to make use of things from the basket of frivolity – picture hats with ostrich feathers like those in a Gainsborough portrait, showy ear-rings – and add thicker make-up, admire herself in the mirrors or parade about in the kimono and wedge shoes he had made.

Edward looked at his models with a direct and concentrated observation, moving round the studio himself to change his angle of view, so that it was often quite some time before he began to draw or paint. He would maybe ask a model to move across the studio, then, suddenly, like Rodin when sketching models, briskly command her to stop and hold a movement which had caught his imagination. Edward once said:

> I know how I always looked at my models; it was in no way threatening or manipulative and certainly not exploitative, but there was at the same time nothing detached or impersonal in my attention, for I needed the model to be not just aware of her sexuality, but rejoicing in it. I wanted to see the old Eve responding in the flesh so that I could get a feeling of sensuality on the paper, naturally, almost as if the sensuality flowed through the brush on to the paper.

In the studio he was always looking for a feeling of heightened sensuality, and he would sometimes strip naked himself to paint, partly because of the high temperature in the room, but principally as a logical step towards putting himself, as he said, on the same plane as his model. His wish was to make his model feel that she was herself participating actively with the artist to produce the qualities he considered essential in his nudes – and, as I discovered from his models themselves, often succeeding in doing so.

When looking through a whole series of his nudes, you have the impression in many studies that the model looks impassively beyond you, that she is exchanging glances with the artist, and with a strong suggestion of conspiracy. One of the more perceptive features I read on Edward and his work was by Tony Warner in *The Artist* (January 1989); one point that he made was that 'Edward Piper's young women were naked, or half-naked; never nude, for that implied a stationary quality, a sense of posing, and being looked at as a professional model.' He also said: 'Edward Piper's young women have the feel of glimpsing one's neighbour's daughter, perhaps with a punk hair-do, undressing before a lighted window. A *frisson* of forbidden but remote eroticism is always present.'

Edward worked carefully over the years to achieve the 'frisson effect' Tony Warner mentions. He sometimes achieved it in nudes drawn with a line so spare as to make the study border on the abstract. But each of Edward's nudes, even in his slightest drawings, has an identifiable personality of her own. Edward always had a most loving respect for his models, which transferred to the nude studies themselves.

From the earliest awakening of his obsession with the female form – the days of his schoolboy collages of pin-ups, his visits to Soho to observe the play of crude lights on the flesh of strippers, to his copies of the *erotica* of the 16th-century mannerist painters of the School of Fontainebleau – Edward was more interested in the body shape than the faces of women. He regarded every female form as having its own distinctive personality.

'I can recognise every model I have ever drawn by the individual signature of her body, and can do so even from an arabesque, just by the turn of an ankle or line of a shoulder,' he said. And though I scarcely needed it, Edward gave me further evidence of his outstanding visual memory when we were going through some of his Matisse-like drawings to choose illustrations for the art book on his work, by identifying each of the models by name.

Edward has been criticised by some art people for his facility, those who distrust his swift attack and easy, assured line. They were doing no more than echo across the years the criticism Edward had first endured at the Slade, and once again they were, in Edward's view, looking for signs of '*graft*', of meticulous and painstaking technique in his nudes, which isn't apparent, so enhancing their joy and decorative quality.

In reply, Edward said emphatically, 'There *is* graft, I *do* work at my paintings, excavating a figure or landscape thoroughly before getting down to draw or paint, but if you can *see* the graft, I have failed, I have lost what Monet called 'instantaneity' and I call immediacy, the seizing of the fleeting moment, which can give a painting magic.'

Edward could, as a matter of fact, complete a nude, or landscape, in anything from a few minutes to four hours, always painting as fast and with as much freedom as he could muster. He employed a variety of techniques, some traditional, some unexpected. He usually applied the colour first and the lines afterwards, thus reversing the normal technique, a procedure which requires self-confidence and judgment. He used a range of differing combinations of material to obtain a myriad of effects – watercolour and pencil for delicacy, for example, acrylic and black ink for the dramatic.

He sometimes used thick strokes, allowing the lines of the figure to sweep across flat patches of colour in recollection of Matisse and Dufy. He showed me one painting of a nude contoured by an especially gossamer-like play of light which reminded me that Renoir, another painter who sought immediacy, insisted that his wife should choose as housemaids girls with skin that reflected the light, so that he could use them as models.

One morning in the big studio at the Old Laundry Edward placed a series of sketches and more detailed drawings of Prue on one of the studio's tall filing cabinets. These drawings revealed the free if still underconfident line he had discovered a quarter-century earlier. And they depicted the whole woman, including a frank drawing of the vulva.

In response to a comment I made on this, Edward said: 'I can remember being resentful that you could look through art and find any number of wonderfully formalised drawings of eyes and noses from medieval times onwards. You could always discover great ways of perceiving eyes or noses as an artist, too – but try to find a well-drawn vulva, and you have had it.'

His resentment went back in time to the days when he bought girlie magazines. He then inked in the outlines of the vulva in the air-sprayed pubic hair of the pictures. It was many years before he discovered, when on a photographic assignment in Ireland, that the 'good vulva' to which he aspired was to be found occasionally in Catholic country churches in the carvings of *Shela na gig*, a Celtic fertility figure.

References to the vulva in paintings are indeed rare, as he asserted. But Edward told me that *he* held as a belief in life that no part of the human body should remain hidden, either by a Cranach kerchief or through a hairless *mons veneris*, as in many paintings of the Middle Ages. The whole should be taken as naturally in art as it appeared in reality.

Edward had in his art library books of etchings of the School of Fontainebleau (which I have always found to have a chilling sensuality) and on one occasion I found him in the big studio with a volume of these etchings open on a table before him, from which he had been copying two of them.

In his own paintings Edward was light years away from the cruel sensuality of the Mannerist images. He had been copying the etchings in order to study through drawing them certain lines that caught his attention. He told me he found something interesting in the lines illustrating the responsiveness of the woman in one, something in the arch of the back, which he had observed when drawing young Somerset couples in the sexual act in his small studio. There was nothing salacious in Edward's studies of the female figure. He thought the artificial eroticism and faked sensuality of soft-porn advertising and publicity completely coarsened natural sexual emotions. He referred more than

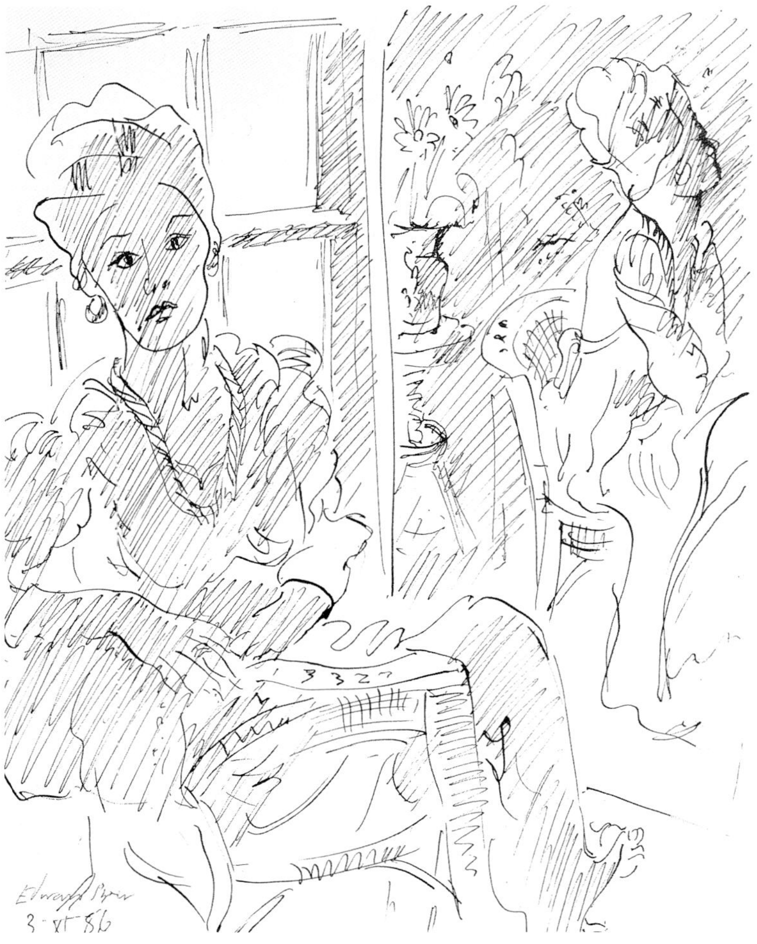

Turbaned Girl and Mirror by Window
Pen and ink, 15½ × 12½ins, 1986

once to his admiration for the way Gustav Klimt had turned, in desperation, to paintings of the female form as a universal metaphor for the hope of continuity of European civilisation in the face of the slaughter of her young men on the Western Front in World War I.

I believe that his unsparing search for understanding of the female figure was to enable him to express, through increased aesthetic authority in his nudes, some of the inner truths he believed in, confronting the sexual imperialism of the *Playboy* attitude with his own natural joy and delight in his nudes.

Nick Hankinson is the director of the Eye Gallery in Bristol, which hosted a major exhibition of Edward's paintings and photographs to mark his 50th birthday; during a discussion of Edward's work Hankinson made these observations:

> Edward Piper was totally fascinated by the sexuality, sensuality and eroticism of the female body. He never spoke of figure painting or drawing, always of his painting of nudes, and I think he always painted women naked as opposed to nude in the sense described by Kenneth Clark in *The Nude*.
>
> But Edward painted his nudes with such sensitivity and love that almost everyone who bought one of his nudes through the Eye Gallery returned later to say how much they loved having his paintings on their walls. His paintings lift the soul, and when you own them, you find over time things in them which make you love his paintings.

I am not sure Edward would ever have theorised about his nudes with any intimacy, but I valued the insights of one of his most intelligent and 'artwise' models, Jacqueline Anstey-Jones, herself a former Slade student and painter. She and her husband, Benny Sirota, a potter and art teacher, became friends with Edward and Prue Piper, and out of her admiration for his painting she accepted an invitation to model for him.

Talking with her in the small studio after Edward's death, I suggested that Edward contrived to turn the modelling platform into a small theatre stage.

She said, 'Perhaps so, but the professional relationship Edward imaginatively built up with a model was anything but theatrical. It was human and sexual, the lovemaking was on the paper, in the eyes, in the colouring he used and in the dialogue he carried on with a model during a painting session.'

Brian Thomas, Edward's companion on the last painting trip before his death, to Malaga and Granada, owns one of Edward's most accomplished *Flower and Nude* studies. He showed it to me in his house near Bath and commented: 'It's in no way sensational, and the placement of the large flower in relation to the genitalia simply sings for me.'

It seemed a natural remark for a man who used to be principal bass singer at Glyndebourne, and whose firm in Frome has printed some of the best of Edward's more recent work. I told him what Jacqueline Anstey-Jones had said, and he nodded agreement. 'It could be like that when I rehearsed songs with my female accompanist. We made love through the music. Isn't there always something sexual at the centre of the creative act?'

A *Guardian* reader himself, Edward was surprised that his pictures did not receive more criticism from feminists. After all, he shows woman as unassertive, dreamy, waiting to be fulfilled. But he claimed never to be manipulative, never to paint his models as sex objects.

One or two galleries where his work was exhibited did endure protests from members of the public, and they sometimes responded by putting aside the painting criticised. What usually caused the anger was the frank representation of the vulva. To Edward, who knew that his view of the body as a whole was far from universal, the censorious reaction was not unexpected and did not perturb him at all.

The Beaux Arts Gallery in Bath gave the first exhibition of Edward's work after his death, in November 1990. The owner of the Beaux Arts, Reg Singh, wrote an appreciation of Edward Piper in *The Independent* (13 May 1990), which was a thoughtful and intelligent measure of Edward as man and artist; in it, he said:

> Edward Piper's paintings have none of the austere or foreboding qualities of his father's. They are light, both in touch and mood. Often unapologetically frivolous, the tone and palette are more French than English. His nudes are fun, they relax or 'display' with a scarf or fan, never self-conscious or coy, a rare thing in English painting. His models radiate a *joie de vivre*, they drape themselves carelessly over chairs or sofas, or abandon themselves to self-admiration in a mirror, surrounded by flowers, plants and – always – sunlight.

How much Edward's continuing obsession with the nude was due to the fact that this was one area of painting which his father had not colonised is hard to say. John Piper did sketch some nudes, particularly in the early 1950s, when he painted and sketched a group of standing female figures against ruined buildings, *Nudes at Wroxeter*, and made a series of life drawings, sketching a seated girl, one leg tucked under the other, with a thick, bold line.

But the figure was not John Piper's primary area of observation. Drawings from his sketch-book of 1971 include those of a girl wearing high-heeled boots of a style that would have appealed to Edward, the figure seen from several angles, including upside-down, the heels of her boots waving in the air, but these are done with a far less assured touch than he brought to architecture or landscape. He had given far less study to the nude than Edward, so that while Edward's nudes are seductive John Piper's are not. 'John has done figures, but he hasn't the same natural freedom as Edward developed,' Myfanwy Piper said after Edward's death, confirming my own view.

Perhaps I can leave the last word on Edward's nudes to his elder son, Luke, now twenty-three, who at the time of his father's death was helping to organise photographic safaris in Tanzania. In some notes he prepared for me Luke wrote:

> My father's paintings have always been part of my life, and I love his nudes, though I suppose I may have found it difficult sometimes at school and in the world beyond Marston Bigot, the world where sex and nudity are often taboo.

It is always something I have taken for granted, growing up in an atmosphere where it is all a natural part of life. I have listened at the Old Laundry to endless discussions on when art is art and soft-porn is what it is, but it all seems a bit academic and precious to me.

What I do know for certain is that the mass media world – of magazines, many films and bestseller books – makes sex ugly and impersonal, against which my father's nudes react strongly. His nudes have never been awkward for me to accept, no matter how provocative the pose or how much on the borderline of the erotic or even pornographic.

The Piper Girl

Edward was a romantic. He gave his women feminine allure: he made them attractive. In the words of Jacqueline Anstey-Jones: 'He painted you as you would like to be. He had no problem finding models – people enjoyed posing for him.'

I looked through thousands of his drawings and paintings, for not only did he paint every day of the year, he kept his work, too, whether he felt it was successful or not. He could learn from his mistakes, he said, as well as from the drawings that still pleased him years later.

He liked to draw girls with long hair, long legs and taut buttocks, who looked lithe and young. There is arguably an Edward Piper type, but it never became a cliché; each drawing was subtly different from others on the same theme. As already discussed, it was Prue, his wife, who released his ability to paint the nude when they were students together. 'I never had to explain anything to Prue from the beginning,' he told me, 'she had an uncanny instinct for the kind of collusion I need to have with my models. She taught me the trick of perceiving the artistic relationship as 'subject and self' and not 'object and other'. Through her, my work acquired its own *imprimatur.*'

Reading back through the notes I made of interviews with a number of Edward's models – all women, he hardly ever painted men, because the male figure did not interest him as a painter – I was struck by a word that kept recurring in their descriptions of Edward, a word I didn't expect: they called him innocent. Plainly they were not implying that he was naïve or ingenuous, either.

They were speaking of the generous kindness of his nature, the sympathy that made it possible for them to discuss any topic in the world with him. Naturally I wondered where the boundaries were drawn, and here there was unanimity: the relationship was not physical, however intense the artistic experience.

I think that here one can allow the models to speak for themselves.

Jay

Jay provided me with a cameo description of Edward's approach to a modelling session.

> We would take some time settling down to work, picking flowers in Prue's garden, as we worked out what we would do in the session. Edward would decide on something and many times between the garden and the studio he would have a fresh inspiration and we would finish up doing something quite different.
>
> I used to bring clothes, a red dressing-gown, a bit of knitting I was doing at the time, in fact, anything feminine, and sometimes the things I brought ended up in the painting. In the studio I had to keep moving about and Edward would say, suddenly, 'That's it', and I would stop in the middle of a movement.
>
> It took quite a while for Edward to know me artistically and then he did what seemed to me fiddly drawings and he would gradually take longer and longer to produce exactly what he wanted. I have sometimes spent a whole day posing with a mask, sometimes he would show me how something small like a woolly leg warmer changed my shape.

Susan

Susan was not a professional model, but had attended art school; when she married she left teaching, and became a designer of textiles and stained glass. It was through her husband, who played jazz with Edward, that she became a friend of Edward and Prue.

In her interview she emphasised Edward's 'exuberant delight' in her nakedness, and recalled how on a hot summer's day they played in the garden at Marston Bigot with a water sprinkler as a relief from posing indoors in the studio – both naked, as unself-consciously as children.

I had the impression from her that Edward enjoyed what the American critic Theodore Roszak called 'a certain enchantment with organic display and pleasure, a celebration of animal nakedness'. Susan put it more simply, in words Edward would probably have preferred to Roszak's description:

> I think Edward was wonderfully unafraid of the human body and had the character to be free in a way one hopes will become the order of the day sometime in the future.
>
> When he talked about painting the genitalia, frankly you weren't embarrassed, especially when you knew how he detested what he called the hurtful masquerade of sexuality you got in the more sophisticated of the *Playboy* style magazines.

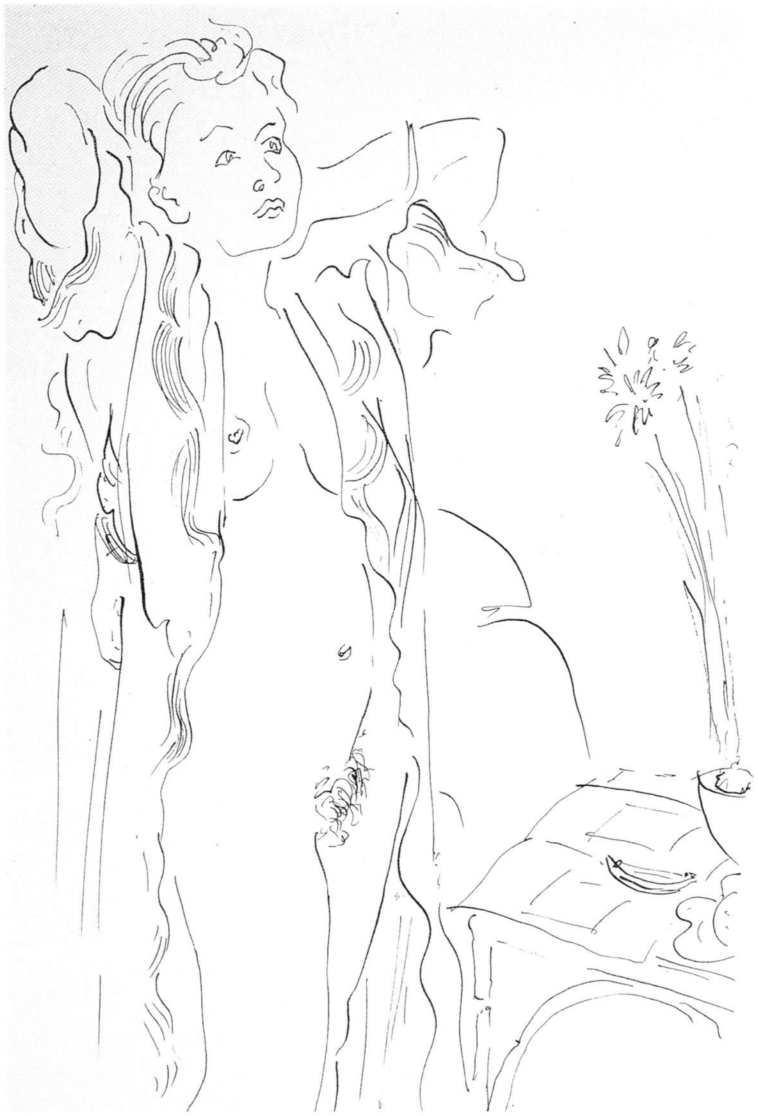

Girl in Silk Dressing Gown
Pen and ink on blue/grey Ingres paper, 18 × 12ins, 1987

Kate

Kate was the young model Edward chose to take to France when he was looking for ambiences beyond the confines of Marston Bigot in which to paint a series of nudes. He recalled that his father in his early years had always resisted pressures by people like Clive Bell, of the Bloomsbury set, to go to France to paint. 'JP always felt that it was somehow wrong for an English painter to slip away into what he described as a foreign pleasure-world to paint – though in saying that I am not implying that his attitude influenced me, at least, not directly.'

When he showed me the Nice series painted with Kate, Edward said: 'I don't know what gave me the idea to go to France, but it was possibly a vote of confidence in myself, a feeling that I had reached a point in my art where I could paint in Matisse and Dufy country.'

He thought he had found in Kate the model he needed to paint in France, setting her languor and fresh youth against the bright and indolent opulence of a Mediterranean seafront hotel. The Nice series with Kate has a radiance and optimism flowing from the model's relaxed *joie de vivre*, and captured by an Edward Piper filled with confidence in himself, painting with superb economy of line and sure sense of colour.

What did Kate herself think of the experience?

> We talked all the time he was painting, and I have never talked to any man as I talked to Edward. We had long discussions, not around but actually quite directly concerned with such things as voyeurism and sexuality.
>
> Everything was said by Edward with a sort of innocence, maybe because he was trying to get clear in his own imagination what these things are really about so that he could handle them better in his painting. I particularly remember the gentle way he persuaded me to put on extra thick make-up, simply because he was curious to see how its effects could alter my features.

Diane

Diane is a professional model – and she is the model in the short video Nick Hankinson commissioned to show Edward at work painting nudes and also a landscape alongside Clifton suspension bridge, for an exhibition of his work called *The First Fifty Years*, at the Eye Gallery in Bristol in 1988. She is a long-legged model with tawny hair and sea-green eyes; she used to stay at the Old Laundry for weekend painting sessions:

> Though he was making nude studies I would often actually *put on* clothes in the studio, clothes I could never wear outside, Edwardian hats and feather boas, enormously tall, high-heeled shoes, all of which were meant by Edward to change the shape and pattern of my body.
>
> I felt I knew my body much better after I had posed for Edward, chiefly because he showed me how to know it from every angle. He would emphasise the chest or ribline with cushions, or get you to pose between mirrors arranged to create reflections in several directions.
>
> I must say that, although I am an experienced model, I could never think of a pose Edward didn't know. And he was always talking to you, often about the differences between art and pornography, and things like the way the body changed its contours, as he said, quite astonishingly in changing lights.

Jacqueline Anstey-Jones

The following interview with Jacqueline Anstey-Jones is given in a 'question and answer' style because I think that is the best way to convey her beautifully vivid and perceptive description of modelling with Edward Piper. She is a former fine arts student at the Slade, a painter herself, and a writer on arts and crafts. She knows the art and craft world of the West Country through her husband who is a potter, and her partner in a gallery in the cathedral city of Wells.

Jacqueline was the model for one of Edward's most striking nude studies, *Girl in a Red Jacket*, a provocative pose owing something to Klimt. I interviewed her in Edward's 'basket of frivolity' studio:

You are a painter yourself. Was this a help in posing for him?
Oh, yes, indeed.

You posed for him here, in this studio?
In darkest winter his studio was a haven. Edward would have had the fire burning for some time so the studio was always very warm.

He created the atmosphere studiously. Did you think it a good idea?
It was certainly special for me, sitting in front of mirrors in flowing garments and silk stockings and things like that – all rather reminiscent of 'the superfine beauties' of Le Bain Turc sometimes. This made me feel feminine, womanly and joyful, and all really quite over the top. I enjoyed being looked at by the artist, enjoyed participating in a piece of art.

Did you choose the poses? Or did Edward?
Edward usually chose them, but having been on both sides of the easel I knew that every pose Edward used had its classical roots, and we would discuss them. This is a bit Bauhaus, this rather Klimt, or a Matisse pose. As I sometimes changed my hairstyle, so the names of the schools from which Edward was drawing his inspiration would change – when my hair was in a short style, for example, we tended to talk about the German school.

The conversation was never dull for a minute.

Did you have a routine when you came into the studio?
In a way. Edward would be fussing around the studio, getting his paints ready, and I would take off what I was wearing and put on the silk kimono and begin to feel myself changing from housewife, mother, career woman – from a Head woman into a Body woman.

Did he talk to you when painting?
Edward talked all the time, sometimes saying 'Oh, it's too difficult, I can't do it.' He would groan about the impossibility of it all, and the struggle. However, there seemed to be opposing forces at work – one was filled with an artist's response to things: 'Look how beautifully the sunlight from the window moves across the rug, the colour tones', he would say, seeing it all clearly; while at the same time he struggled with a feeling of underconfidence in his practical skills as a painter to get it down on paper.

Did he work fast?
Very fast. Much of the time was spent in finding the pose he wanted and then moving flowers or a pottery jug to just the right place. Once satisfied, he would take a long, long look. He would then block in the colour, just get the brush and go. He could do five paintings in a day when things went right.

You liked the way he approached his relationship with a model in the studio?
As a painter I knew the relationship could make a painting special, and with Edward, posing gave one a sense of baring a mystery, of co-operating in a relationship to make a piece of art, and the fancy dressing-up was all surprisingly innocent and perfectly natural as a preliminary to the painting. It all helped to give Edward a sense of inner security to enable him to paint.

What do you think is special about his paintings?
They are alive, physically alive, and I think Edward enjoyed the female body in a way that was never remotely voyeuristic so that his paintings have an innocence, a deep pleasure in living. I know that after a painting session he always made me feel that I had made a vital contribution to what was happening in his paintings.

Pop Art Time

In his mature period Edward felt no compulsion to paint on a large scale, believing that what he had to say could be said in a canvas as small as two feet by three feet. But Edward was always ready to change his views on his art, particularly when he felt that, as far as *he* was concerned, he had exhausted a subject's aesthetic potential. You cannot even say that he would never have returned to large compositions such as the giant 'Sharon Tate' painting of female figures in startling red outline in pin-up poses, which hangs in the main studio at Marston Bigot.

The painting belonged to the 1960s when Edward

was prominent in the pop art movement, producing some work as fine and enduring as any inspired by the movement. I do not think it was any accident that this was, perhaps, the only time in his career that his work chimed with a fashionable trend.

Richard Hamilton, a writer on pop art, defined its criteria: Popular (designed for a mass audience), Transient (short-term solutions), Expendable (easily forgotten), Low cost (mass-produced), Young (aimed at youth), Witty, Sexy, Gimmicky, Glamorous, Big Business. The emphasis – that art should be less exclusive and instantly pleasing to people without any art training – was always near to Edward's heart.

To what extent he would have subscribed to Richard Hamilton's other criteria in his later years, is again a subject only for speculation. Edward himself wrote in a catalogue note accompanying some of his pop art paintings in an exhibition:

> My recent work is the result of many drawings (and photographs) of one or two models and, more recently, of drawings I have made from all kinds of photographs. I have also gained from looking with great care at nudes in art, Cranach, Rubens, the late drawings of Rodin, Matisse (especially his collages), and Bill Brandt's photographs of the nude.
>
> I am involved with the actual business of painting, and try, while giving my images of the nude a life of their own, to make them part of a balanced and coherent surface pattern in which area has its descriptive role as well as being an integral part of that pattern. I find that as a particular painting progresses, this sort of balance can only be achieved by a series of visual hunches.

The nudes of his pop art period in both paintings and collages were outlined with firm precision. One painting of Prue looking at her reflection in the mirror, her flaxen hair set off by orange, pink and apricot colours is as good as anything in Edward's pop art portfolio, a composition softly lit with a tender affection that never slips into the sentimental.

Another of his pop-art works, a frieze of seven girls, was in an international exhibition at the Galeria Milano in Milan in *The London Under-40* show in 1966. An Italian art critic said of the frieze, with its easy jazzy rhythms: 'Edward Piper's nudes in brilliant colour steer a middle course between an odalisque and a pin-up. What gives individuality to the images is that they form part of a gentle, flowing motif in which each feature has a descriptive role.' This suggests that for the Italian, Edward had brought off one of his 'visual hunches'.

It was also in 1966 that Edward's work was on exhibition in America for the first time, with other young British artists – Terry Setch, Brian Yale, Norman Toynton, Tom Phillips and Richard Allen, among others. Roland Penrose, friend and biographer of Picasso, said the groups of British painters revealed a great variety in methods, but the message they had in common was a vigorous desire to communicate emotionally through their paintings. He added: 'Edward Piper brings a lightness of touch and boldness of colour to his compositions, which are lyrical odes to girls, a theme that colours our lives traditionally and yet with him is forever being celebrated with delight.'

Elegant as the Roland Penrose praise is, it does not suggest any of the meticulous application Edward brought to his pop art creations. It took him many hours to maintain an exact distinction between female flesh and background in the 'hard edge' techniques he was using. In this period, Edward's main inventiveness in pop art nudes went into the colouring, which was often somewhat strident yet without losing its great charm, largely through some surprising harmonies.

The six silk-screen prints that were commissioned by the Marlborough Gallery in 1970 on the recommendation of the artist Robert Melville – also an authority on Picasso – represented the apogee of Edward's work as a pop art painter. Edward himself regarded the silk-screen prints as his farewell to pop art, considering he had followed this direction as far as he felt it would go.

The prints are of collages of outstanding skill and ingenuity. Like those of Matisse, the master collagist, they are never static. The lines are graceful and vibrant, and the counter-positioning of bright colours gives them a luminous quality, especially evident in the figure of the long-haired blonde, whose tanned body contrasts with her lacy vest, clipped from a doily, and her high-heeled shoes of rippled silver.

All the six girls share a sense of litheness and delight. A slim redhead stands in full spotlight, theatrically posed as if at the end of a dance. In three collages Edward makes use of marbled paper background. A figure in burnt orange, head flung back, kneels as if against a curtain. The most slender of the posing figures set against a vivid blue background was, in fact adapted from a postcard of nudism on the Isle of Levant.

The whole series has a note of affectionate comedy. The pubic hair of the girl who stands in her orange peep-toe shoes and green beads against a blue marbled background is made from newsprint, discreetly trimmed. That in itself is a visual joke, since Picasso and Braque, pioneers of *papiers collés*, used newsprint in the shape of guitars and shadows to change the texture of a picture.

It is astonishing to think that these decorative prints had no great sale in 1970; though like much of Edward's work, they may well have been ahead of their time. Certainly they show how Edward had perfected a highly disciplined technique which in less skilful hands can look simplistic or boring.

The True Jazzman

Looking at Edward's work, you feel the constant rhythms of jazz, so much a part of his life, are never far from his paintings, both his nudes and his landscapes, and especially in the best of his pop art work. In the Nice series of paintings, with young Kate as his model, you actually feel that she is listening to jazz, perhaps something played by the jazz pianists Edward loved – Errol Garner, Art Tatum, Fats Waller, or maybe a piece played by his greatest jazz love, Earl Hines.

Even as students in London, Edward at the Slade and Prue at University College, the young Pipers always had a piano in their flat. A piano was a necessity of life for Edward. The one he kept in the drying-room studio at the Old Laundry was a Weber, an Edwardian pianola with a fat body which had once held a piano roll mechanism, and had stood in the saloon bar of *The Bear* pub at Holwell in rural Somerset. My last memory of Edward is of him strumming *Georgia Brown* while we talked of pop art, just before his death.

The jazz band with which Edward played jazz keyboard for years always comprised a mixed social group. Mike Henning was a physicist, who played trumpet: what Edward brought to the band, he said, was not just a good technique, but energy, verve and enthusiasm. The band played gigs regularly round Somerset pubs on music nights, and Ron Weldon, another trumpeter – and husband of novelist Fay Weldon – said a 'pub gig' always had more excitement when Edward was playing. Weldon was not the only one with this feeling: 'Edward's exuberance always gave a gig a "night-out" feeling; and whatever time the band got back to the Old Laundry Prue would have made something fabulous to eat, Danish pastries or a meat paté,' said Neil Mantell, the rural studies teacher, who played harmonica and sang with the band.

Edward grew up in a home where classical music was appreciated, and music, in fact, provides another of the shadowy parallels between the lives of the Piper families, John and Myfanwy at Fawley Bottom, and Edward and Prue at the Old Laundry. John Piper played piano with an amateur dance band in the 1920s, though usually in staider settings than Edward's pub gigs.

What sort of music did Edward's jazz band play? According to Edward himself: 'Nothing jazz pompous,

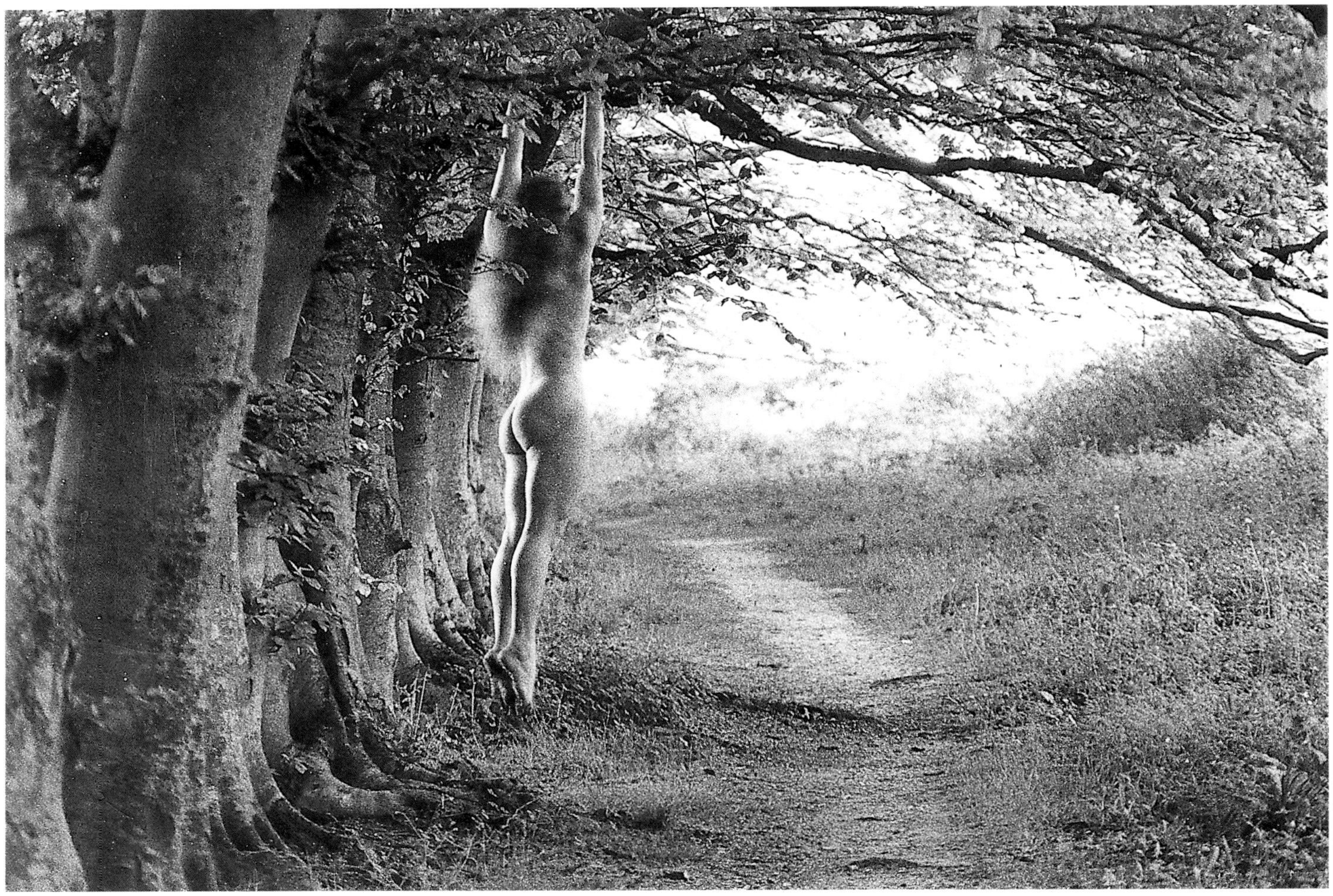

Girl in Beech Trees, 1979

nothing purist, but middle of the road jazz. Twelve-bar blues, big band numbers from the 1940s which went down a treat with Somerset pub audiences, and half-comic numbers like *Back of Town Blues*,' he broke off to sing in his light voice, *I'm gonna move to the outskirts of town, I'm gonna buy my own groceries*. 'It was a sort of Jealousy Blues, railing against grocery boys making a pass at the wives, all great fun.'

Neil Mantell also has good memories:

> The last gig we played with Edward, only two weeks before he died, was at the Yarlington pub, not far from Castle Cary. He was wearing a black coat, black trousers, and black hat because of the hair loss induced by his medical treatment. And he used his 'black box', a gadget he had recently acquired to enable him to synthesise the piano sound. The Yarlington has a small bar, not much bigger than a sitting-room but the atmosphere was special. People kept crowding in. Edward played that night with what I can only describe as a wonderful and hopeful vivaciousness for the future it turned out he didn't have.

I have often tried to work out the relationship between Edward's jazz and his painting, for he left only faint clues. He preferred the individuality of jazz, he once told me, that way no two performances were the same. Curiously enough I found that Ralph Ellison, the black novelist who wrote *The Invisible Man*, had made a point in an essay on the great jazz guitarist Charlie Christian, which established a link between Edward's art and his jazz:

> True jazz is a contest in which each member of a jazz group challenges the rest, each solo or improvisation representing *like the successive canvases of a painter* [my emphasis], a definition of his identity.

When I remembered the thousands upon thousands of variations on the female form that Edward drew over his thirty years of daily committed work, the jazz variations, created for fun and entertainment, seemed another illustration of his creative equilibrium. And I think his son Henry had it right when he said his father worked in his single-minded way to make himself what Duke Ellington used to call a true jazzman.

The Face of Sorrows

One of the finest portraits he ever painted – the 'face of sorrows' as Edward referred to it – hangs beside the big open fireplace in the studio where he kept his jazz piano. Often, visitors to the studio would walk round looking at Edward's works on the wall, pause at the portrait, and then at the end of their tour of the studio, would return for a second, longer look. It is a 'face' which could well be associated with one of Edward's favourite blues numbers.

It is the portrait of a young woman living on a council estate in Frome and depicts a noble-featured face, framed by glossy black hair, painted with the use of a few brush strokes, a patch of green shadow on the left side of the face contrasting with the flesh colour of the right side to convey her expression. In technique I was reminded of Matisse, but the portrait has always seemed to me an entirely original personal statement about someone of extraordinary serenity, who has found peace after personal storm.

Edward described how he accomplished the portrait, and his encounter with its subject, with such intensity and dramatic truth that I thought afterwards 'Moravia would have made a story of this', and determined to give his account pretty well verbatim, by way of text to accompany a reproduction of the portrait. First of all, however, let me explain that Edward came to portraiture relatively late in his career. He said he liked to work with faces outside any conventional rules, 'trusting his eyes', and experimenting with line and colour to obtain the mood or expression of inner meaning in a human face that had taken over his imagination – '*the look*' as he described it.

He said he found the 'great thing about heads', when he turned his artistic attention to them, was that they were quick. They had just a few elements, and you knew straightaway whether you had painted a successful portrait or not. In his final phase he was tending to simplify his portraits, like some Léger heads done in a couple of colours with a black line; in his own words:

'You can produce a strong image of a face in ten minutes, providing they are the *right* ten minutes for you as a painter.'

He was more concerned with capturing a likeness and an inner tension in the face – '*the look*' – than with the conventional aesthetics of portraiture. The models he liked to use for portraits were, as you might imagine, those of the young women to be found in the main streets and supermarkets of Somerset towns – like the original face of sorrows, whom he first saw at a concert at his boys' school. He first mentioned portrait-painting as an illustration of the way he could become absorbed to the point of irresistible obsession with something, studying a subject, photographing it from every angle, enlarging details; then making innumerable studies in different materials, always in the hope of finding the core secrets of the subject so he could express them in line alone, or line and colour.

I hadn't expected to find this obsessive streak in someone as controlled, balanced and engaging as Edward. Strange as his account was in one or two details, never for a minute did I distrust its truth. We were sitting in an overheated studio taping a preliminary interview for his voice-over commentary when he said, in a burst of candour:

> Look at my painting of what I think of now as the 'face of sorrows'. Her name is Christine. I actually first set eyes on her at the school my boys were attending in Frome, at an end-of-term concert. She was a young mother then. I tell you I couldn't take my eyes off her face, I was so amazed to find it among an audience of ordinary Frome parents.
>
> I decided I must speak to her, but she vanished, and I found it most difficult to find out who she was or where she lived. The school wasn't helpful, naturally, I suppose. I told one of the boys, Henry probably, that I wanted to use her as a model, and he managed somehow to get hold of her address.
>
> I went round to her house on a Frome council estate and with my heart in my mouth knocked at her door, which she answered holding a baby in her arms. I said: 'I'm a painter, and though it may sound cock-eyed to you, I want to try and sketch your portrait. 'Oh, yes, that's what I said and she, rather to my astonishment, replied, 'Well, I suppose that's all right.'
>
> Later I discovered her straight-out reply was in character. You once asked where I found my models. Well, not exactly where one might expect.
>
> Although the details don't matter here, she had rather a sad life, and I found her face marvellous. I think her face was the first time I came across a concept of beauty in the abstract. Abstract? I suppose I mean abstract in the way people talk of the beauty of a sunset, or birdsong at dawn, or a memory of an old love.
>
> It was all absolutely extraordinary!
>
> I would leave here to drive down to Frome on a Monday morning, sometimes when it was pouring with rain, and I would go into her house and simply spend about half an hour studying her face. She didn't speak much and sometimes seemed rigid with fear and mystery, not fear of me in any way, but fear of some deep mystery of existence.
>
> She seemed to like my visits, though she never said so directly. All I can say is that I could leave her house after looking at her face, and I mean just looking at her face, sort of dancing and whistling and really pleased with myself and life.
>
> It dawned on me that seeing her face, sometimes shadowed with gloom, depressed almost, was sheer beauty for me . . .
>
> No, I did no drawing of her face at her house, I just looked at it, and eventually I got her to come here to the Old Laundry so that I could do some work on it. I had at that time never seriously tried to do 'faces' and my first Christine drawings were no good at all. I took rolls of photos of her face and spent hours enlarging them and looking at them. I can show you boxes of these studies in my files.
>
> I would spend a couple of hours getting the lighting conditions for a photo of her face right, and I think I finally came pretty close to achieving in a photo the kind of structure I could use to draw from.
>
> The point here is that I didn't know the *rules* about drawing faces – I mean, people who do theatrical make-up probably have some guidelines. You know, where you shadow a different colour on a face or add a make-up line, which may not change the face much but can actually change its entire mood.
>
> Through Christine's face I found that to draw a face at all you have to become obsessed by it, realising that expressions are fleeting, inscrutable, but that the structure remains. I was saying to the printer I have been working with on the lithographs of my work for my one-man show at the Catto Gallery, that I can only learn about things by actually doing them. I cannot learn rules, art school rules, you know what I mean – block in the shape, draw this, do that. Not for me.
>
> The face of Christine taught me that I can only draw a face well if I have studied it, sketched it from several angles, and if this sounds strange, loved the face for itself.

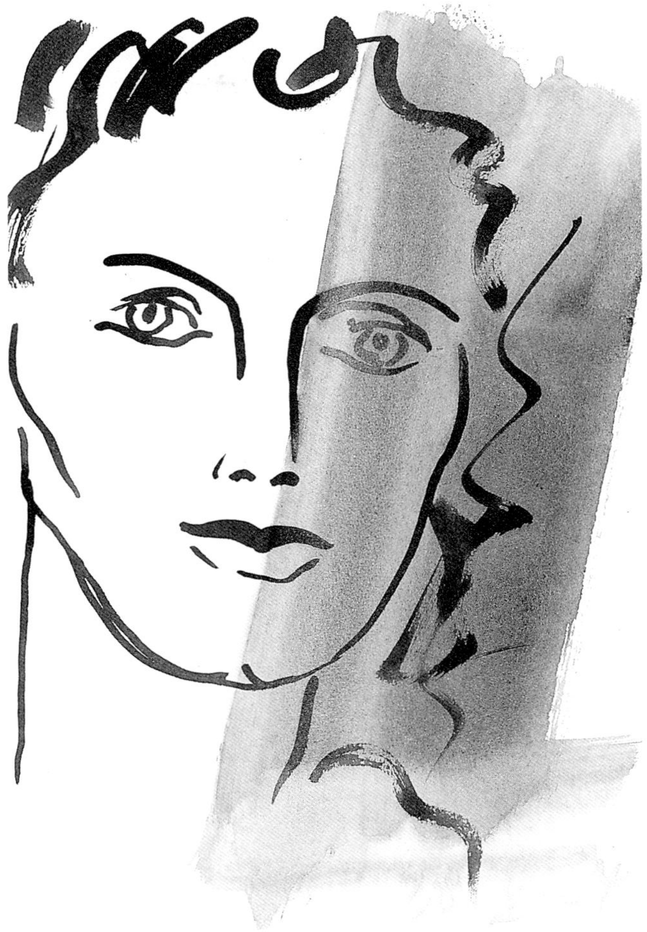

Portrait Head Brush and ink wash, 11½ × 8½ins, 1984

He was too tired for further questions, but the vision of her face lives on in beautiful tawny-coloured paintings like *Christine with Flowers*, in which her thoughtful face is illuminated by a jug of sunflowers and other high summer blooms. You may even eat at the Old Laundry from blue-and-white plates that Edward has decorated with her unforgettable features.

An Englishman's View

Less than a mile from the Old Laundry at Marston Bigot, patches of Somerset landscape have in the last few years been changed irretrievably. Edward's attitude to these changes in his immediate environment reveals his thinking as a painter and as a man. In this corner of east Somerset not far from Frome, a massive programme of road building and traffic re-routing has altered the shape of the fields and lanes. Roundabouts have eaten up the grass with concrete, trees have been cut down, hedges have disappeared.

Edward Piper was a dedicated motorist, far from antagonistic to road building. He liked to drive fast and to explore roads by car. In the last week of his life when he was, in his own words, 'weak as a kitten', he drove himself to hospital at Bath because he found it 'relaxing to be behind the steering-wheel'.

But he was primarily an artist whose eyes feasted on

the countryside, and who saw that landscape threatened. Through his photographic work for the Shell guides he had gained a prodigiously detailed knowledge of different parts of England, and he resented what he saw as callous development or mindless government planning.

To help the groups of people resisting such development, he would take photographs and make drawings. He never asked for a fee for this type of work. He was practical, too – for example he saw the necessity for a 'slurry lagoon' (as farmers call the complex where manure is converted into bio-gas) *but* he wanted it to be sited where it would not destroy a memorable view, and he offered precise suggestions to planning committees. His concern for the environment made him oppose any nuclear development, and most emphatically the building of another reactor at Hinkley Point on the Somerset coast nearest to his home.

Though he was aware that any part of the landscape he knew might be destroyed, this never occupied the forefront of his mind. He painted as if such possibilities did not exist. What he wanted to communicate was the immediate joy he found in the shape of a Dorset coastline, of a Corsican village framed by blackened trees, a village in Tuscany alive with sunflowers, a fountain in a city square guarded by ancient Roman goddesses and geraniums in flower.

Nor was there anything religious or symbolic, he said, about the way he looked at landscape; although his pictures are far from a literal record of the scenery. In the view of Bath gallery owner Reg Singh, talking after Edward's death: 'In the last five or six years he displayed an individual freshness and confidence in his approach to landscapes. He often positioned himself on a hilltop or coastal promontory and managed to capture a breathtaking width and depth of vision, always with the same lightness and dancing light he caught in his paintings of nudes.'

This confidence is evident in his Menorca paintings in 1987 and in a series of paintings he made in Corsica where he followed in the footsteps of Edward Lear, using Dorothy Carrington's award-winning book *Granite Island* as a guide. He was using – with a masterly skill – the technique of Gothicising a painting, which involves compressing a wide-angle view of a scene into a picture with a relatively small area. This confidence in his skills can also be seen in the charming touch with which he painted a miniature landscape seen through a window behind one of his nudes.

Edward himself divided his landscapes into two categories, British and Continental, and he had subtle, but markedly different approaches in the handling of each one. In a British landscape, his sensitive understanding of light was a dominating factor; this is illustrated clearly in his paintings of the Dorset coast, where a rocky foreshore meets the English sky, in compositions with a secure line and subdued watercolour washes. In his Continental landscapes, almost invariably he captures a holiday feeling of sun and warmth. These pictures evoke a feeling that, while you are familiar with the scene, you are seeing it for the first time – the kind of feeling you get when re-reading a favourite lyric poem.

When we were discussing the paintings he would like to see in an art book about his work, he said of his British paintings: 'My later landscapes are getting there and showing my deep joy in the British countryside.' Of his Continental ones he said: 'They are really a very English Englishman's view of foreign parts.' And there I think he *was* expressing a truth, for his 'very English view' may well be the quality which enables his Continental landscapes to absorb the influences of his favourite French painters, and yet come through as paintings that are original and bear the unmistakable marks of Edward Piper.

Edward was always more ready to discuss his nudes than his landscapes, yet his later period landscapes attracted an enthusiastic art public, not only in the UK, but in Europe and America, and recently Japan. The nude studies to which he added his mastery of landscapes in views seen through a window in the composition, or as an actual context for the nude, proved particularly saleable. For instance, the CCA Galleries, one of Europe's leading publishers of contemporary prints, commissioned several, including *Hôtel de Calais à Nice* in an edition of 150, which quickly sold, many bought by Italians.

All this was material reinforcement of his own conviction that he had finally developed into a landscape painter in his own right, emerging at last from the long shadow of his father. Shortly after Edward's death I was discussing his painting with his mother at Marston Bigot. She again expressed her view that Edward had taken time to break through into landscape because his father had so thoroughly explored the genre. She said:

'Edward undoubtedly had to fight his way through to the painting of his own landscapes in his own style. But he remained in many ways John Piper's son, uncompromising, following his own path without paying overmuch attention to current trends or criticism. I'm absolutely sure he didn't embark on landscapes for exhibition until he was ready to paint good landscapes in his own fashion.'

In one of our last conversations Edward had said, 'You may not credit it, but it was the combine harvester that provided my real breakthrough into landscape.'

Apparently, Edward was driving home to Marston Bigot one summer afternoon in 1981 from London, where he had been discussing the selection of paintings for an exhibition of his work at the Savile Club; it was to succeed an exhibition of John Piper's work. The organiser of the Savile Club exhibition, Nigel Foxell, had said he would prefer to have some landscapes, to balance against Edward's studies of nudes depicted with flowers or reflective mirrors. 'Possibly Nigel Foxell thought the Savile Club might have found my nudes rather much,' Edward said.

He was pondering what landscapes he had in hand at the Old Laundry, which would be suitable for the Savile show, when his eye was caught by the threatening shape and menacing movement of combine harvesters at work in a field – 'like bloody great red monsters' – just outside the village of Buckland Dinham near Frome.

He returned to the gently sloping field first thing next morning to sketch the combine harvesters in the landscape. Describing the venture, he said:

> You see those red monsters rattling past, and the whole concept becomes exciting. Storms of dust, glittering in the heavy summer atmosphere. I expended a lot of energy charging round the field before I began to feel I was actually getting down on paper the relationship between the path taken by the combine harvester and the harvest scene.
>
> You get one sketch down with some truth in the line, and the combine harvester moves to a fresh path – it may have moved by twelve feet in its path, and everything changes, the shape of the field, the angle, the light and shadows. Everything!
>
> When I got back to Marston Bigot to study my day's sketching of the combine harvesters I suddenly realised that, without any conscious thought or controlled effort on my part, I had, in fact, been making a landscape. Nothing planned, it just happened, all as I say a happy chance.
>
> I have always had this facility to get references down on paper swiftly, and in my sketches I saw – *I mean I saw for the first time in reality on the paper* – what my imagination had seen in the harvest field and my hand had automatically sketched: a Piper-like church in the background, trees heavy with leaf and the summer shadow you find in the trees on the edge of my sketches, with a track from the top of the field to a big double gate holding the entire landscape together.
>
> Yes, I had a landscape, in which I found what I call my fantasy, the bit of magic I mentioned to you earlier, and which may well be that 'further' they used to talk to me about at the Slade. I felt I had

painted a landscape in a way nobody else would have painted it.

I had been so completely spellbound in my physical efforts to catch the combine harvester in relation to its constantly changing angle that I had at the time failed completely to recognise that I was creating a landscape, *my* landscape – not to mention a landscape they might approve of back at the Savile.

I have always believed that the unexpected turns up in different lights and sometimes creates defined moods and unique subjects to paint in scenes you may well have observed scores of times. You see the way shadows fall from a building or a tree differently with a change in light – and the combine harvester showed me that you can even find something different in a Somerset field that has been cultivated for centuries, and that you have seen so often.

The experience with the combine harvesters convinced me that you have to have a direct response to a subject if you are going to paint it with any life or truth – what you see intellectually and objectively is *not* what is actually there. And I believe these are all things which gave me the confidence I needed for a breakthrough into landscape.

His experience with the combine harvesters at Buckland Dinham was, in its way, as valuable an artistic epiphany as the one he had experienced over twenty years earlier, when his sketches of his wife gave him the proof that he *could* draw figures with the freedom of line that had eluded him at life classes.

He continued his work on combine harvester paintings when he went with Prue, Luke and Henry for a late summer holiday at the cottage in Pembrokeshire, which the Piper families use as a holiday home. The harvest is made later in Wales than in Somerset, and this enabled him to do more fieldwork. Because rainy weather also intervenes more often in Pembrokeshire, he was able to draw combine harvesters sitting still in the landscape.

These paintings enabled him to isolate relationships and natural accents in the landscape, which – excellent photographer though he was – he could never have hoped to capture with his camera, and which provide the psychological and imaginative insights that resonate with the continuing relationship of man to the land. Edward also said:

'When you are following your father's profession you may well inherit something of his method and even his lifestyle. What I must repeat is that by the time I had finished with combine harvesters, I knew I could paint landscapes which I could sign with my name, knowing they were mine entirely.'

From the combine harvester studies he turned to other landscapes, with verve and animation and sensual delight in nature and in the act of painting it, using a light, bright palette (in contrast to the black and emerald and dark greens used by his father). Edward applied the colour first as an independent element, adding detail in a black line which varied in thickness, and leaving white spaces, all with a sure instinct for the dramatic.

It was sometimes said in criticism that one could see too much Dufy or Matisse in his Continental landscapes, a fact which did not move him. Shortly before his death he told art writer Tony Warner:

'I am now trying to find out how simple an approach you can get away with; if that gets confused with great names it is not deliberate imitation, but more a case of people coming to the same conclusion artistically . . . all the Renaissance artists used one another's ideas and subjects all the time . . . I know now that I am doing something worth doing in expressing my own feelings in my art about the external world.'

In some notes on Edward, Kate, the model for his *Hôtel de Calais à Nice* paintings, gave me a pleasant word-picture of Edward at work. She wrote:

> He would arrive at a scene in his old estate car in which he carried a short stepladder, and he used the car's tailgate as a table for his paints, water and sponges. He then sat on top of the ladder with his home-made easel and painted away, having devised a method of getting a scene down from a high angle, and he painted with a fierce concentration.

In his landscapes he was always striving to find 'the instant moment' in a scene: the mist rolling down through a valley in the Forest of Bavella in Corsica, the lightning-swift change in texture of the grey and green leaves of eucalyptus in Spain, or the quivering of huge palm-fronds in the breeze at Hyères. He was always wanting to marry light and movement and, as he once remarked to me, he liked to create a sense of the trees in his landscapes actually growing, and the flow of fountain water actually bouncing in its basin.

Edward's impulsive decisions would often dictate the course of events; one such occurred in Malaga during the final 'painting swing' of his short life, and it seems to me to say as much about his attitude to his art as anything I heard or read during my research for material for this monograph. He was driving round Malaga looking for subjects to paint, when he found himself in a town square with a terrace of yellow houses down one side. He recognised the terrace: Picasso had been born in its end house; with the capital raised by the sale of two of his paintings, it has been endowed as a centre for Picasso scholars.

Edward was thinking of visiting the centre, when his attention was engaged by three or four new wooden shop kiosks, and their possibilities as the subject of a painting; they were dark olive-green in colour, one selling newspapers, magazines and cigarettes, another with fresh fruit and vegetables arranged in colour shapes – orange, tomato red, the purple of aubergines, the russets of apples and pale yellow melons – and a florist's shop with pot geraniums in flower standing like full stops on the square outside. Edward took his short stepladder from the back of his car, set it up, and when perched on top, took out his sketching pad.

He worked for so long that he found when he finally shut his sketching pad, the Picasso centre was closed for the day. And he left early the next morning for the interior of Granada with Prue, before the centre was open for visitors. However: 'I reckon old Pablo would have agreed with me in thinking that I was better employed sketching his square than listening to some arty bullshit in the Picasso centre,' Edward said to me.

Art Photography

Landscape with Figures

In 1977 the Fox Talbot Museum of Photography at Lacock Abbey in Wiltshire presented an impressive one-man exhibition of Edward Piper's art photography. The exhibition was organised by Bob Lassam, then director of the museum. In his view, if Edward had put the full force of his creative energies into photography he would have made a reputation for himself comparable to those of Fay Godwin and Bill Brandt. He believes that Edward took some of the finest studies of the female figure against a natural background to have been produced by any British or European photographer in the past fifty years.

Bob Lassam said: 'Edward Piper managed the extremely difficult and elusive effect of merging the realism of landscape with a frank and lively enjoyment of the female body with a perfect artistic equilibrium. To do this he undoubtedly drew deeply not only on the wealth of information he had accumulated as a painter about the female figure, but also from his experience of working closely with models, who understood his methods and were always ready to co-operate with him in some quite fantastic, yet absolutely right poses, relaxing on rocky seashores in Dorset, pressing their bodies hard against a rough stone arch at Stourhead, or coiling themselves lazily on coarse reeds by a river.'

Edward's practical skills enabled him to produce first-class vintage prints, that is, photographs taken, developed, retouched and, where necessary cut and

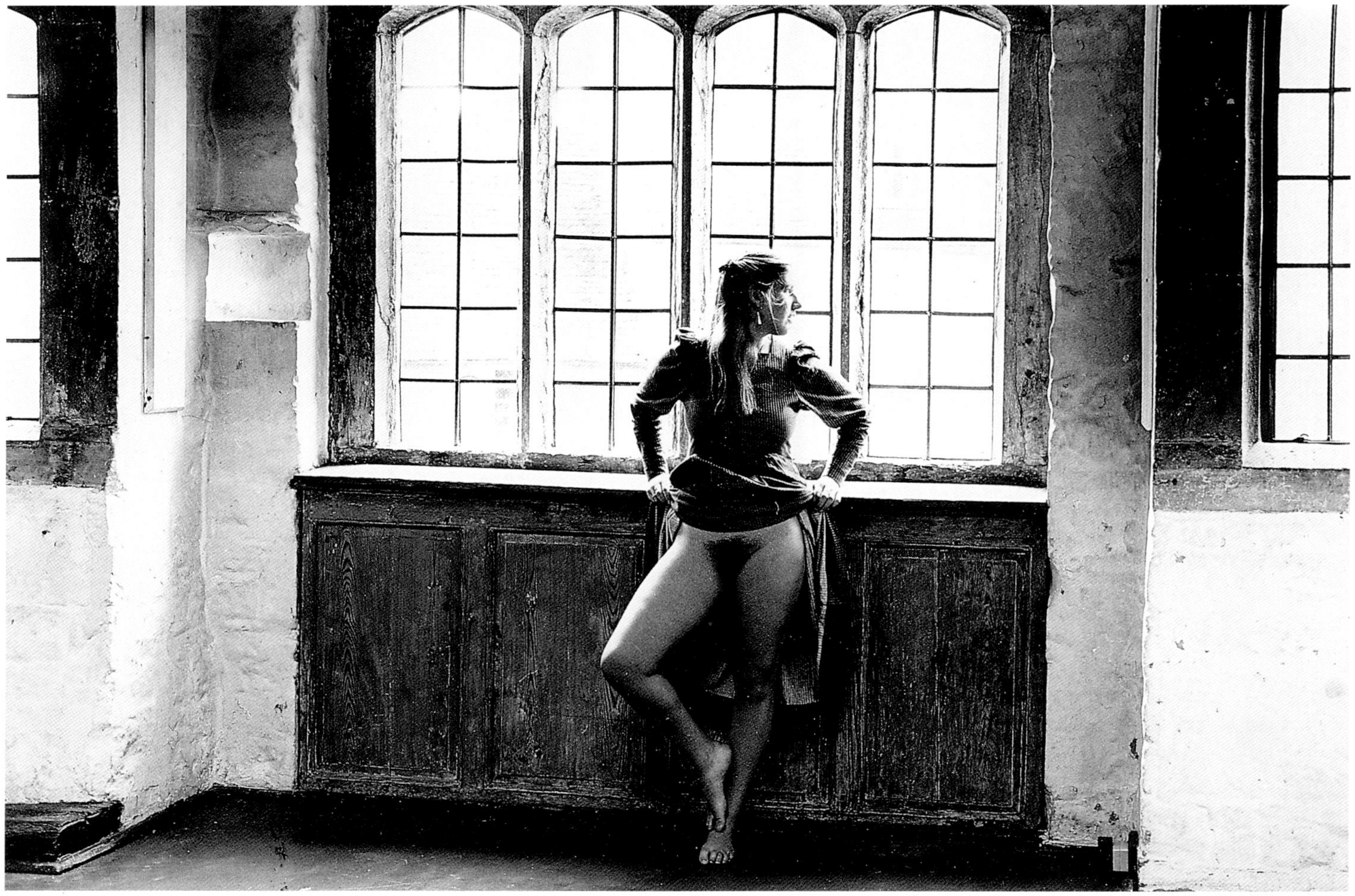

Girl at Window in Sherborne, Dorset, 1984

trimmed by the photographer himself for issue to the public in signed and limited editions. Some 'name' photographers, such as Cecil Beaton, hardly ever processed their own photographs. Edward would not let anyone else involve themselves in technical photographic processes which he could control and carry out himself.

What were the essentials to be found in Edward's vintage prints which made them so outstanding? To answer my question Bob Lassam, now retired, took down one of Edward's vintage prints from the wall in his sitting room at his home in Bath. He had chosen the print – a landscape – when Edward invited him to choose a print from the exhibition's portfolio in return for his help in planning and organising the exhibition. Bob Lassam chose the landscape because he thought it illustrated so completely Edward's photographic talents.

Bob Lassam said: 'I chose this print because you cannot fail to be struck by the sensitivity of his responses. When I heard of his death I looked at the print again to remind myself of the beauty of its composition. The relationship of space to sky, Masterly! Look at the emphasis given to meadows and trees, all leading quite lyrically through the misty middle section to the prominent centre.'

Edward was far more reluctant to talk of his photography than he was of his nudes, but I know he had clear in his own mind the boundaries separating photography and painting, between the representational and the artistic image. He constantly used his camera as a tool, something to parallel his painting and drawing both in the field and in the studio. When eventually he turned his attention seriously to portraits, he would shoot roll after roll of film – as with Christine, the model for his 'face of sorrows' – looking for insights into the way a certain angle or flicker of expression could change the entire mood of a portrait. He concerned himself more with identifying the factors which made even the most sensitive photograph less truthful than a painting, seldom painting directly from a photograph of a 'head', a nude or landscape.

He spent hours in his dark room at the Old Laundry, working on different technical processes – printing negatives, making huge enlargements, and experimenting with solarisation, which deals with changes in photographic images in relative darkness during a long exposure. He distrusted colour in photography, thinking that it imposed a reaction on the viewer which made it useful in publicity photography but a trap in art photography. He was, however, fascinated by the effects of colour enlargement and colour photocopying. In his own words:

> The entire point of doing a painting is to do something the camera cannot do: to put across what you, as a painter, know is in a nude study or landscape, as opposed to what the camera lens records is there. The camera is altogether too literal, and often makes its own selection of things, and even when you take pictures of a pose for reference, somehow the information is not always the information you want, particularly for a nude painting.

He made the same energetic preparations for taking landscape photographs as he would for painting a landscape. He would cross the scene by car or on foot, quartering it swiftly and thoroughly, to discover the exact spot to place his camera tripod for the best angle. Then, despite his natural impetuosity, he would wait as patiently as a hunter, and would not shoot until the light was exactly right.

Yet he was an adventurous photographer too, ready to break accepted rules and take artistic risks. He preferred to use natural light when most professionals would have found it far safer to use artificial lighting. Mike Gray, present director of the Fox Talbot Museum and himself a talented photographer, said Edward would 'go against the normal grammar' of photography in his compositions and would mix tungsten, flash and daylight for special effect. According to Gray:

> Few photographers have the knowledge or enterprise to take such chances, and it is even more surprising, perhaps, with Edward Piper, when you remember that he never had a lesson in photography in his life. What he knew he taught himself, and one can only think that he was born with a gift for photography.

The Mock Tudor Maid

I had come across examples of Edward's visual wit; this was mainly in his pop art period, when he would sometimes use bits of newsprint torn into triangles to represent female pubic hair, or small patty pans to cover the nipples of a nude; the underlying intent was serious, questioning how much a line in a nude could take before losing its meaning.

It was, however, in researching his photography that I

came across what must be a prime example of the sardonic side of his wit, a side to which he rarely gave play, and usually only to startle some conventional group in provincial society.

For a celebration of the first photograph taken by the Victorian pioneer photographer, William Henry Fox Talbot (1800–1877), the National Trust sponsored a competition for photographers at the Fox Talbot Museum. Fox Talbot's first photograph featured a window, which made a window shot a logical theme for the competition. Edward entered a print of one of his models, Susan, backlit against a Gothic window, looking flirtatiously over her shoulder.

It could be described as a photographic tease. The pose refers back to Elizabethan times, with Susan apparently waiting by the window for a Tudor beau. In the photograph Susan has the expression of a demure wench, and wears a dress cut on Tudor lines. It takes a few seconds to register the fact that she is nonchalantly holding up her dress to show the thick pubic hair of her sex. The judges of the Fox Talbot competition regarded it as an ingenious and strong image, but some members of the National Trust considered it was 'not quite National Trust', and asked the judges to invite Edward to withdraw the picture; which he did.

Neither Edward nor Susan was in the least taken aback by this censorship, and both regarded the picture as outstandingly good; which it is. As so often with Edward, his 'quite rebellious gesture', as he spoke of it, was for some reason accepted without fuss, possibly because of his charm, and seemingly without any lingering ill-feeling.

The National Trust was quite happy to continue taking Edward's pictures – of the more conventional kind – for its publications, and only too happy to have him plan firework displays for events in the grounds of some of the properties it manages for the nation in the South West.

Edward said that he had a 'puritan honesty' in his approach to landscape painting. Even when he 'gothicised' a scene, he was scrupulously careful not to disturb the objective truth in his painting. Even more than in painting, probably, photography can be based in illusion. Someone as technically resourceful as Edward would have had no difficulty in composing landscape views bathed in perpetual sunshine, but he disliked resorting to any tricks or fakery in his photographs.

He would wait all day, for example, for that unusual moment when the light off the water is brighter than the sky, for a view of a river with clouds – as in his picture of Cuckmere Haven in Sussex. In this photograph, the light on the sun-dried grass draws the spectator into the scene and, unusually for Edward, the image is shot from a low angle. Characteristically he gave the original print to Mike Gray's wife, Barbara, an interior designer, when she said how much his photograph reminded her of her childhood memories of Cuckmere Haven.

In photography as in his paintings, his serious approach to the subject matter was sometimes masked and under-valued because of his *légèreté*, and the smooth assurance of technique that is evident in his photographs. This assurance and the sound judgement with which he chooses the reference points in his compositions, can be seen in the way the flowers of a wild briar or a tree in a field relate to, for example, a manor house, and so define the location. Bob Lassam again:

> You find a magic in his photographs as evocative in its way as in any of his landscape paintings. His talents with a camera were God-given, but he sharpened and tempered them with his application to basic technical skills, an application he took care to hide from the world . . .
>
> . . . I wouldn't think that Edward Piper ever took a careless picture in his life, whether a landscape or building for a Shell guide, the opulent interiors of brochures for 'millionaire's row' property, or a champion billiard player looking along a cue for an export catalogue. He wasn't just a good taker of pictures, he was a good finisher, who must have delighted any art editor he worked for.

Commercial Photography

The Hidden Angle

On leaving the Slade, Edward made his living chiefly through commercial photography. For several years he worked with John Piper on the Shell county guides. John's photographs look stately, monumental, like backcloths for serious drama. Edward's emphasise the romantic play of light and shadow on landscapes and church brasses, transmuting the Regency architecture of Brighton Pavilion into a building that exists between dream and waking.

Edward was versatile and wide-ranging in his commercial work, illustrating firework catalogues, exploring opulent interiors along Bath's Royal Crescent, photographing elegant railway bridges. 'For every subject there is an obvious angle,' he said, 'but you have to dig for the hidden angle to get the indelible image.'

His painter's expertise informed his photography. His colourist's eye helped to produce luminous images of Gloucester Cathedral's stained glass. Mark Girouard said Edward's photographs were invariably true to the spirit of a building or place. His guidebook to Stonor, a medieval manor house near his boyhood home, captures both its historical splendours and its secrecy as a centre of recusancy.

The range of his camera skills is best displayed in the series of studies he made of the Celtic stone circles in Britain and Ireland for Aubrey Burl's book, *Ring of Stone*. Burl says of the enigmatic rings: 'We shall never see the circles' dancers, the painted sunlit bodies, the dark figures against the moon. Yet the symbols and the dreads are constant. Death is always there.' Reading Burl's words soon after Edward's death, it struck me as poignant and remarkable that Edward, who so loved life, should have caught in every image the elegiac quality of the circles.

Zigzag Ceramics at Queen Camel

In his studio at Marston Bigot Edward kept, alongside his 'basket of frivolity' a small selection of beautifully crafted pots carrying a zigzag potter's mark for use in his nude paintings. The zigzag mark symbolises the earth, fire and water elements of the potter's craft; the pots were created by Douglas Phillips, a gifted studio potter and one of Britain's best kiln-makers, at his Ridge pottery at Queen Camel village in Somerset.

When Douglas Phillips and his wife, Jenny – a textile designer by profession who has most successfully adapted her skills to ceramics – visited the Old Laundry they thought how beautifully the suave, sinewy lines of his nudes would fill plain pottery shapes. They discussed ceramic decoration several times with Edward before he agreed to decorate a series of plates Douglas would prepare for him.

The description by Douglas and Jenny Phillips of the ease with which he moved into the field of decorative pottery might suggest that Edward had long been aware of the aesthetic potential in his painting as decoration for pots, and of the way in which the pure line of his nudes would provide an elegant motif for ceramics. The discussions with the Phillips occurred in the mid-1980s, when Edward knew that his lightness of touch and swift drawing techniques would work most effectively with the pottery's flowing curves and create the finest of ceramic decorations, comparable with those leaving any other artist-potter's studio.

Edward did not make ceramics part of his artistic

repertory until the mid-1980s, and his output was limited: half-a-dozen small firings at Queen Camel; some pots made and decorated in partnership with David Garland at his Oxfordshire pottery, which include the plates decorated by Edward with Christine's 'face of sorrows' and are in regular use in the kitchen at the Old Laundry; firings of vases and plates at the Fulham pottery for the Catto Gallery; some decorative jugs; and the single porcelain teapot. From chance remarks, I believe that had Edward lived he would have created more ceramics.

The Right Thing to Do

Edward Piper's grave in the churchyard of St Leonard's, Marston Bigot, less than half a mile from his home, is marked by a headstone carved by his younger son, Henry, a philosophy student at Sussex University. It was the first lettering on stone he had ever done, but he has the Piper versatility in artistic matters.

The inscription could not be simpler: *Edward Piper, 1938–1990.* The slab is a piece of freestone, which Prue and her two sons hauled from the Marston brook that runs through the garden of the Old Laundry. The funeral, a brief service conducted by the local vicar, was kept private; only close relatives attended. Edward's parents, John and Myfanwy were present, though at 87, John Piper was in failing health. They were practising Anglicans, as Edward and Prue were not, though Edward had never actually renounced the faith that had briefly once meant much to him at public school.

Many of those in Edward's wide circle of friends wanted his death to be marked by some rite of passage – they wanted the opportunity to bid him farewell. His death, although he had been ill for months, came suddenly at the end, and he had never expressed views on how his passing should be commemorated, even when he knew he was mortally ill.

After a discussion, Prue and his sons decided to hold a celebration at the Old Laundry, which would follow closely the style of the many parties Edward had hosted there; this meant with good food, wine and home-brewed ale, the sounds of jazz, and with a crowning firework display – and nothing resembling a speech.

It was held on Saturday 9 June 1990.

Guests at the reception who had walked to the church of the scattered parish of Marston Bigot, St Leonard's, found Edward's grave under the wall facing the landscape which, in his own words, he was 'building to paint in his old age'. The grave was clad with sun-scorched turves and carried a large cushion of yellow marguerites, with a treble clef of maroon flowers from 'The Band' and a posy of wild flowers at its head.

In mid-afternoon Nick Hankinson, of Bristol's Eye Gallery, returned with a van laden with paintings and vintage prints from Edward's one-man show at the Malvern Festival, the last exhibition for which the artist had himself chosen the works he wanted to represent his art. His mother Myfanwy and his sisters, Clarissa and Suzannah, arrived; his nephews were pitching a tent in which to spend the June night, in the shelter of an enormous rootball of a big tree blown down in a spring gale. Edward had thought it might have been one of the last few trees surviving from Selwood Forest, which the monks of Witham Friary had once hunted.

The Old Laundry was once again alive, as Edward liked to see it. Luke and Henry marched out of the main studio carrying crowbars like spears, to punch holes in the ground to take the rocket sticks for the fireworks display they had designed. John Piper was not well enough to attend the commemoration of his elder son, so the Piper boys had put some fireworks aside by the jazz piano for their Uncle Sebastian to take to Fawley Bottom to set off, so that John would not feel left out.

One guest asked Edward's sons: 'Why did you choose a party to commemorate your father?' I heard them reply quietly, incisively: 'We just felt it would be the right thing to do.' No explanation, no apology, just a statement of fact, in typical Edward Piper style.

Through the studio windows you could hear the sound of a jazz break by a trumpeter, coming from the jazz marquee. In the studio, Prue phoned Bristol Weather Centre to check that the rain would have cleared Marston Bigot by 10pm, when the fireworks were due to begin. Food began appearing on the trestle tables – salad dishes, chicken, woodpigeon, pâtés of all kinds, Indian and Malaysian curries, Greek yoghurt dip, cakes and biscuits and cheeses.

The friendly neighbours who had sold the Old Laundry to Edward and Prue in 1967, arrived with freshly baked loaves hollowed out and filled with home-grown asparagus spears. As dusk began closing in, Patrick Reyntiens, the stained glass artist, was to be found, presiding elegantly at a centre table in the studio, saying: 'I feel that while we are mourning an artist who has left us too soon, we are also celebrating the marvellous years he was with us'; which was as near a speech as the occasion came. And in the kitchen you found the pearly glazed plates decorated with Christine's 'face of sorrows' in Edward's favourite cobalt blue; they were carrying pyramids of the fattest, reddest strawberries I have ever seen.

One of Edward's fellow artists expressed a view that he preferred Edwards later landscapes to his nudes, for which the poses were sometimes too contrived for his taste. 'Can you tell me of any nude poses that are not by their nature contrived?' inquired Grahaeme Barrasford-Young, a bookshop owner who had accompanied Edward on a painting trip to Scotland. Some of Edward's models could be seen looking at the nude studies he had painted of them.

At precisely 10pm the sky above Marston Bigot was lit by flashing colours from a volley of Roman candles, and the garden was filled with the mood music specially composed for the display by Sebastian Piper. Then the Roman candles were overtaken by a barrage of 'Bombettes', followed by clusters of dazzling shell-bursts high into the night, to the sound of rapid fire-shots like Chinese fire-crackers.

To a chorus of exclamations from the guests looking on, the shell-bursts were lost in a blaze of shooting stars which left long comet tails of coloured light trailing across the inky sky – only to be over-ridden by 'aerial bombshells' fired even higher into the sky, to explode in a blaze of silver rods, lighting up a silhouette of Prue watching her sons fire the display. Then four whirling crown wheels, spinning with lights like a fairground pin-table, lifted, slowly, to four or five feet high – an eye-catching prelude to one of Edward's best-liked fireworks, a giant Catherine wheel, the 'Big Wheel', spinning for ever in a blaze of colour.

Had it been a less formal occasion, the Piper boys would have ended with a 'big-bang' firework, as John Deeker, the director of Pains Fireworks explained to me later. As it was, they had planned a special finale: first a firework (named 'Goodnight') which produced a breathtaking waterfall of golden rain some fifteen feet high, this merging with one called the 'Falls of Zambesi' (once 'Victoria Falls') which threw off a shimmering and sparkling curtain of silver rain. It was reflected in the black mirror of Edward's lake until finally it disappeared, thus bringing down the curtain on the display.

I had arrived with a pocket tape recorder intending to record my instant impressions, but the tape recorder went unused.

While guests uttered cries of delight, I had become 'a solitary individual enclosed in my own world, time suspended'. In giving this celebration in loving memory of Edward Piper, the artist and man, his widow and sons had without doubt done the right thing.

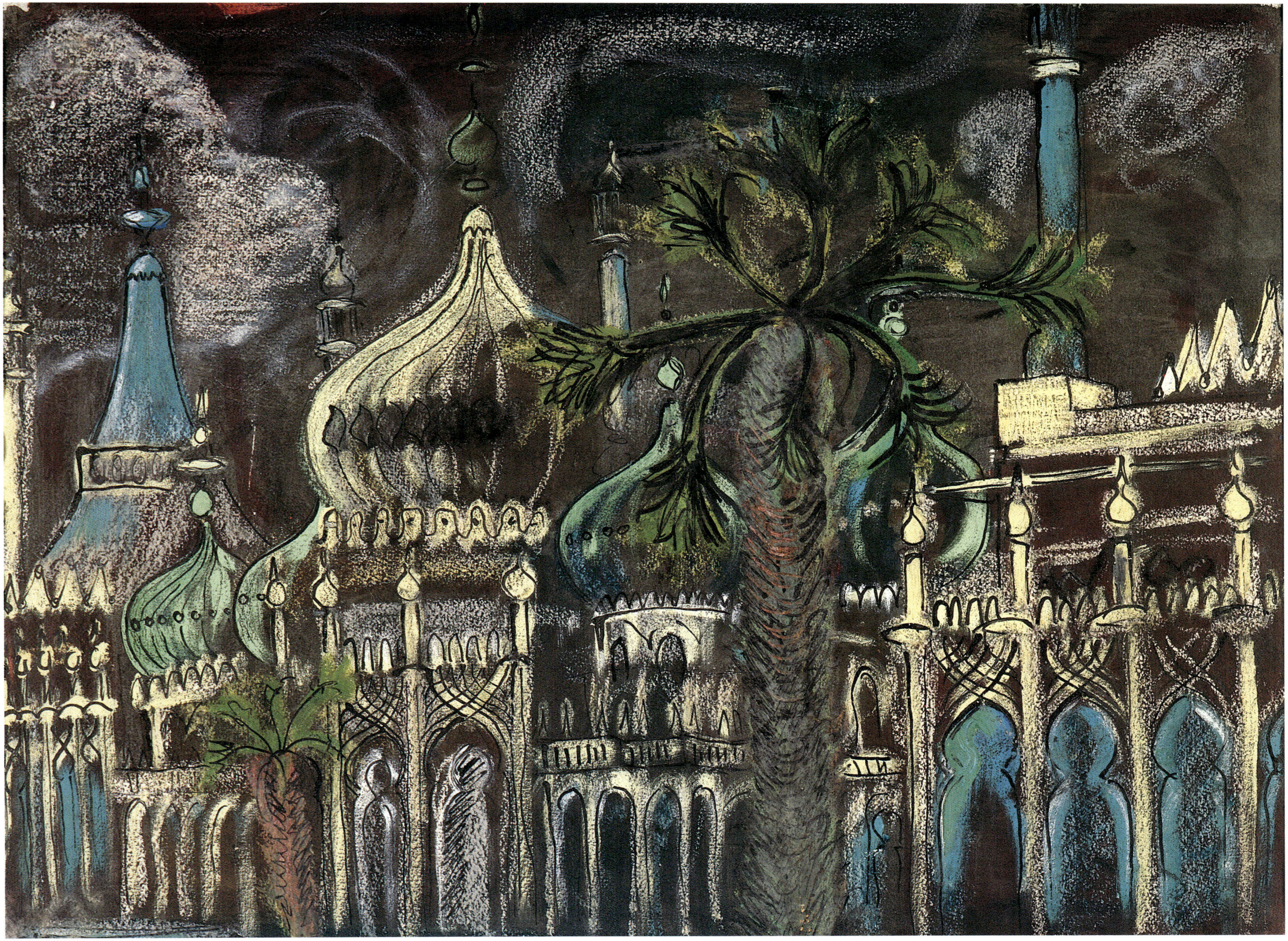

Brighton Pavilion
Ink, chalk and watercolour, 15 × 20ins, 1955

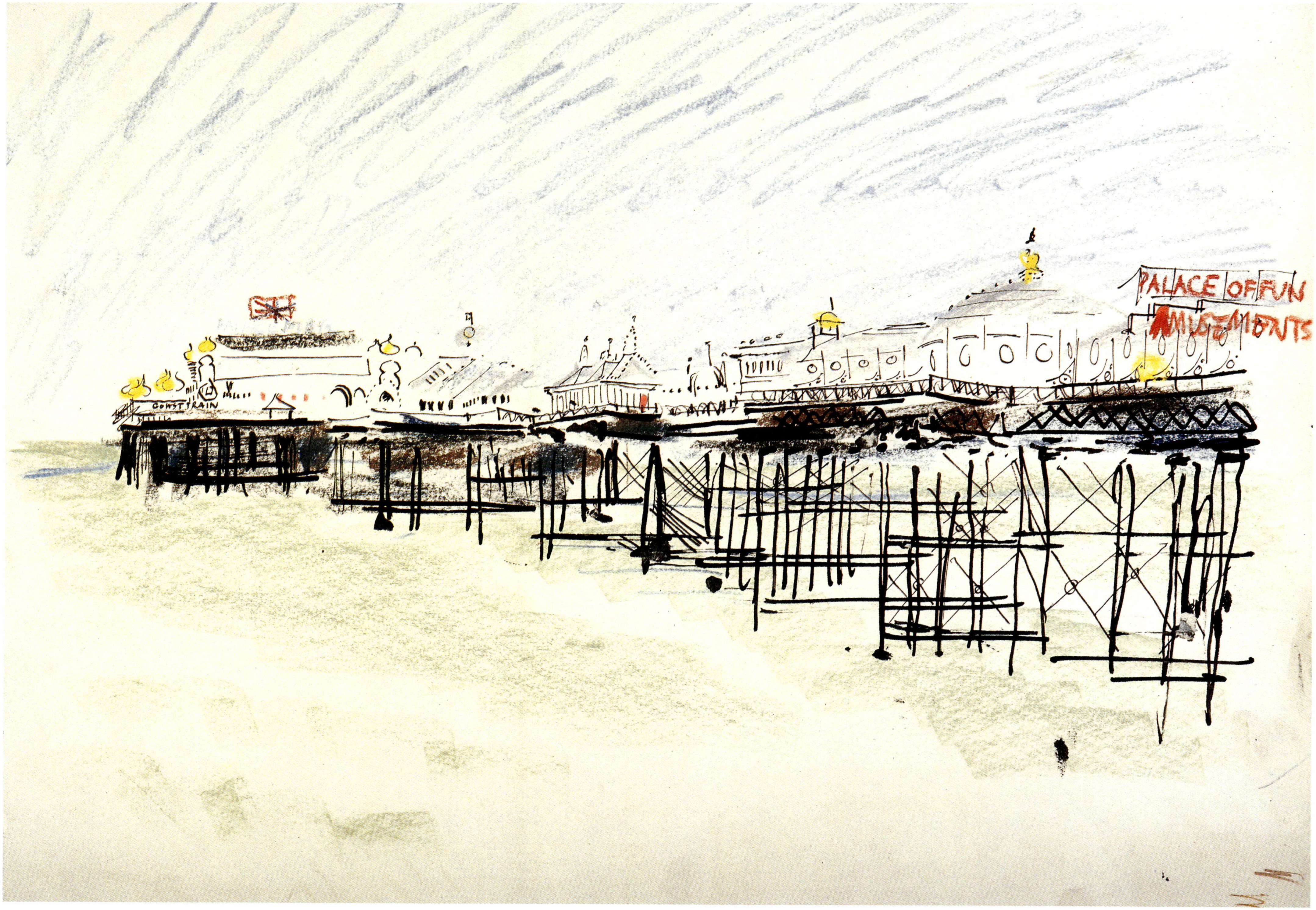

Palace Pier, Brighton
Ink and chalk, 14 × 20ins, 1957

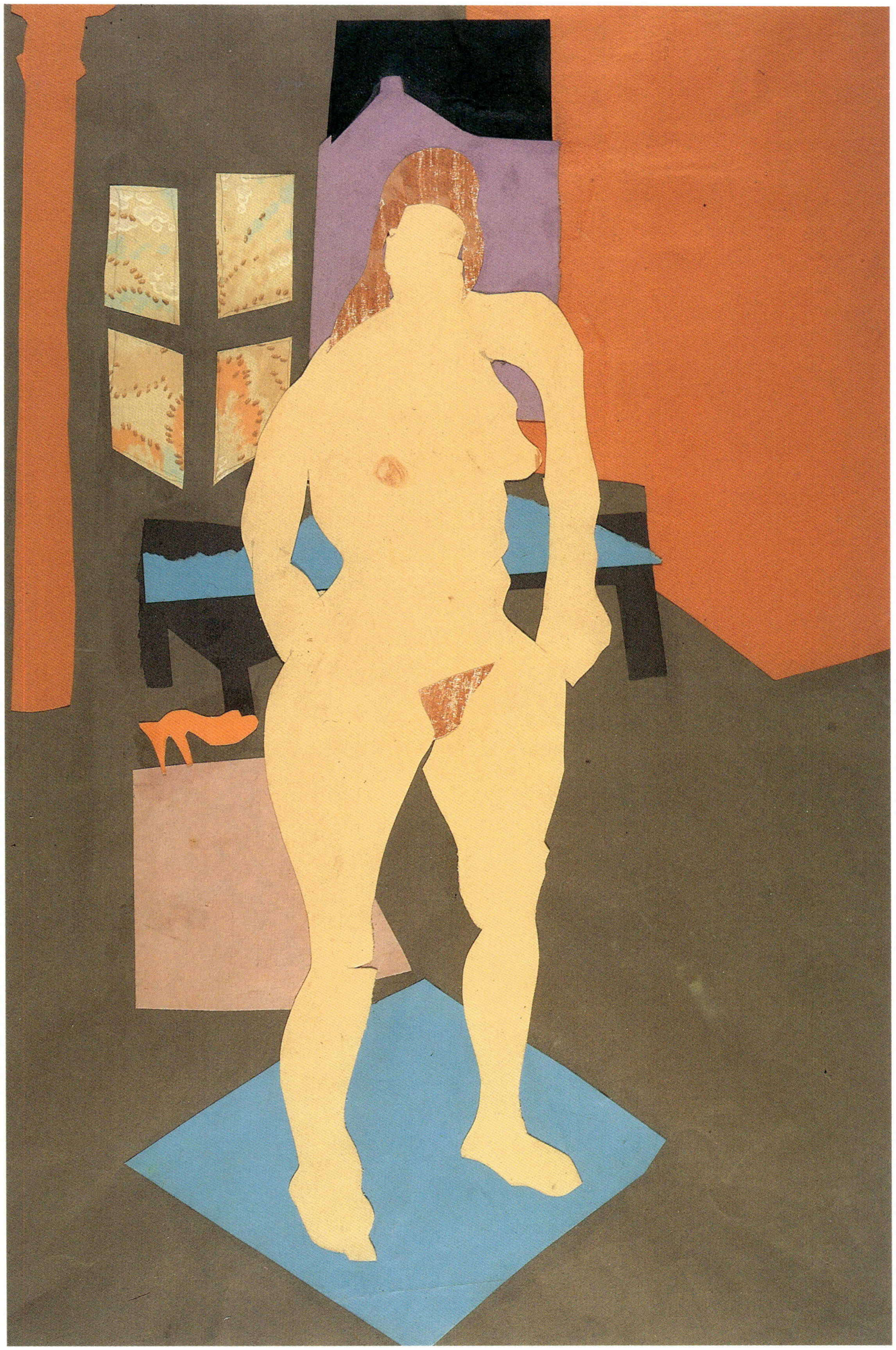

Life Room at the Slade
Collage, 21½ × 14ins, 1959

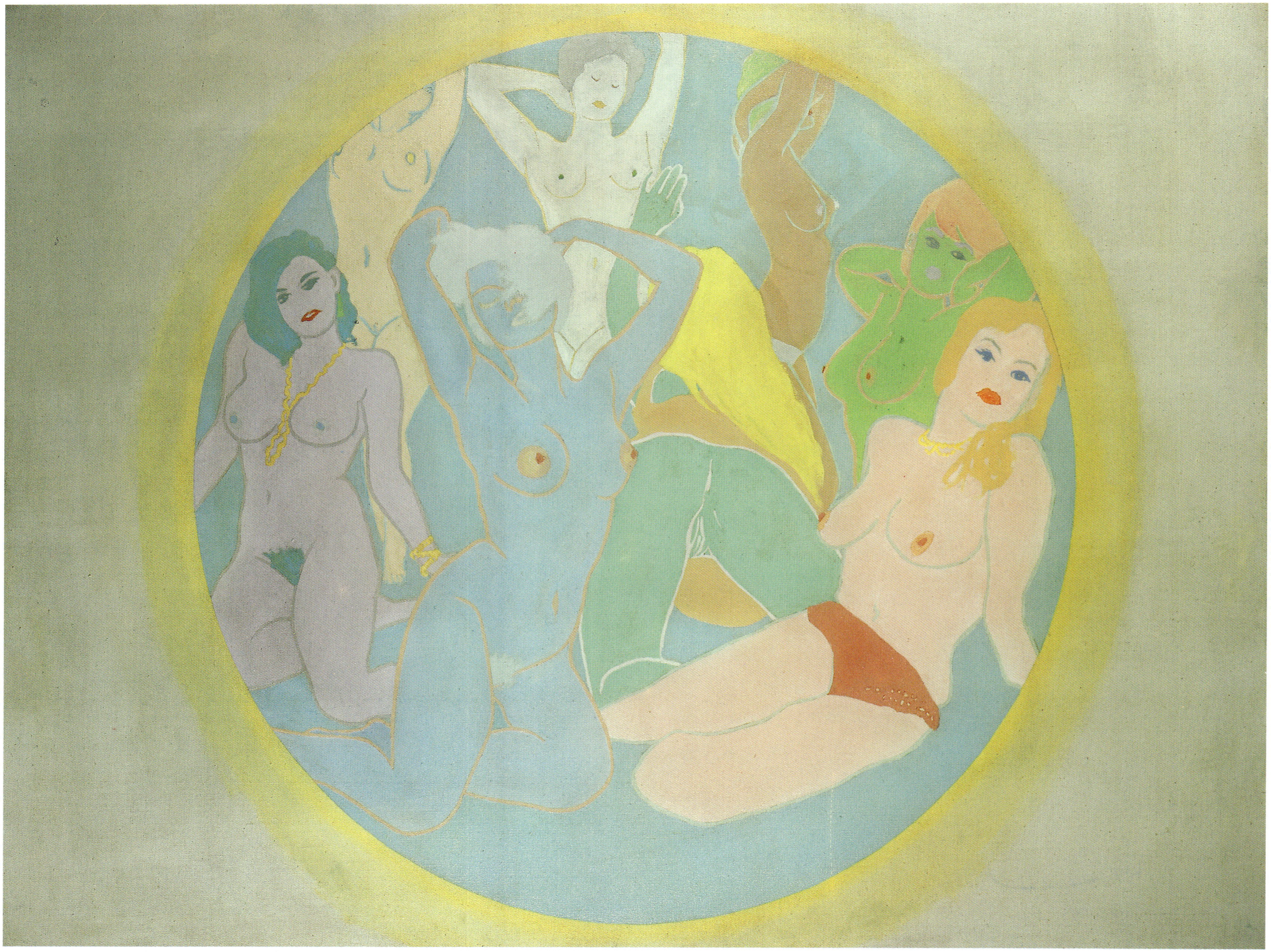

Nudes, after 'le Bain Turc' (pin-ups)
Oil on canvas, 36 × 36ins, Early 1960s

Reclining Girl on Bosnian Rug
Chalks, 22 × 27½ins, 1957

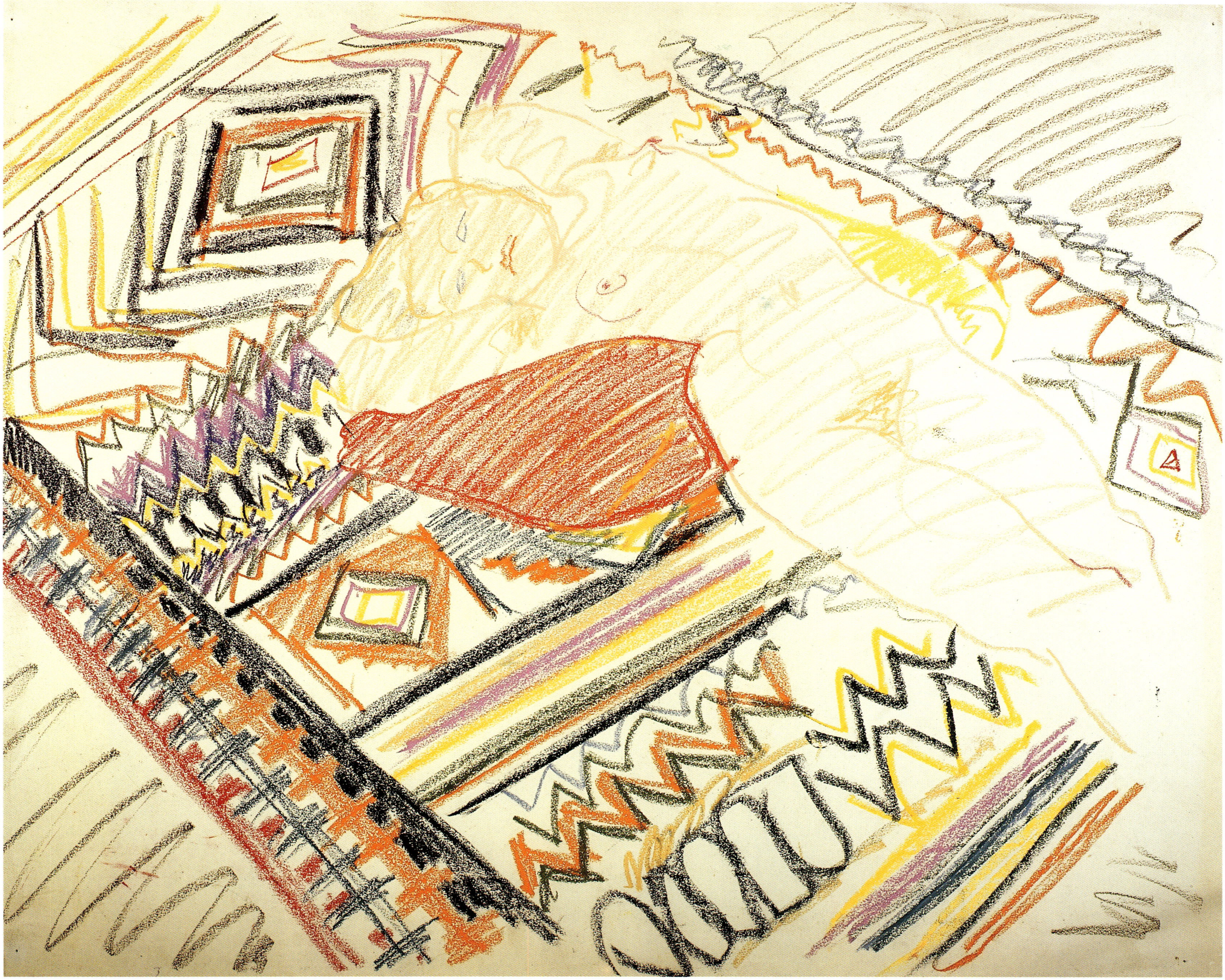

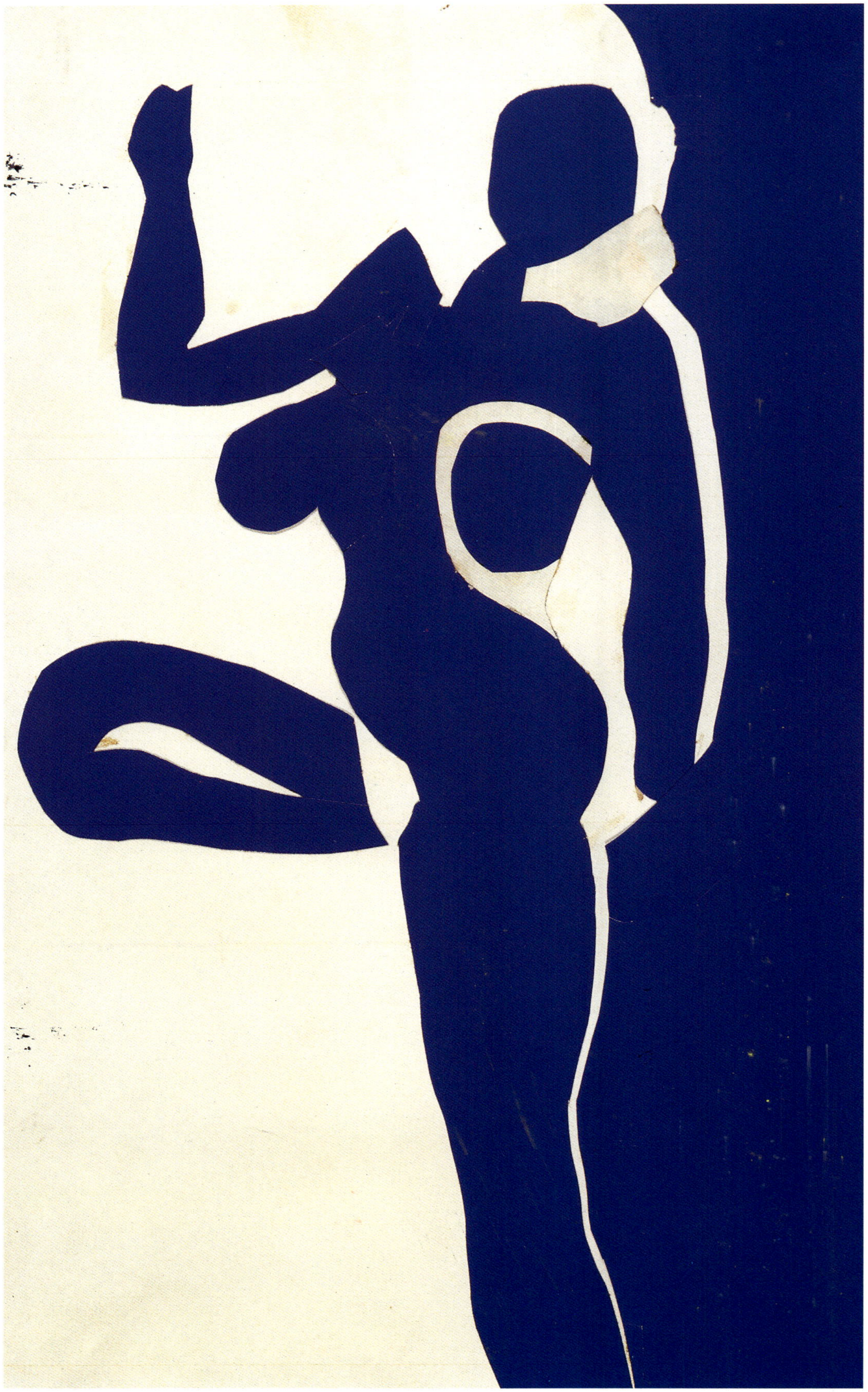

1960s Pin-up
Collage, blue and white paper, 17½ × 10½ins, 1960s

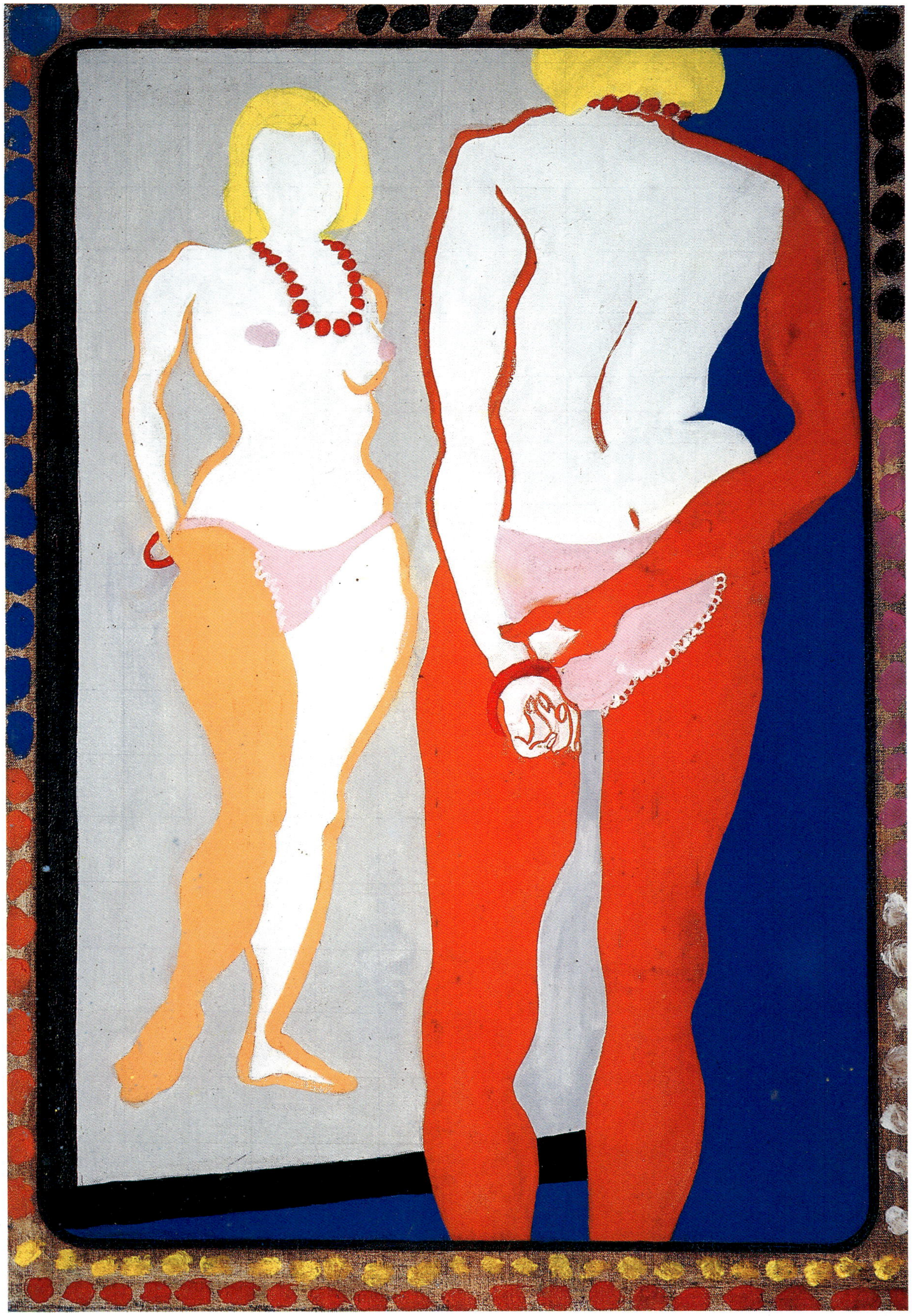

Girl and Reflection, Spotted Border
Oil on canvas, 36 × 25ins, 1962

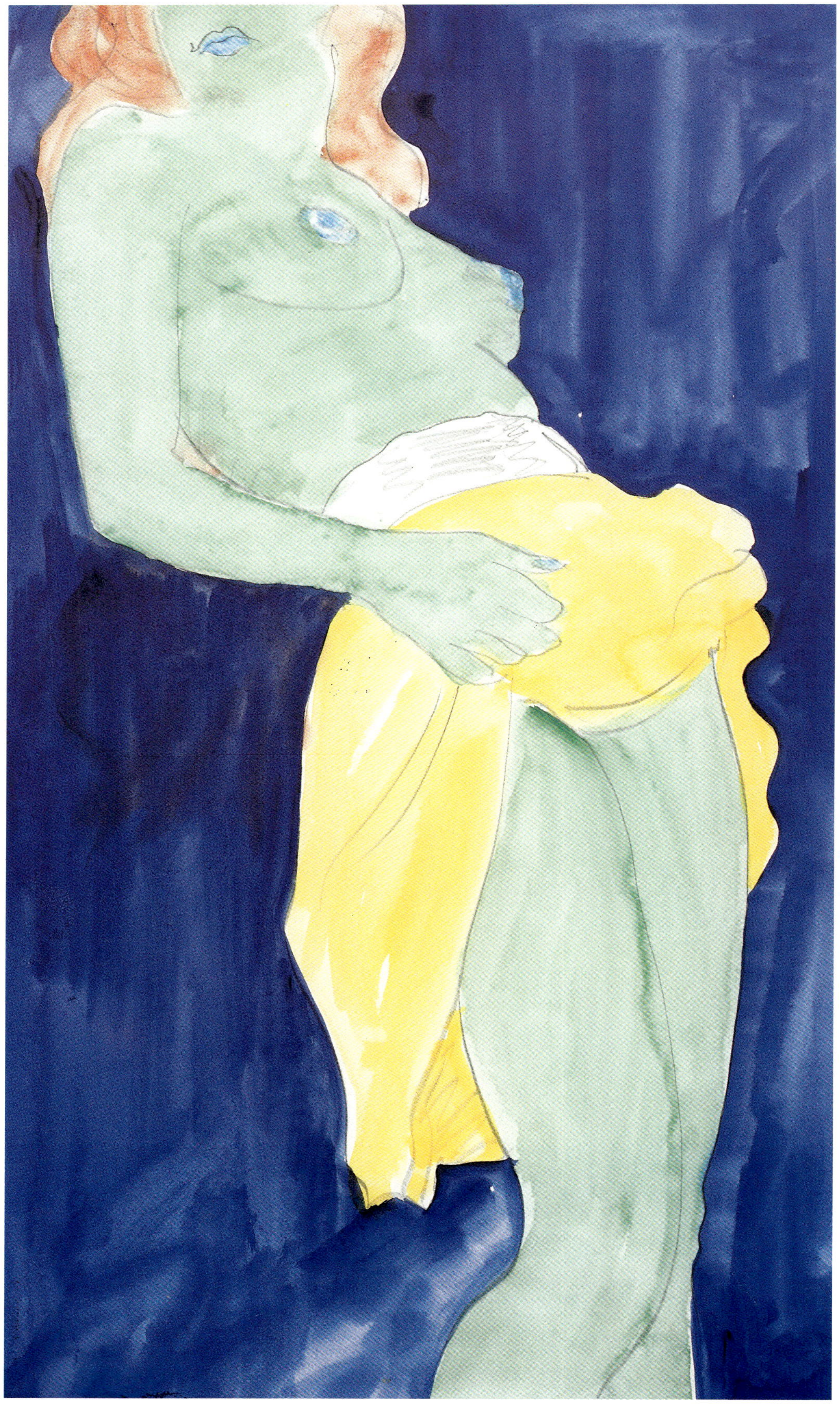

Pin-up
Pencil and watercolour, 19 × 11ins, 1962

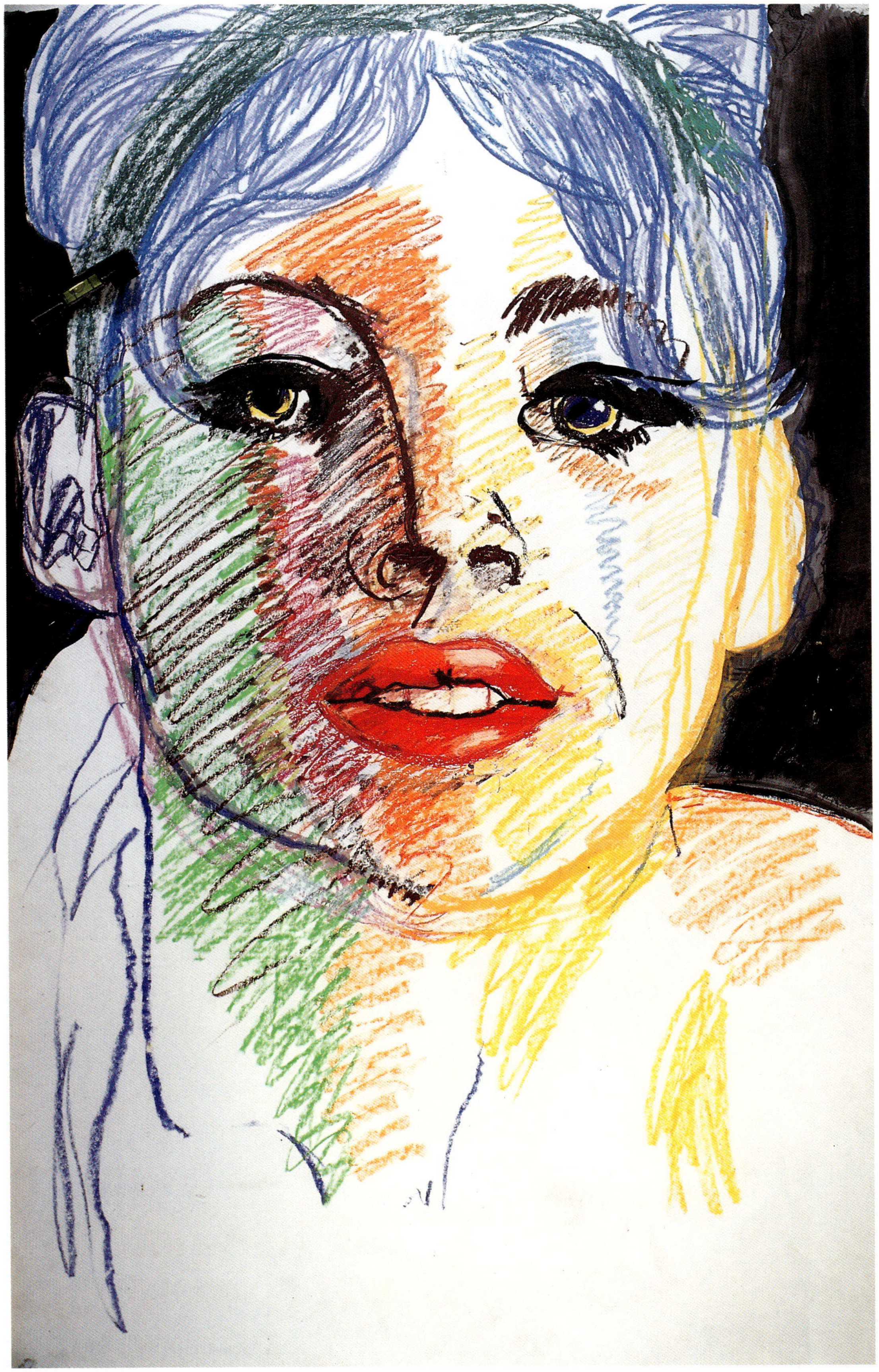

Sixties Face
Chalks, 36 × 24ins, 1964/65

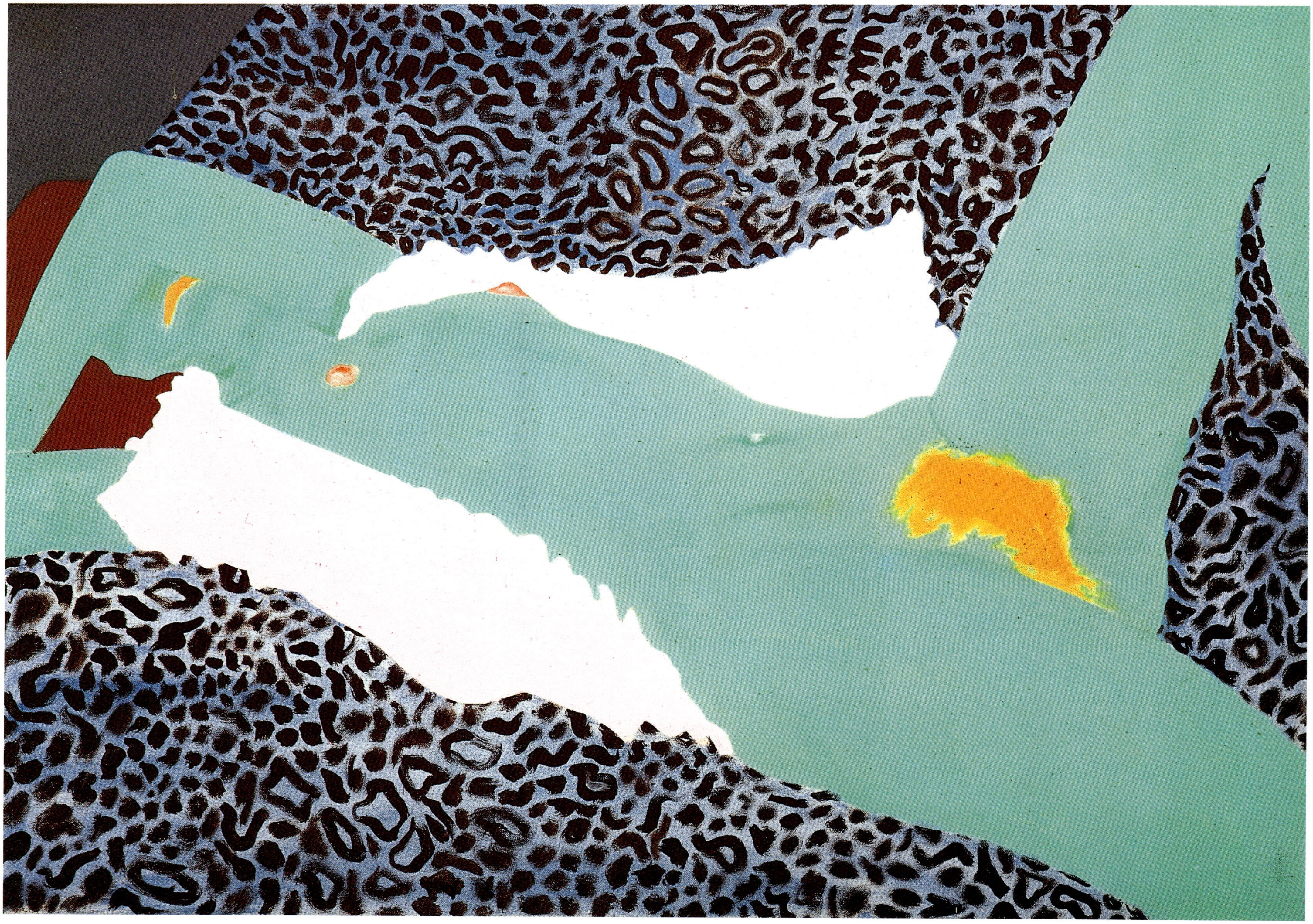

Nude on Leopardskin (pin-up)
Oil on canvas, 25 × 36ins, late 1960s

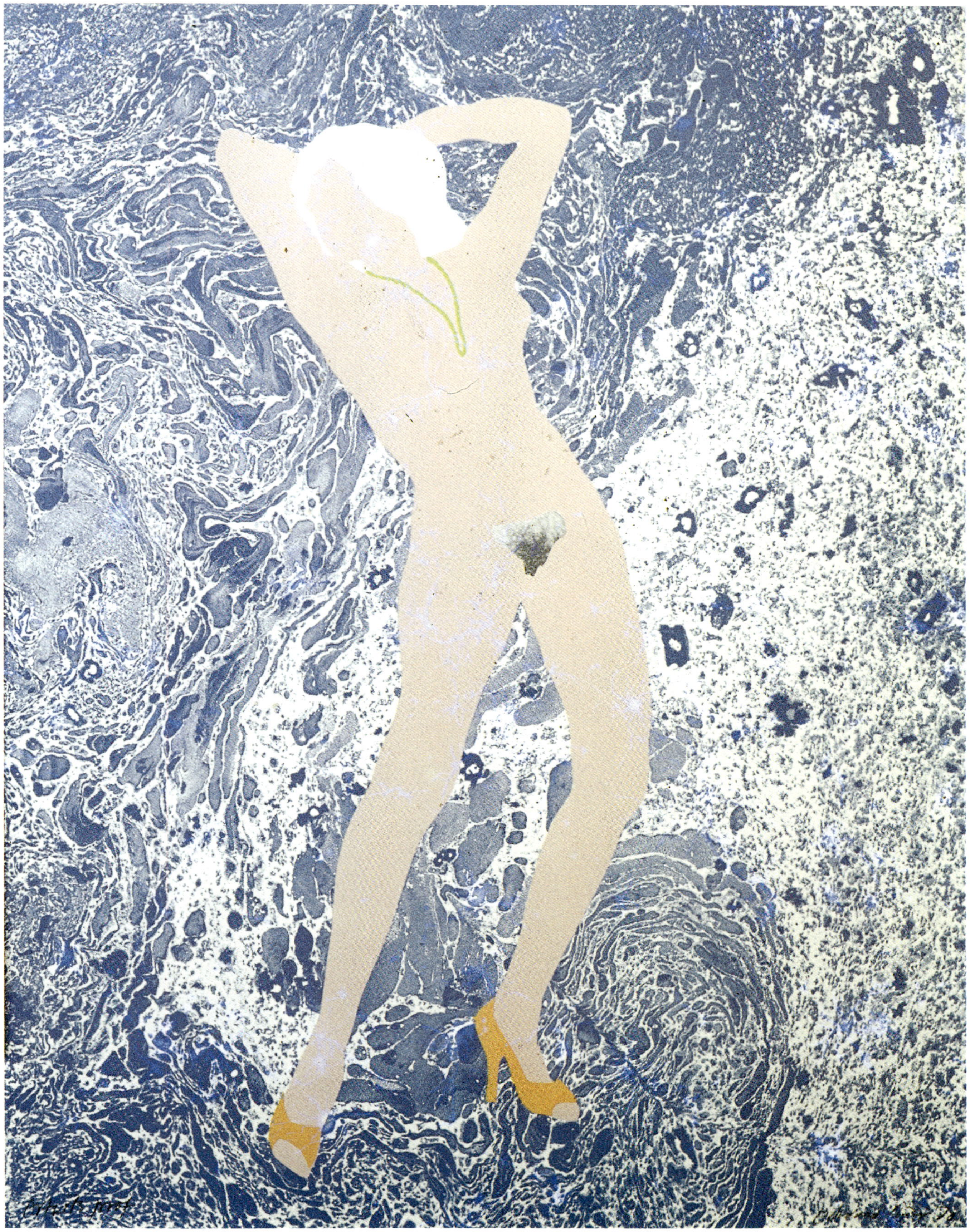

Nude 5
Silkscreen, edition of 70, Kelpra, 27½ × 21ins, 1970

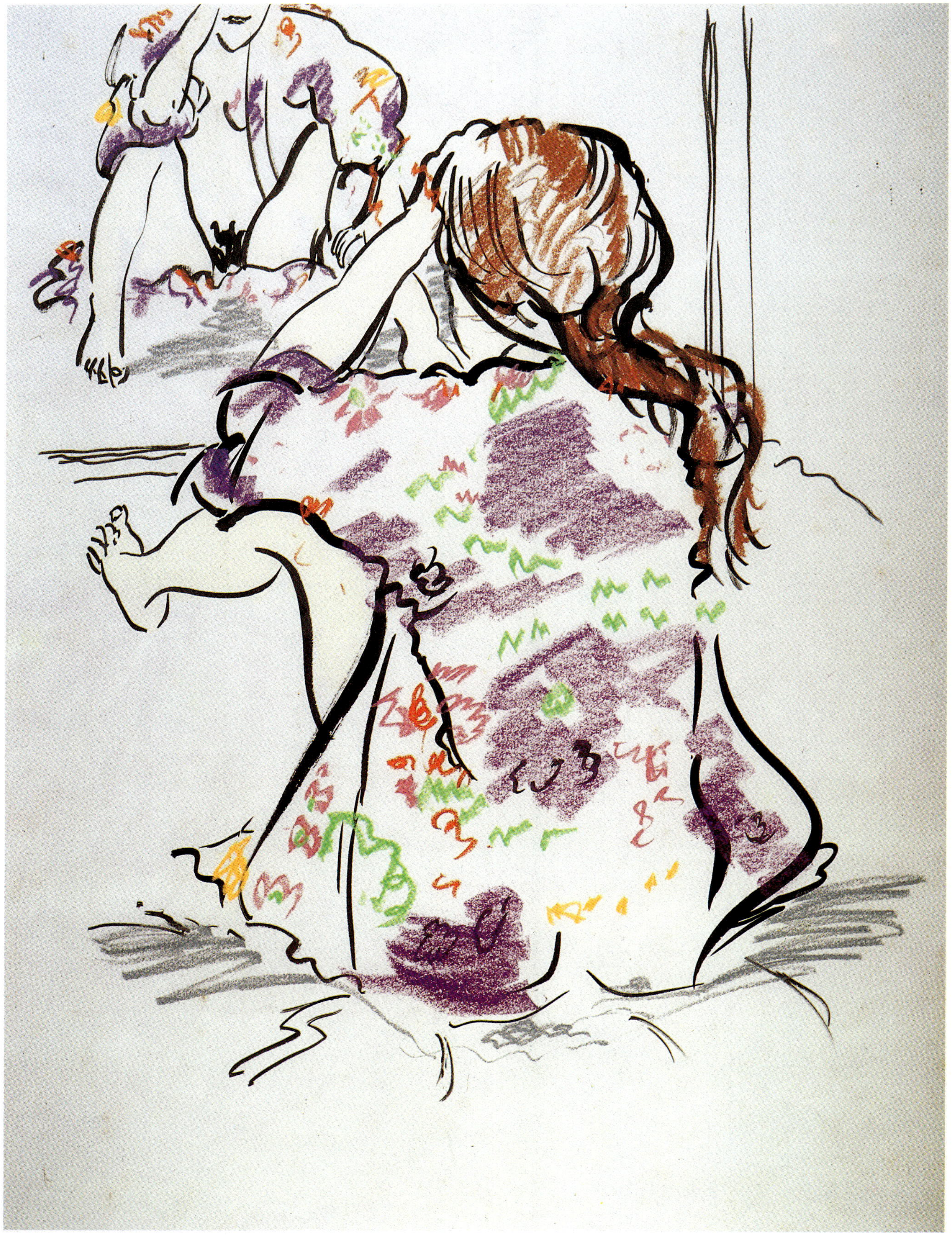

Seated Girl and Reflection
Ink and chalk, 23½ × 16½ins, 1974

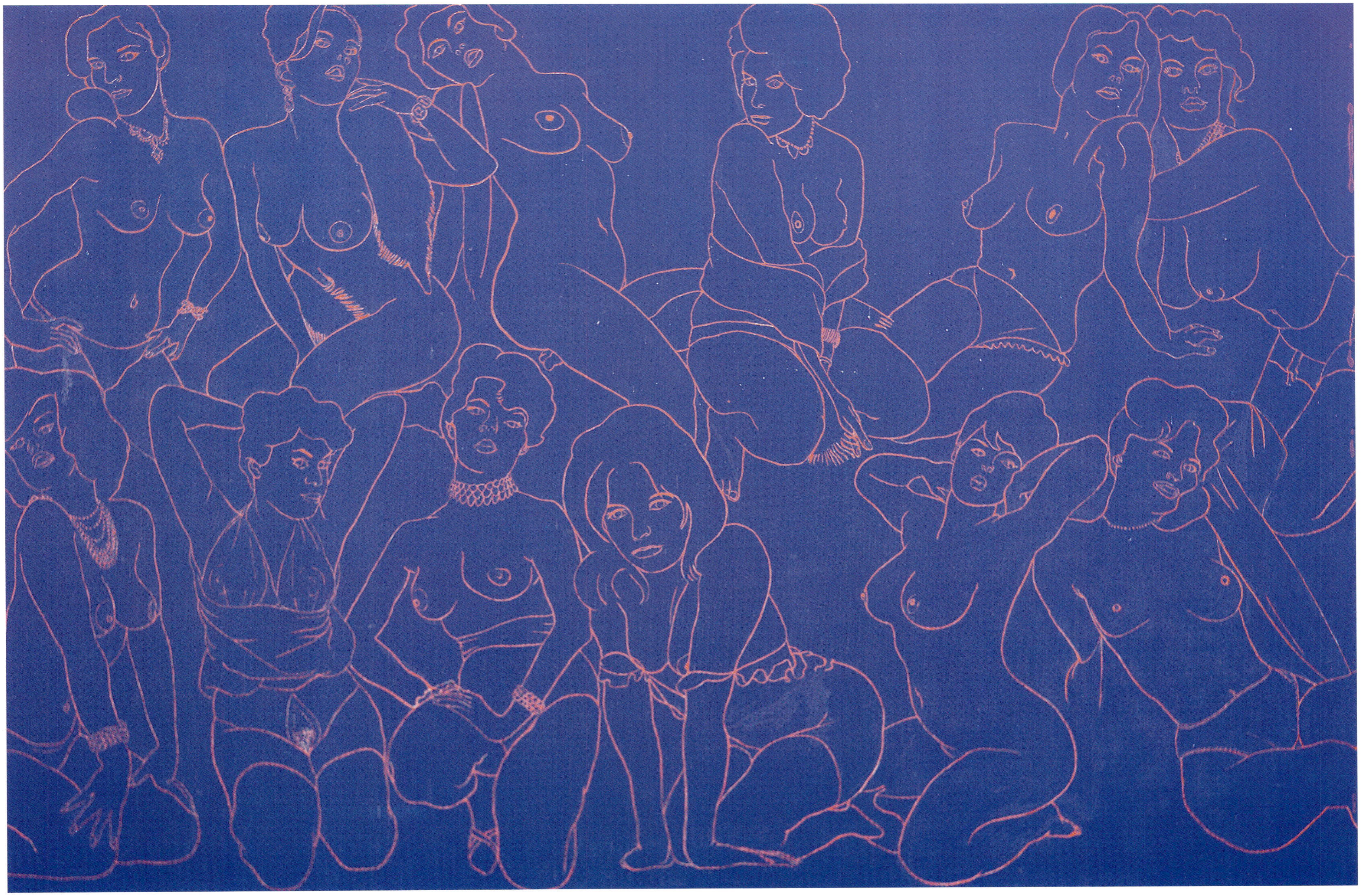

Nudes 2
Oil on canvas, 54½ × 84ins, 1975

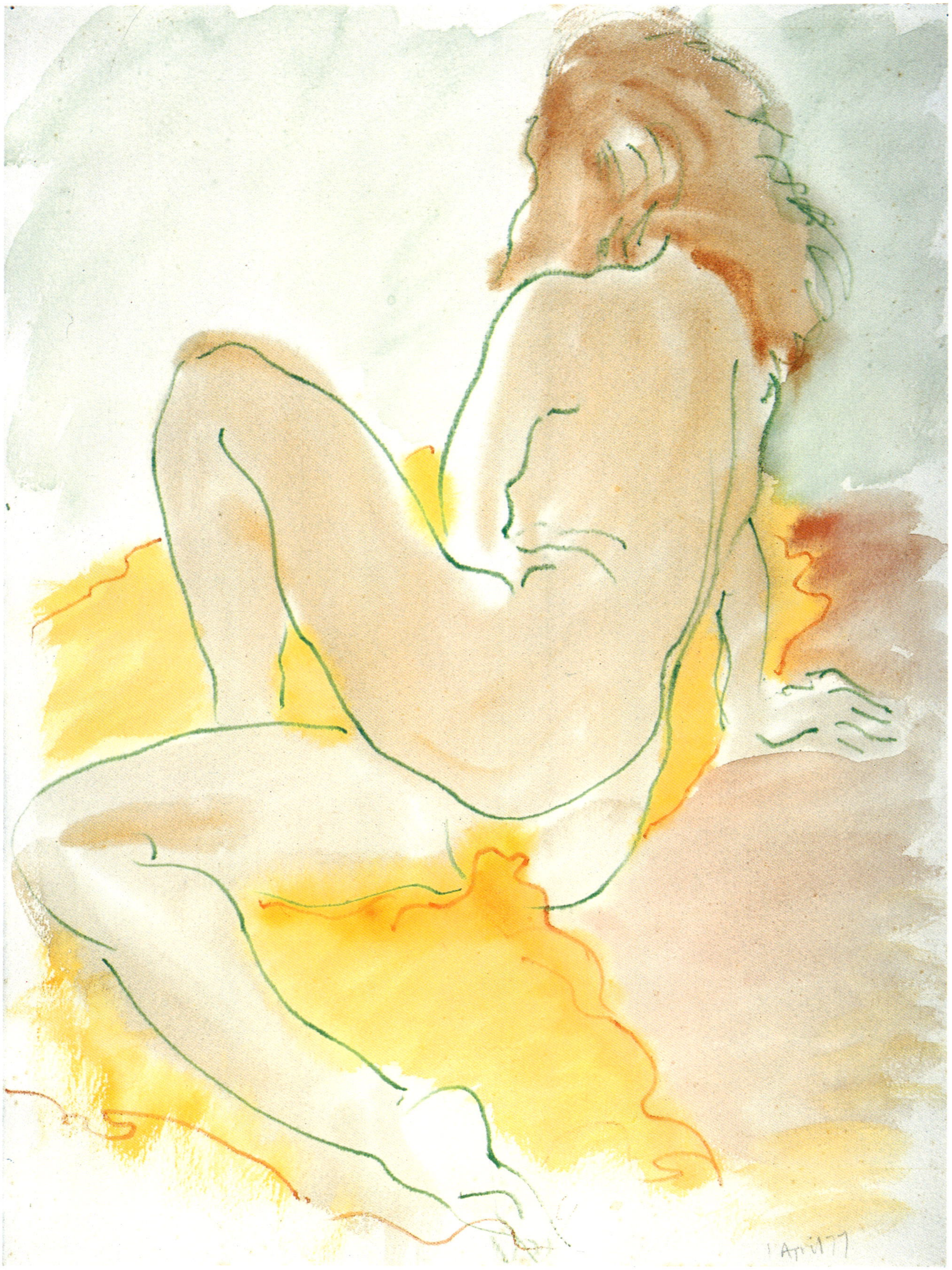

Seated Girl
Watercolour pencils and watercolour, 15½ × 11½ins, 1977

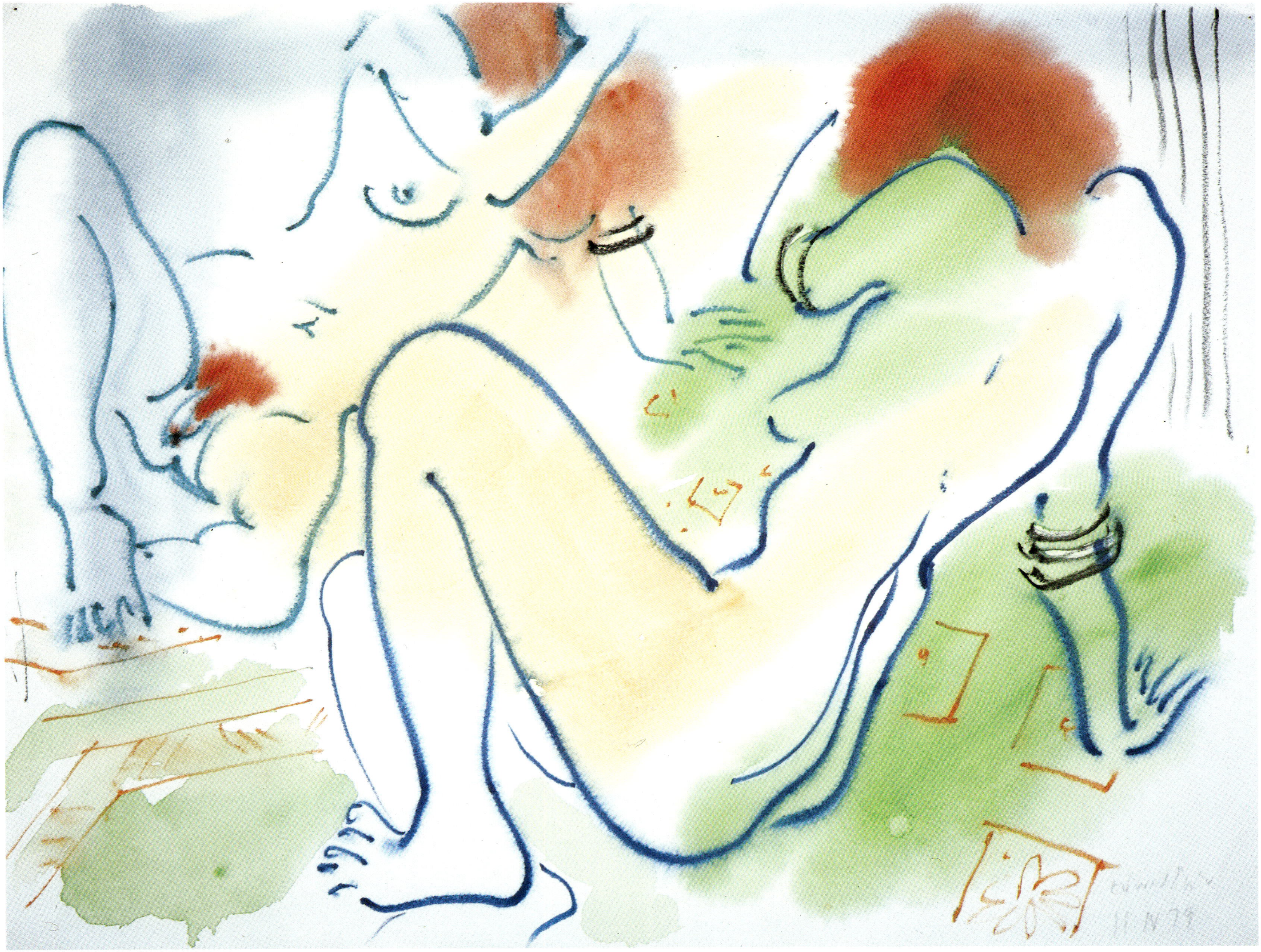

Girl with Red Hair, Seated by Mirror
Watercolour pencils and watercolour, 15 × 20ins, 1979

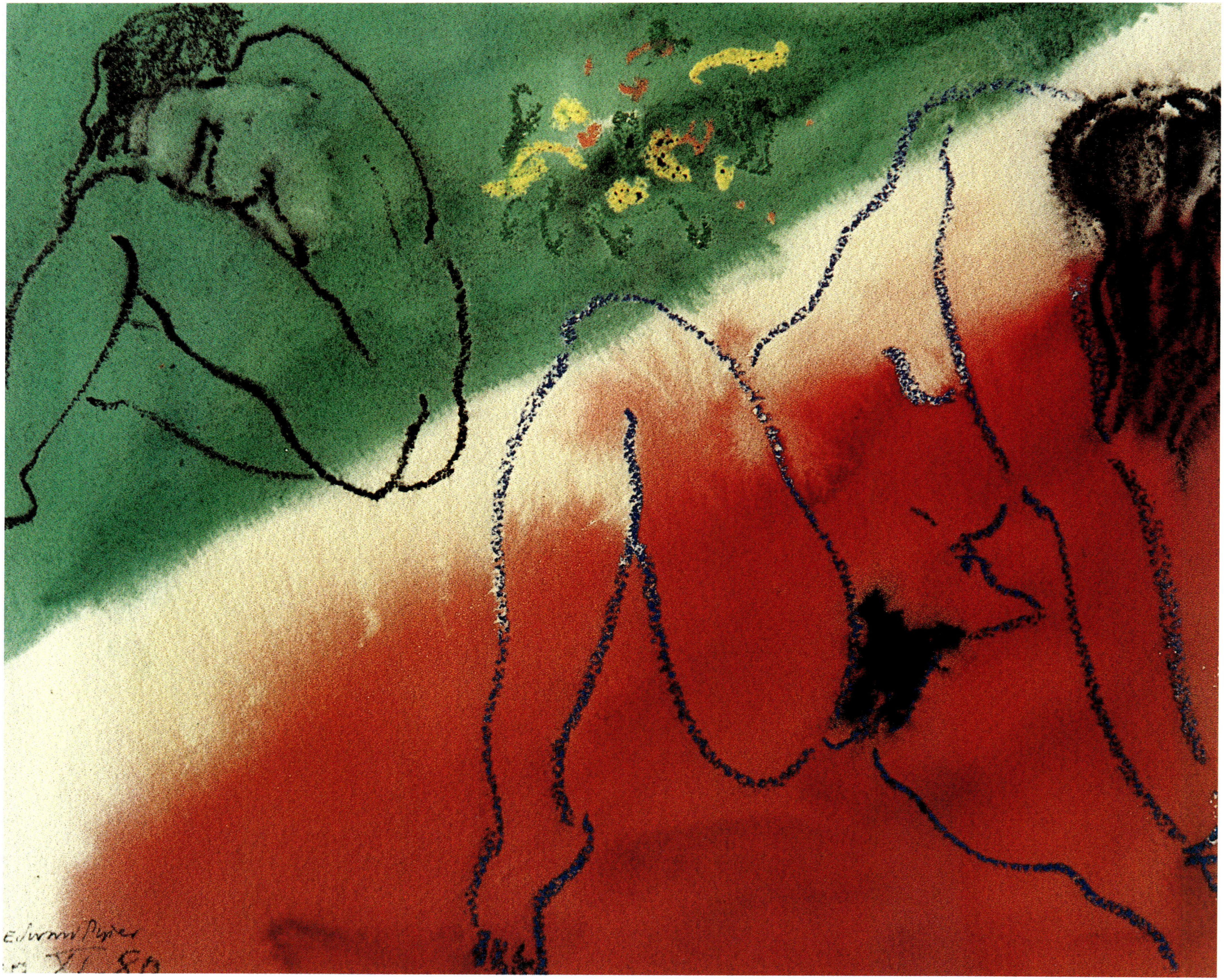
Edward Piper

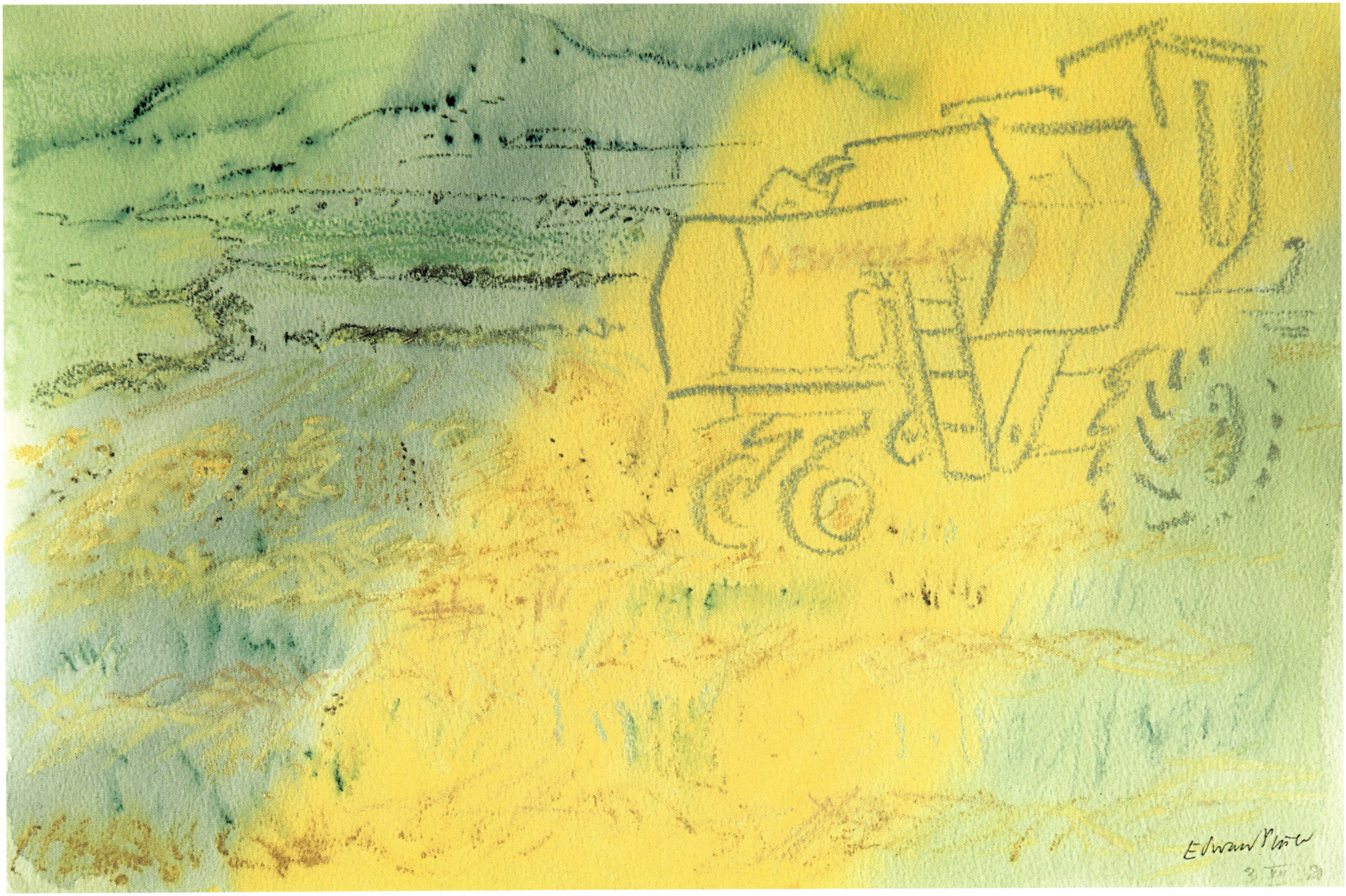

Combine at Strumble Head, Pembrokeshire
Watercolour, 15 × 20ins, 1980

Seated Girl and Reflection, Green and Red Light
Watercolour pencils, chalk and watercolour, 15 × 20ins, 1980

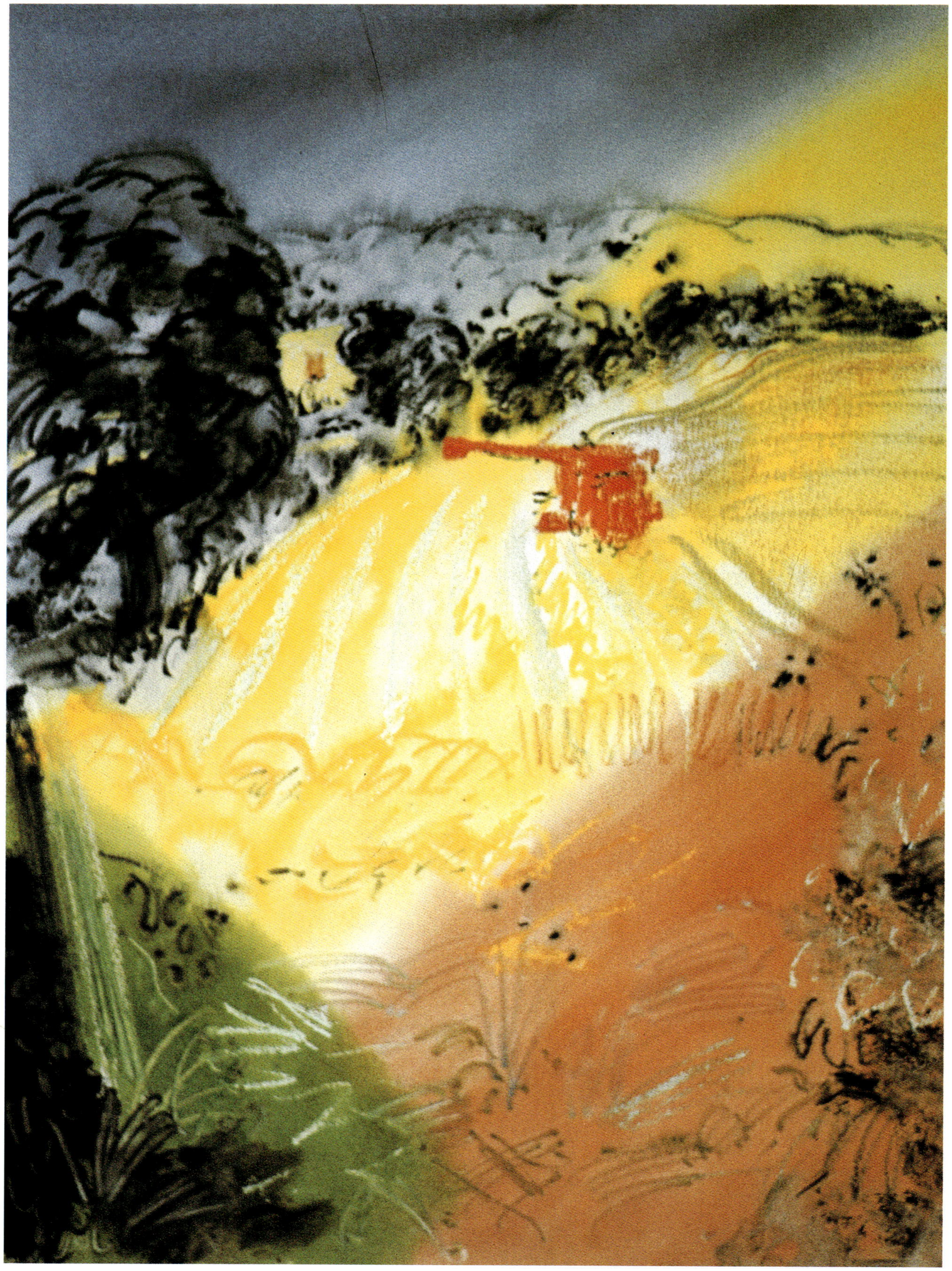

Combine at Hardington, Somerset
Pencil, watercolour and chalk, 20 × 15ins, 1981

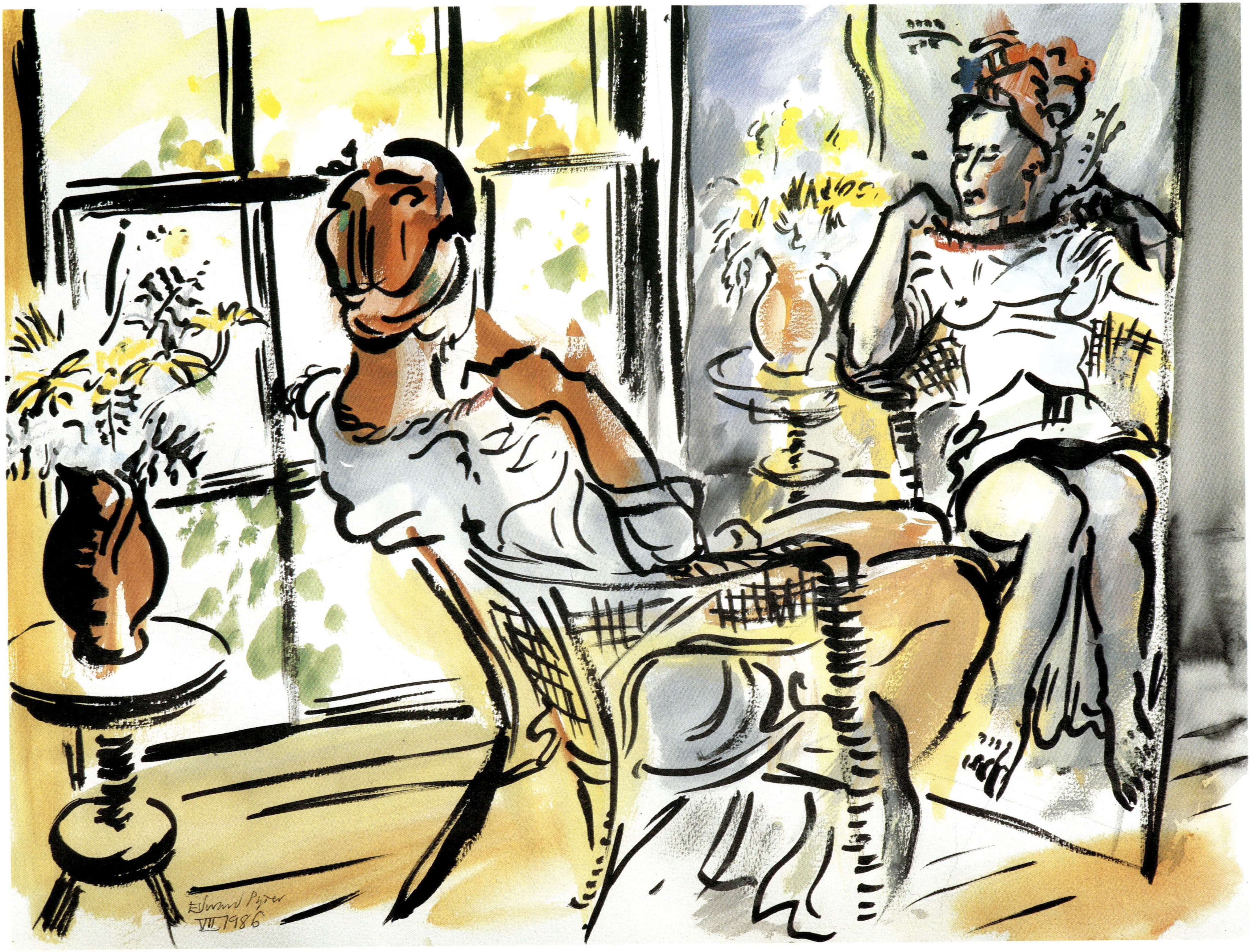

Turbaned Girl, Seated by Window, Reflection
Ink and acrylic, 18 × 24ins, 1986

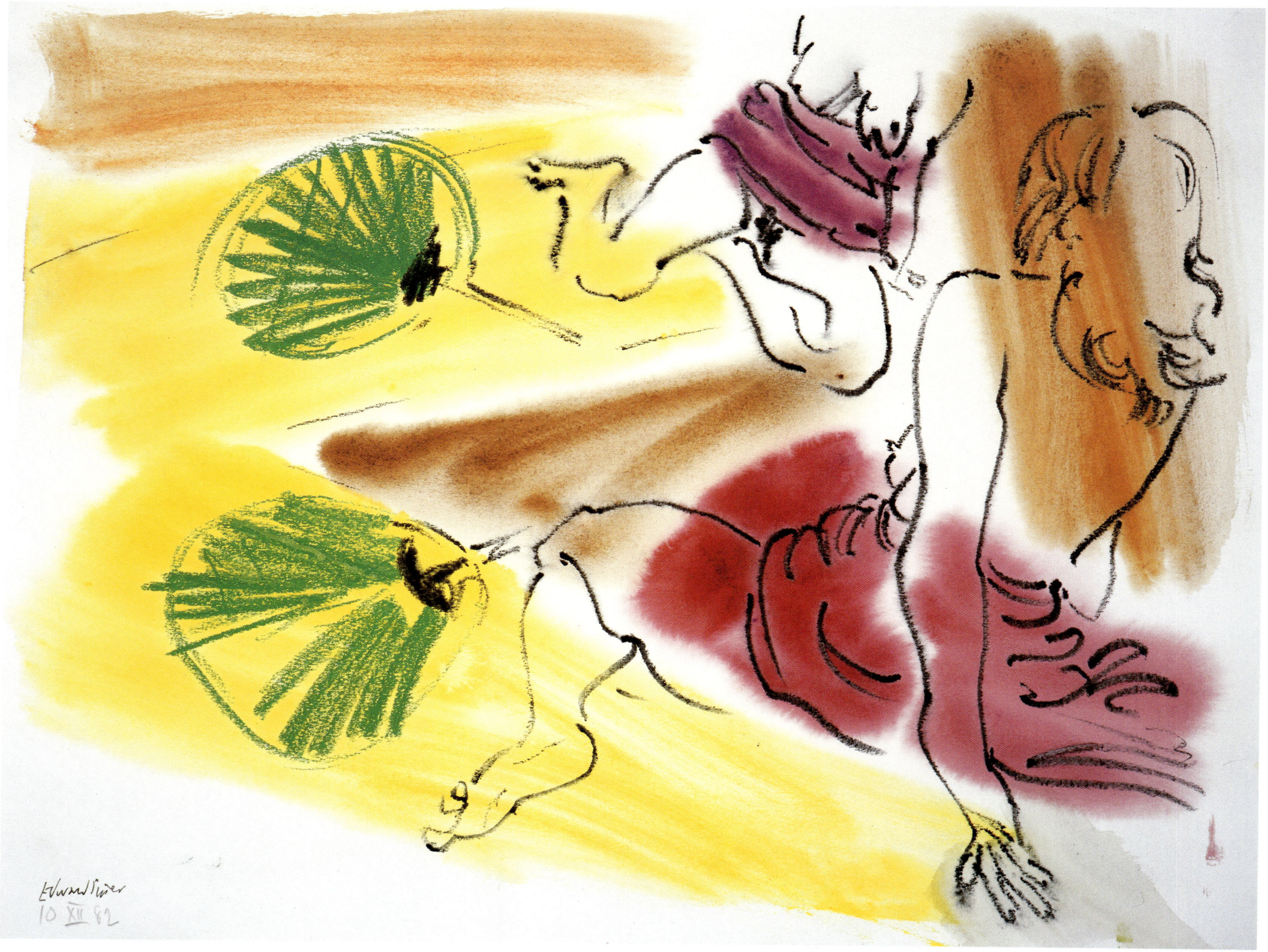

Seated Girl in Red Skirt, Green Fan
Pencil, chalk and watercolour, 15 × 20ins, 1982

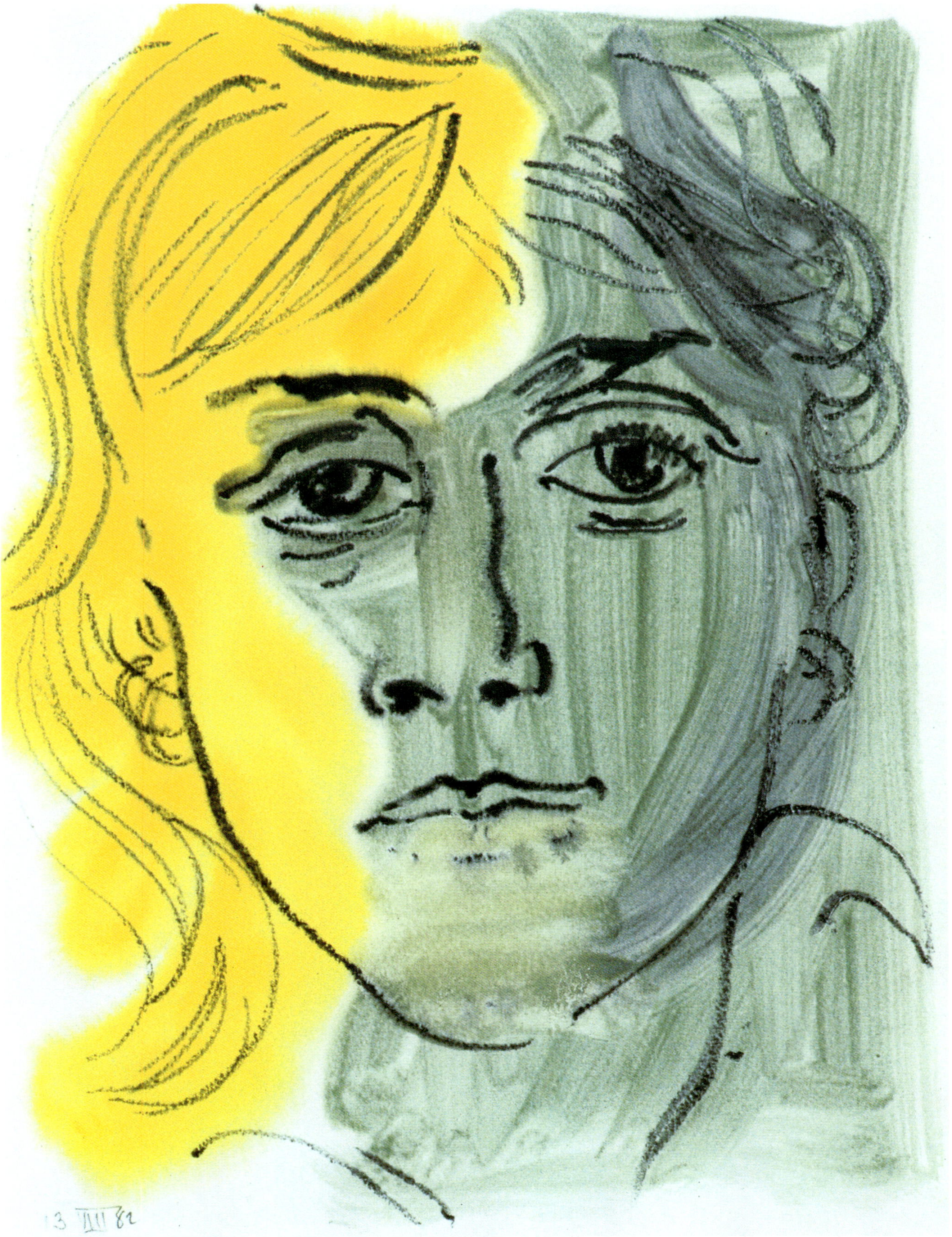

Portrait of a Girl with Yellow Hair
Pencil and watercolour, 20 × 15ins, 1982

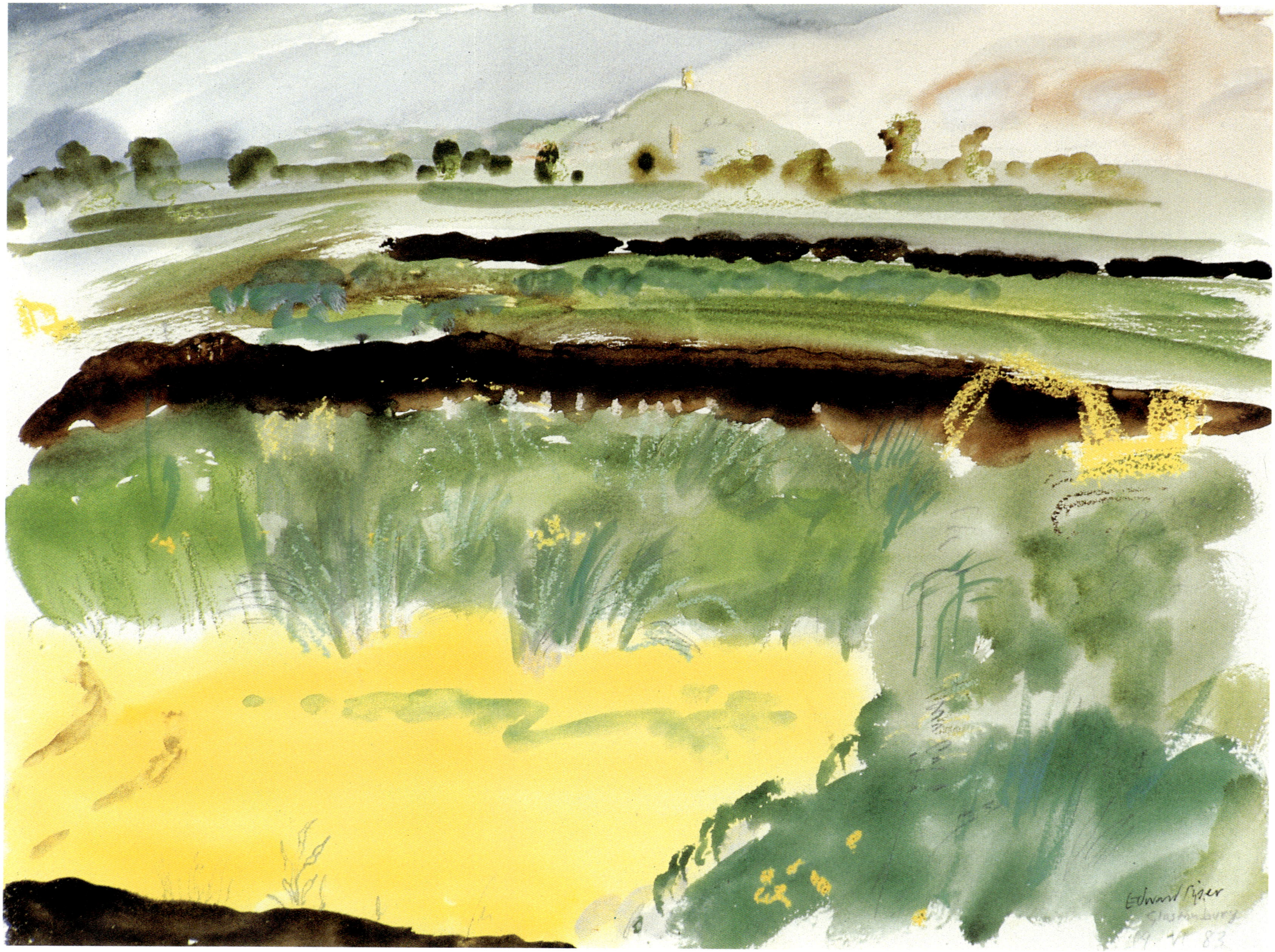

Peat Beds at Glastonbury
Watercolour, chalks, 15 × 20ins, 1983

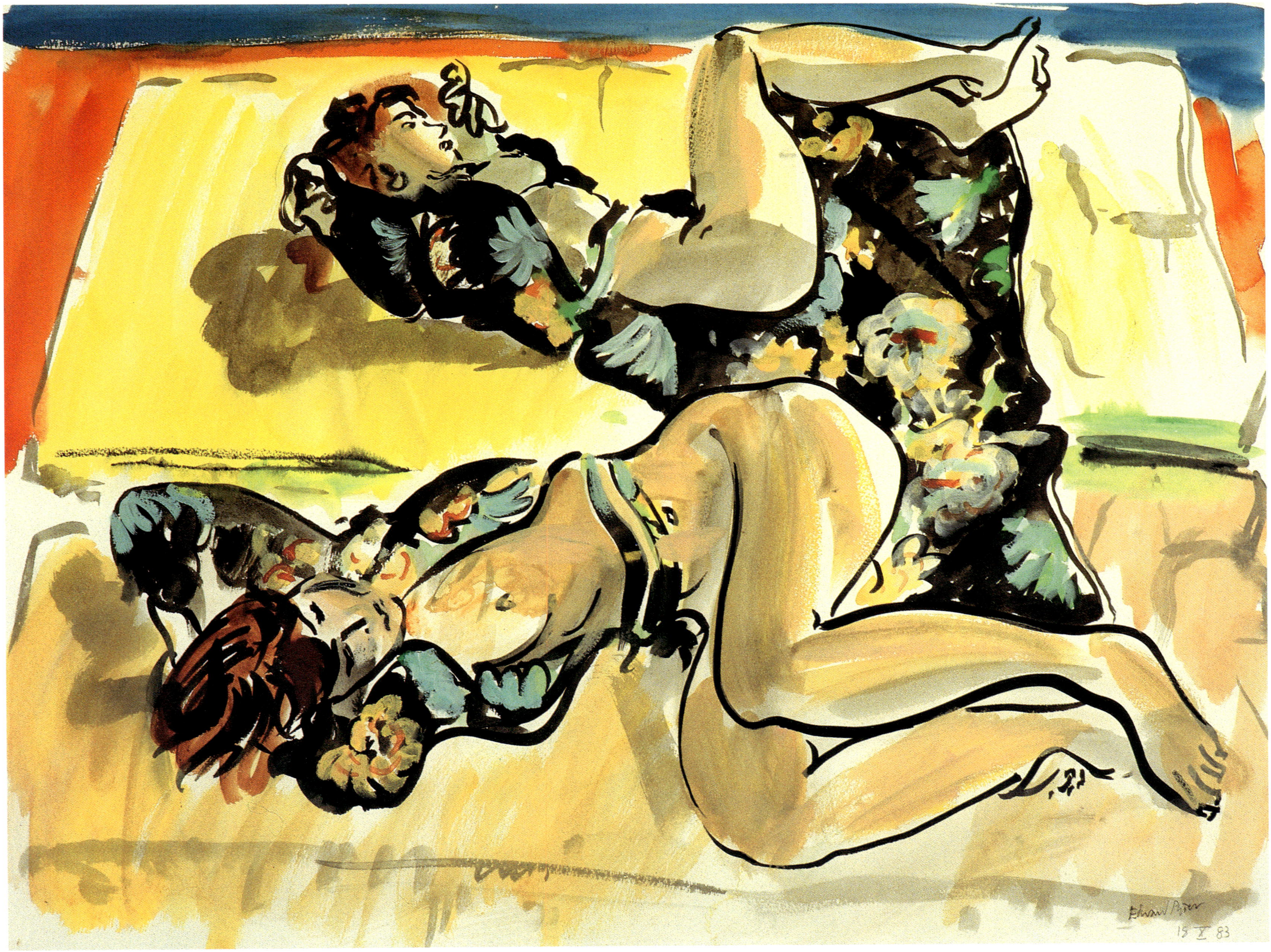

Reclining Girl in Flowered Kimono, Reflection
Ink and acrylic, 18 × 24ins, 1983

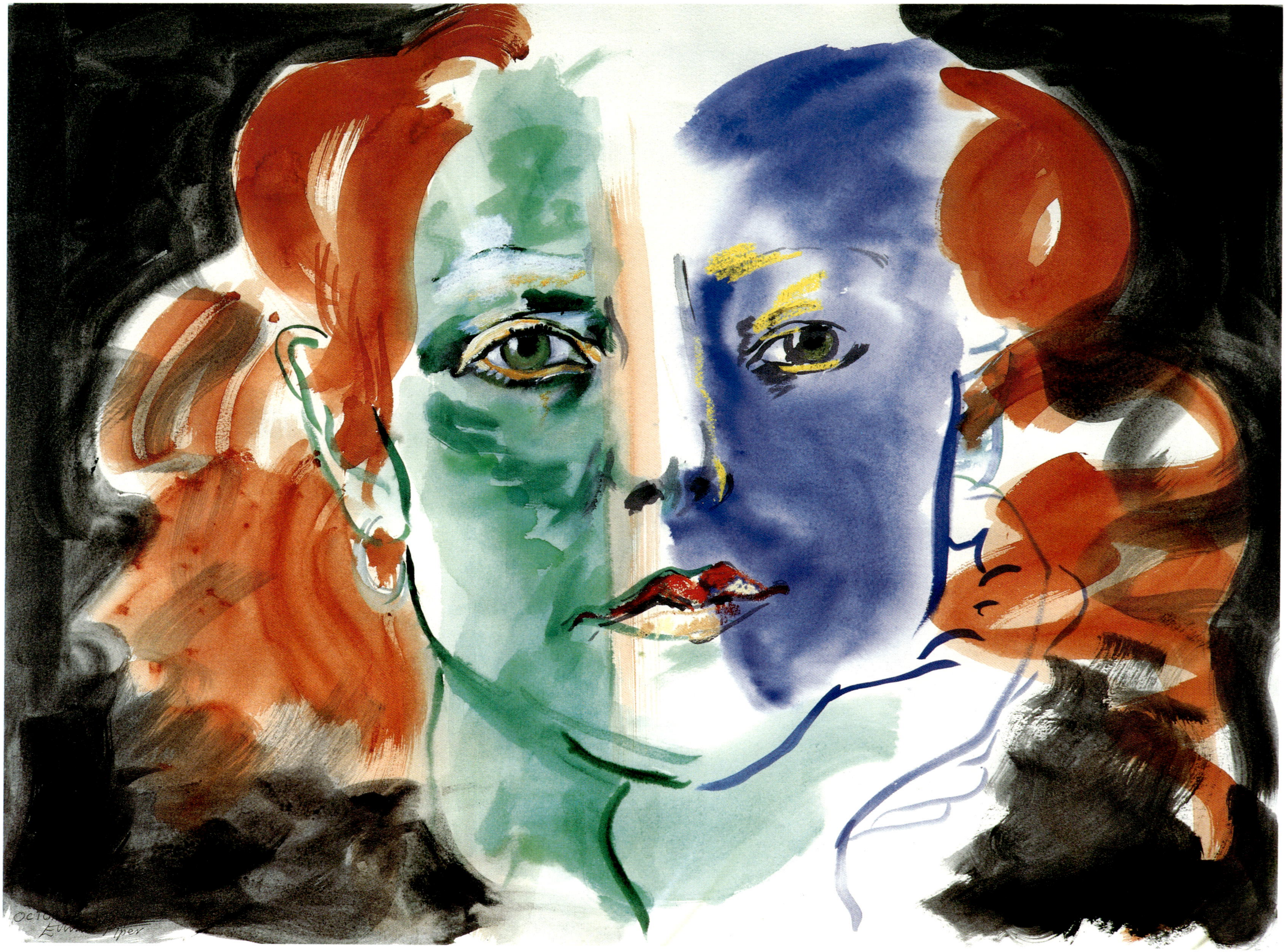

Head of a Girl
Ink, acrylic and chalks, 18 × 24ins, 1984

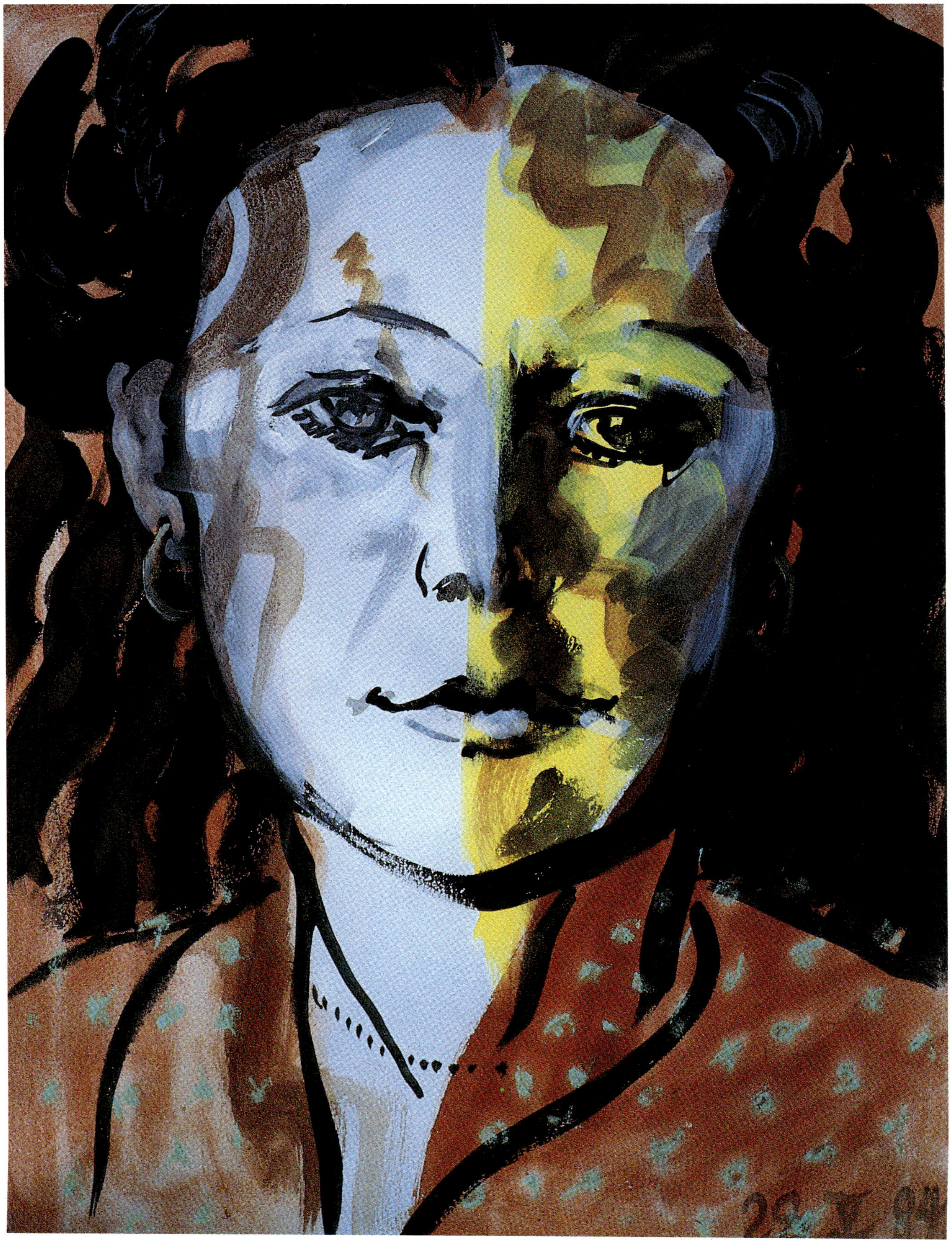

Head of a Girl in Pink Spotted Dress
Ink and acrylic, 20 × 15ins, 1984

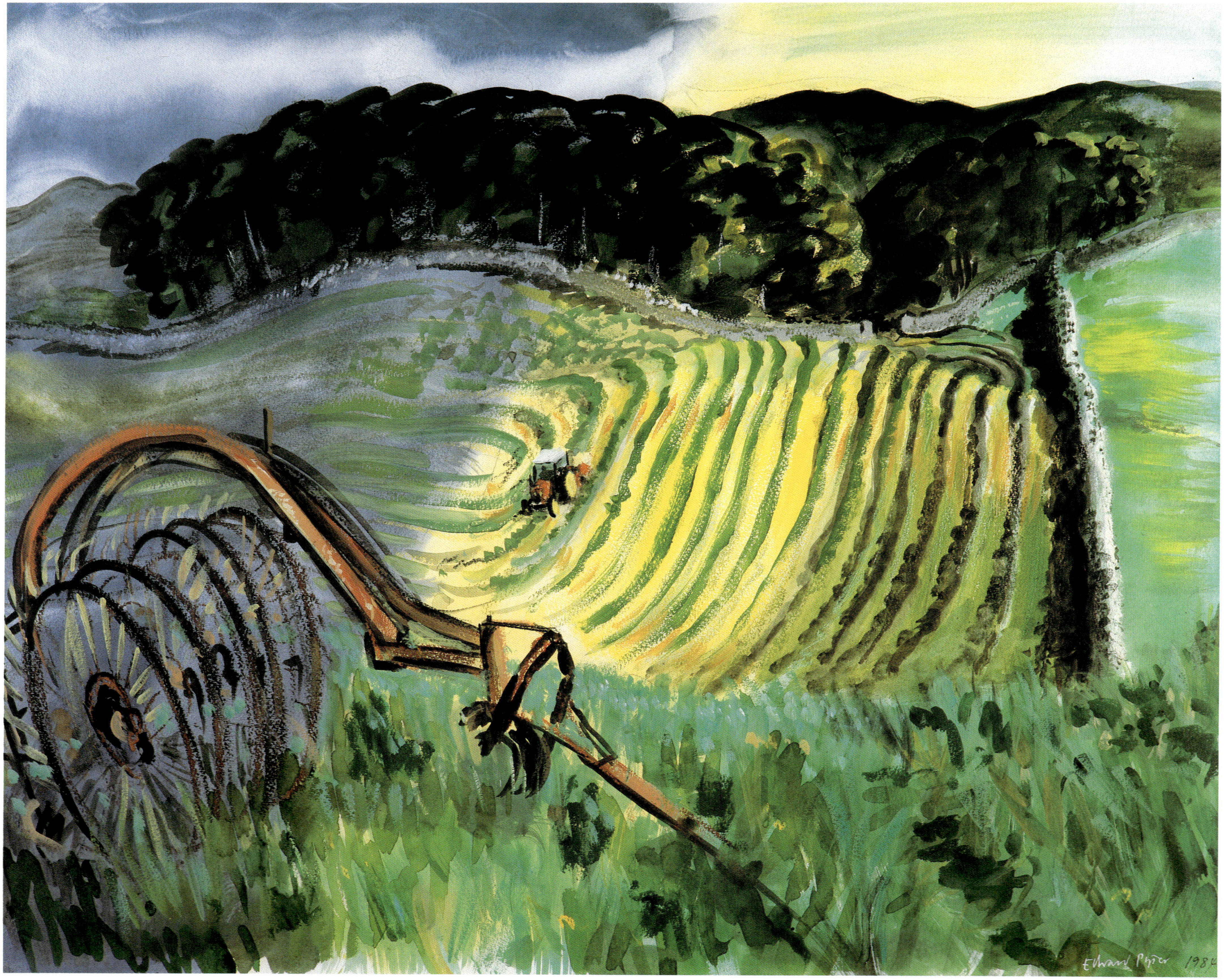
Edward Piper 1984

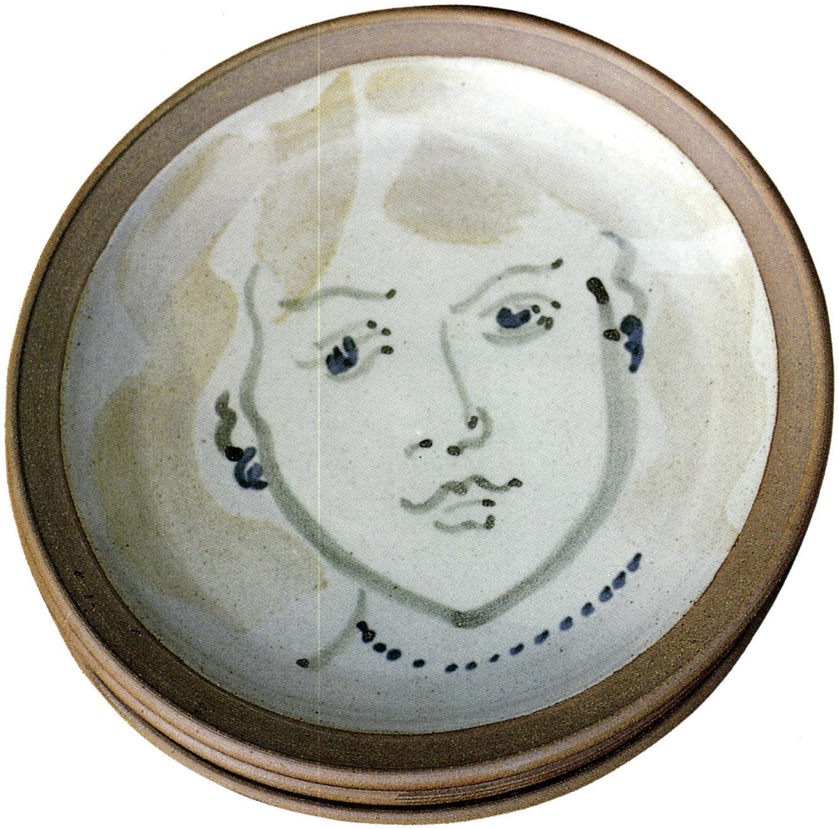

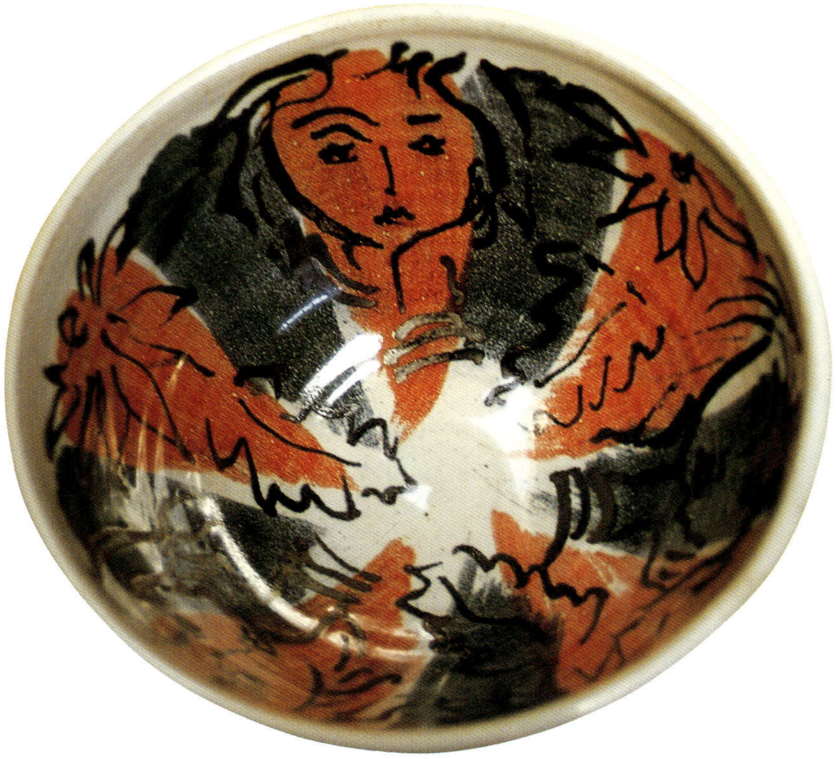

Above
Plate made in collaboration with Douglas Phillips
Woodfired Stoneware, Slipped with on-glaze decoration, 10ins diameter

Top right
Bowl made in collaboration with Fulham Pottery
Earthenware, on-glaze decoration, 7½ins diameter

Bottom right
Dish made in collaboration with David Garland Earthenware,
majolica, 10½ins diameter

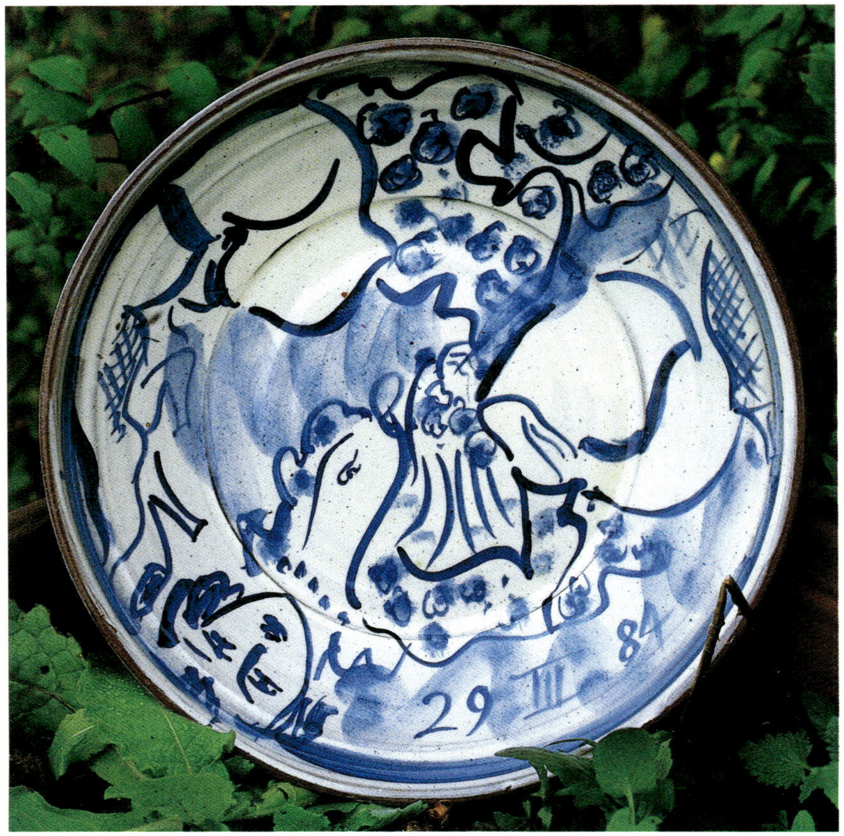

Swaledale
Ink, gouache, chalks, 18 × 24ins, 1984

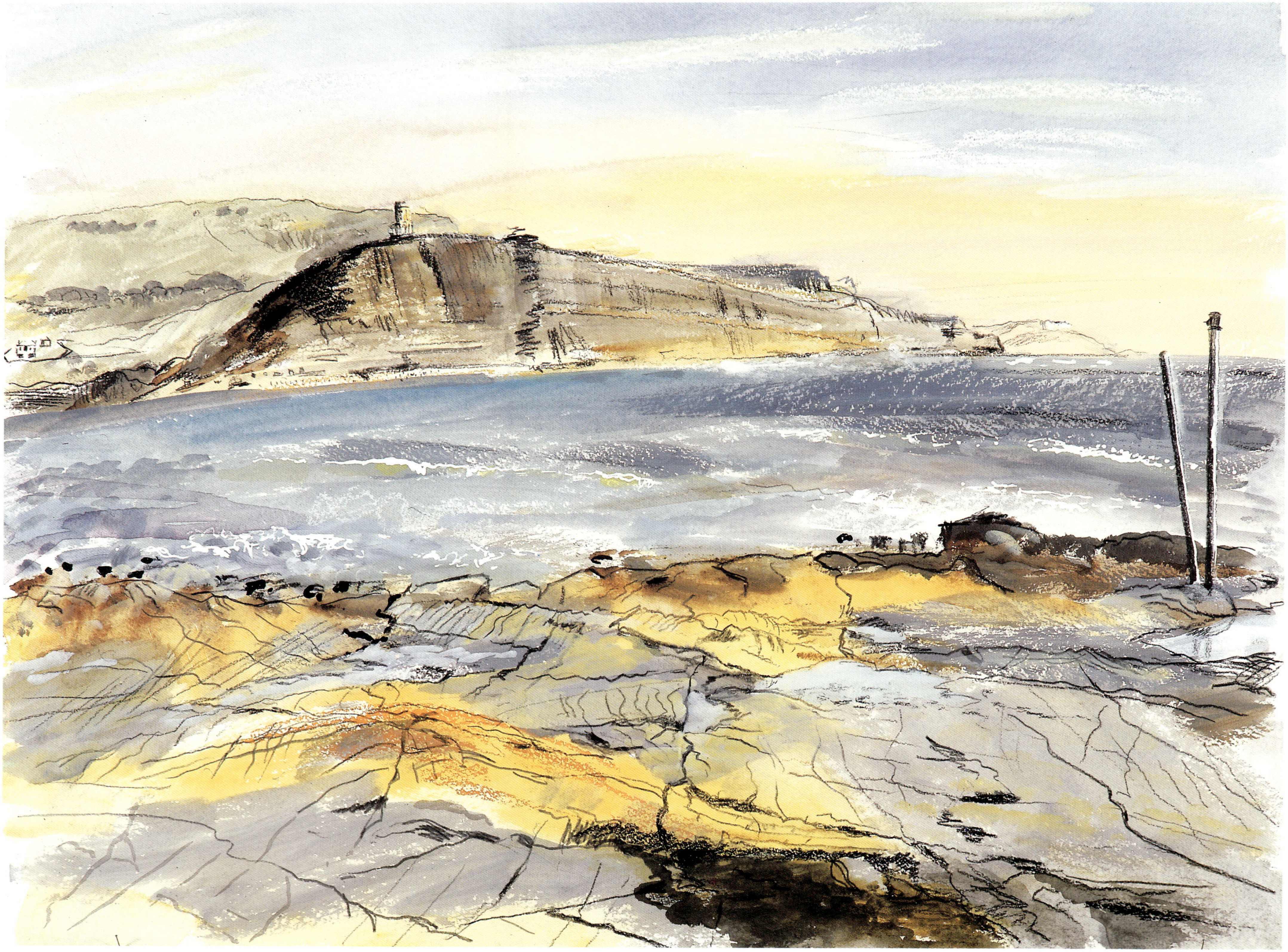

Kimmeridge Bay
Pencil, watercolour, 18 × 24ins, Autumn 1985

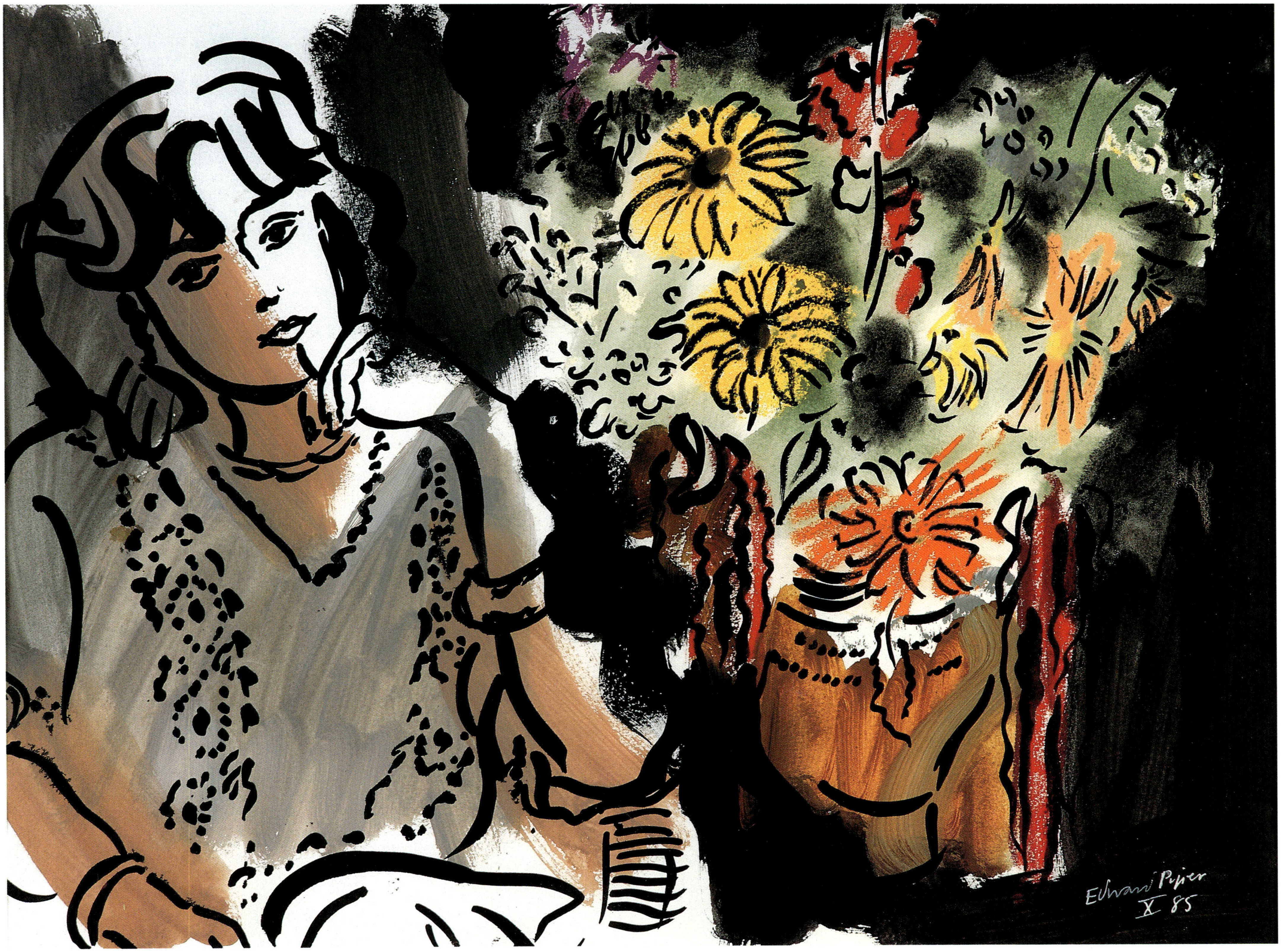

Portrait of a Girl, Lace Blouse and Autumn Flowers
Ink and acrylic, 18 × 24ins, 1985

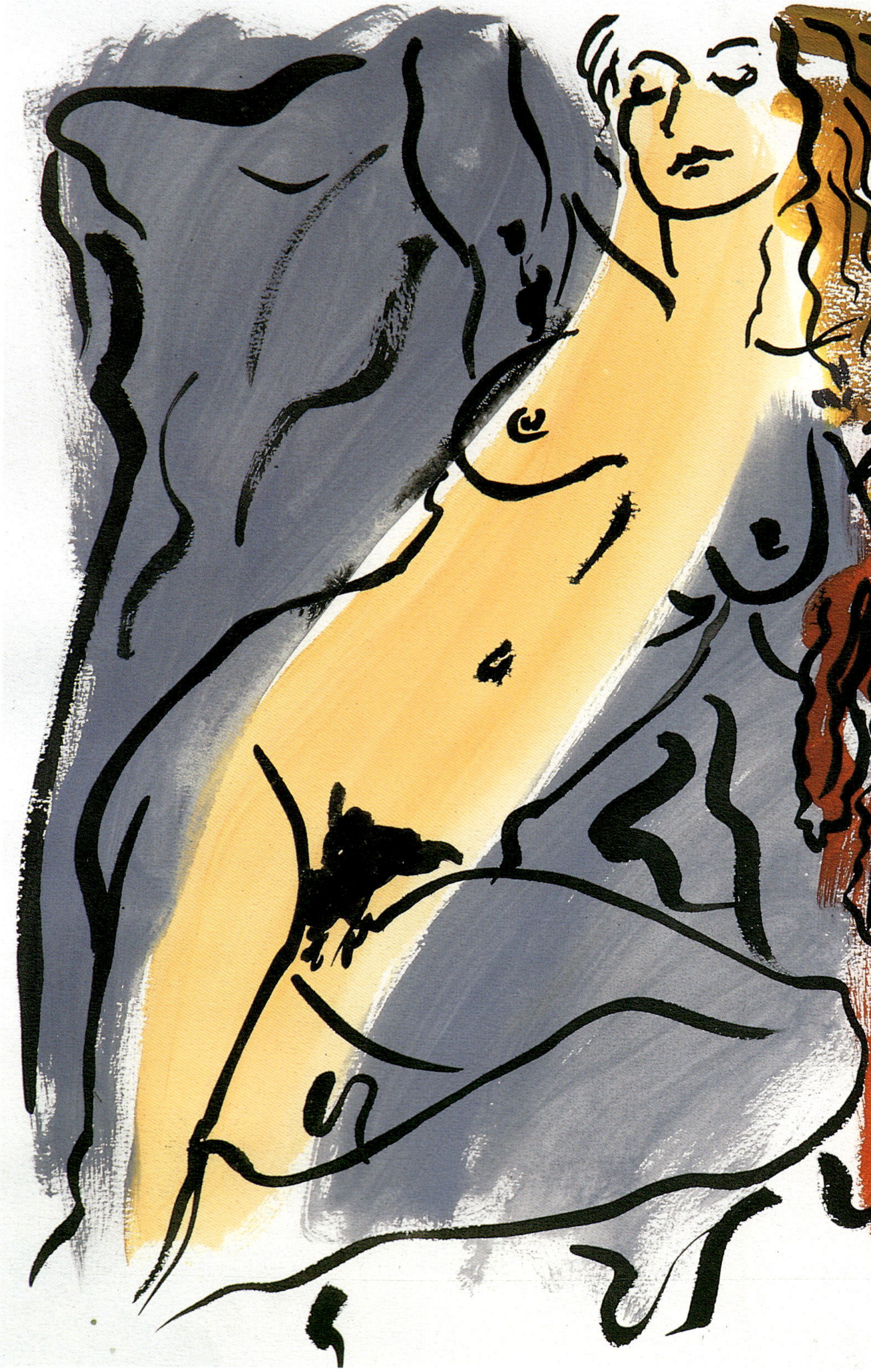

Seated Girl in Blue with Bright Flowers
Ink and watercolour, 15 × 20ins, 1989

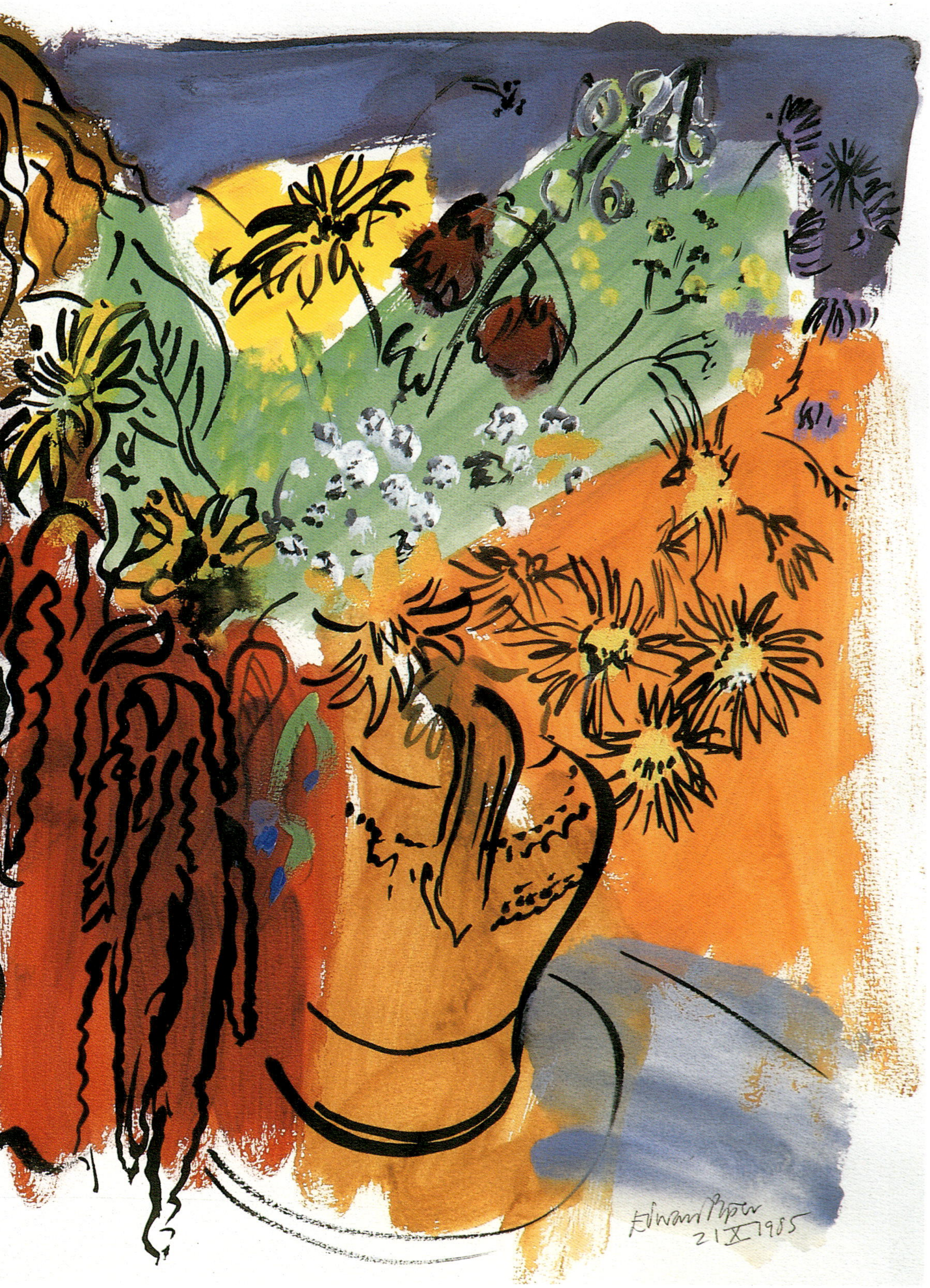

Portrait of Christine
Oil and acrylic on canvas, 20 × 24ins, 1985

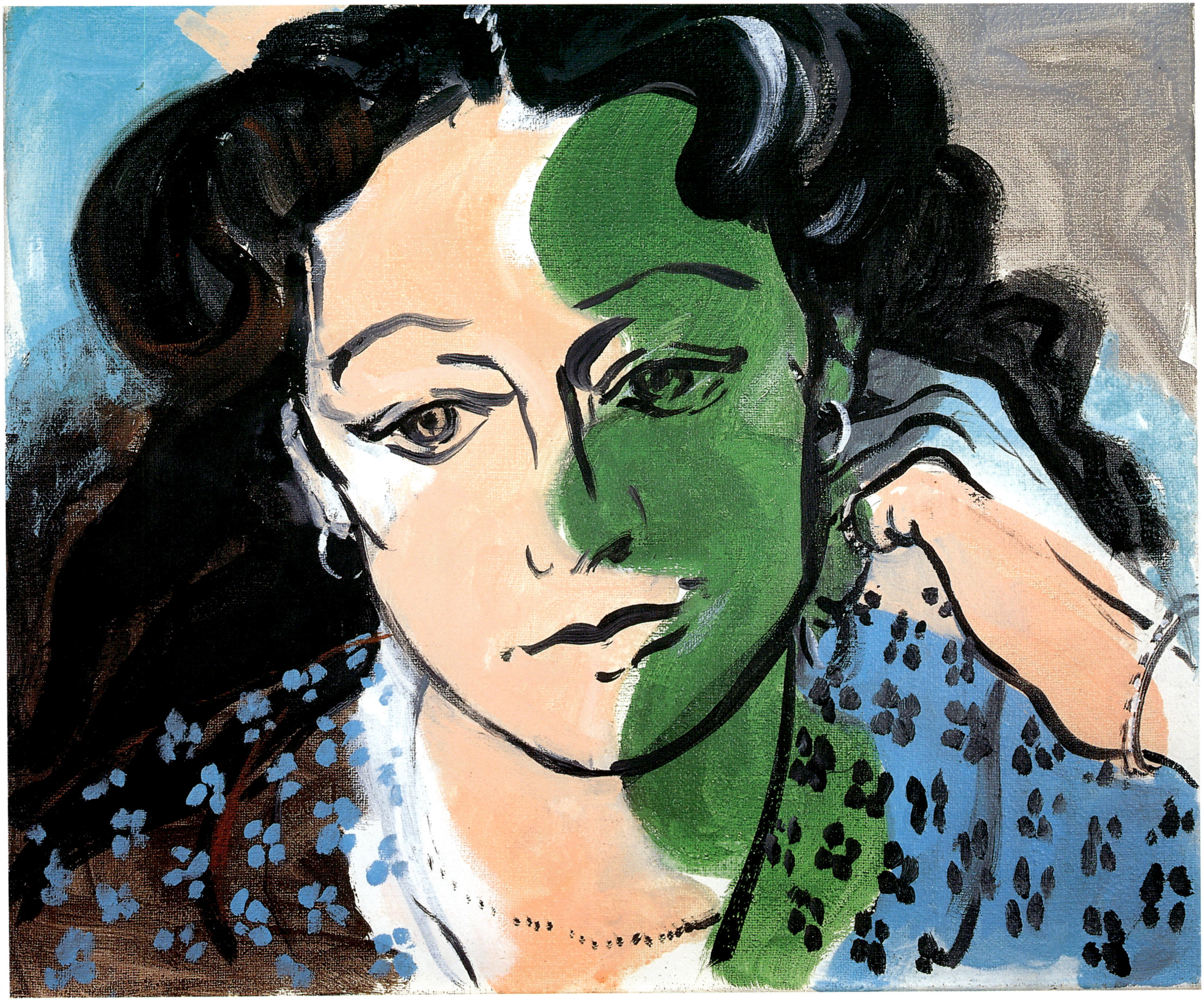

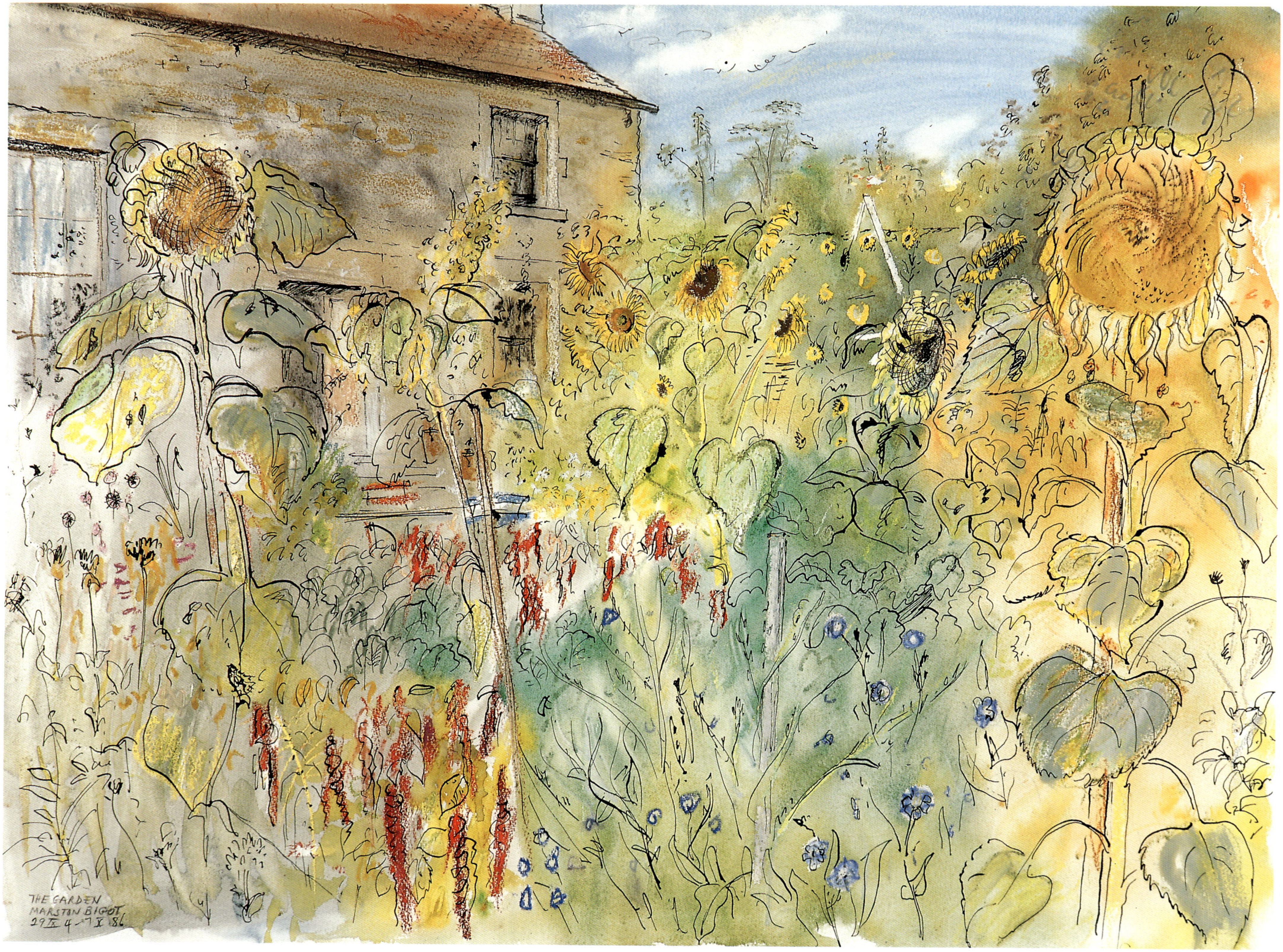

Garden at Marston Bigot
Mixed media, 18 × 24ins, 1986

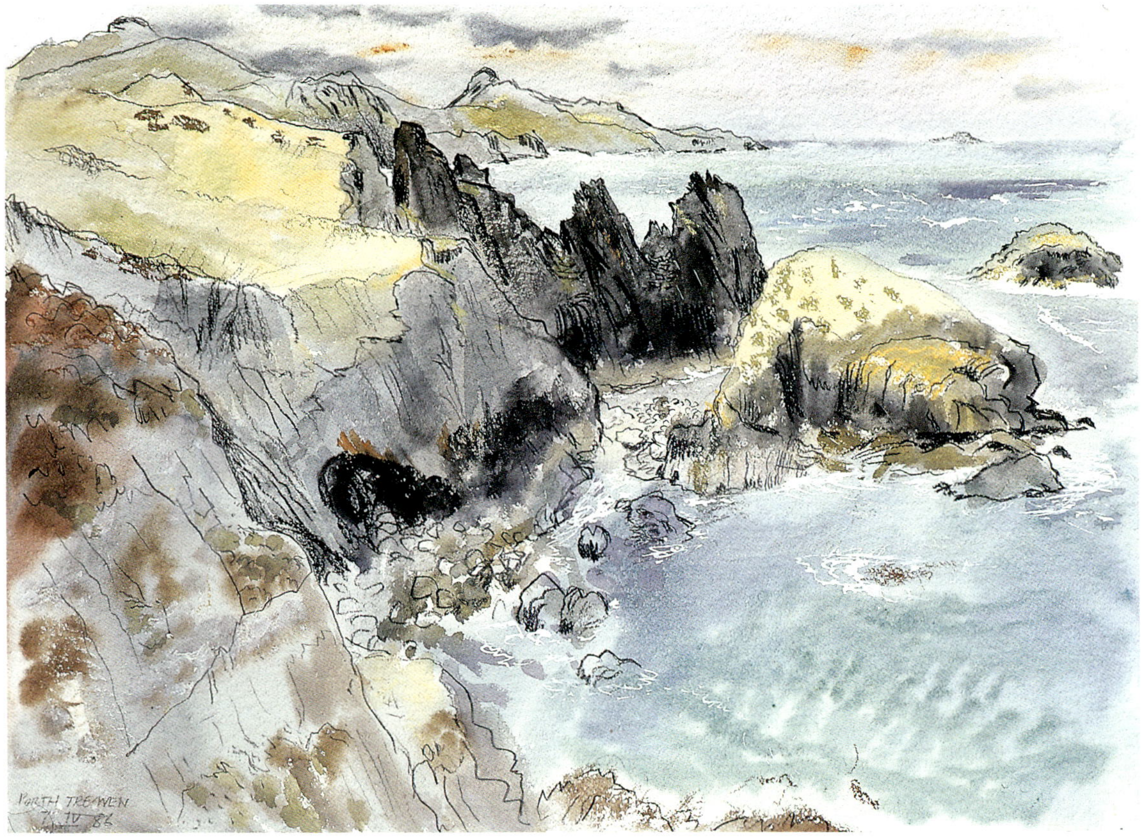

Porth Tre-wen, Pembrokeshire
Pencil, mixed media, 18 × 24ins, 1986

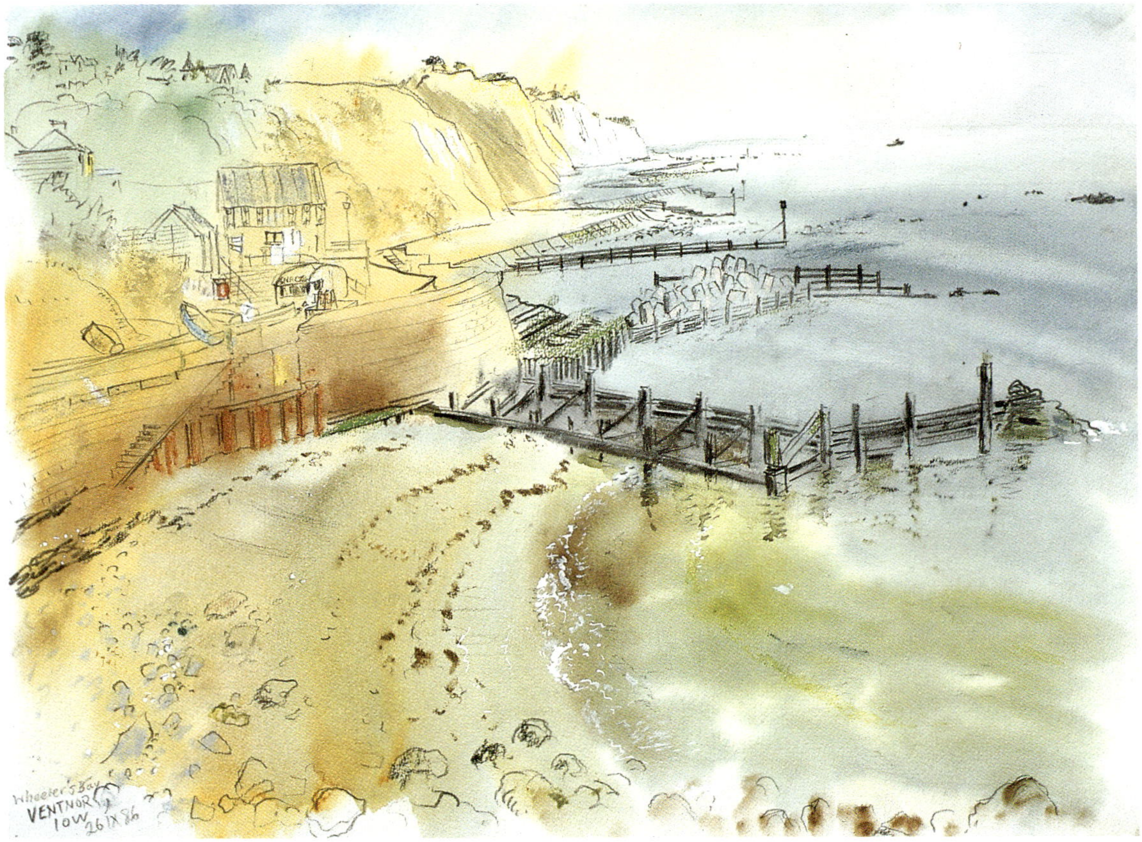

Wheeler's Bay, Ventnor, Isle of Wight
Pencil, watercolour, 18 × 24 ins, 1986

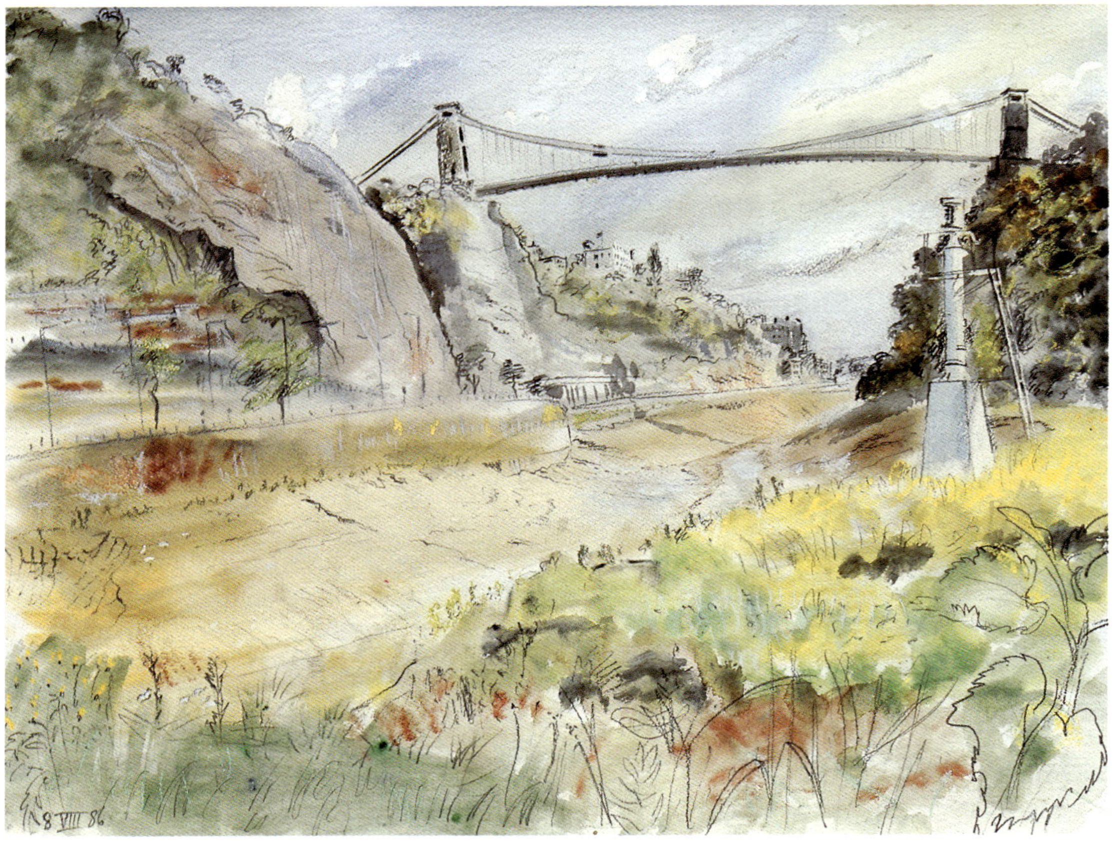

Clifton Suspension Bridge, Bristol
Pencil and watercolour, 15 × 20ins, 1986

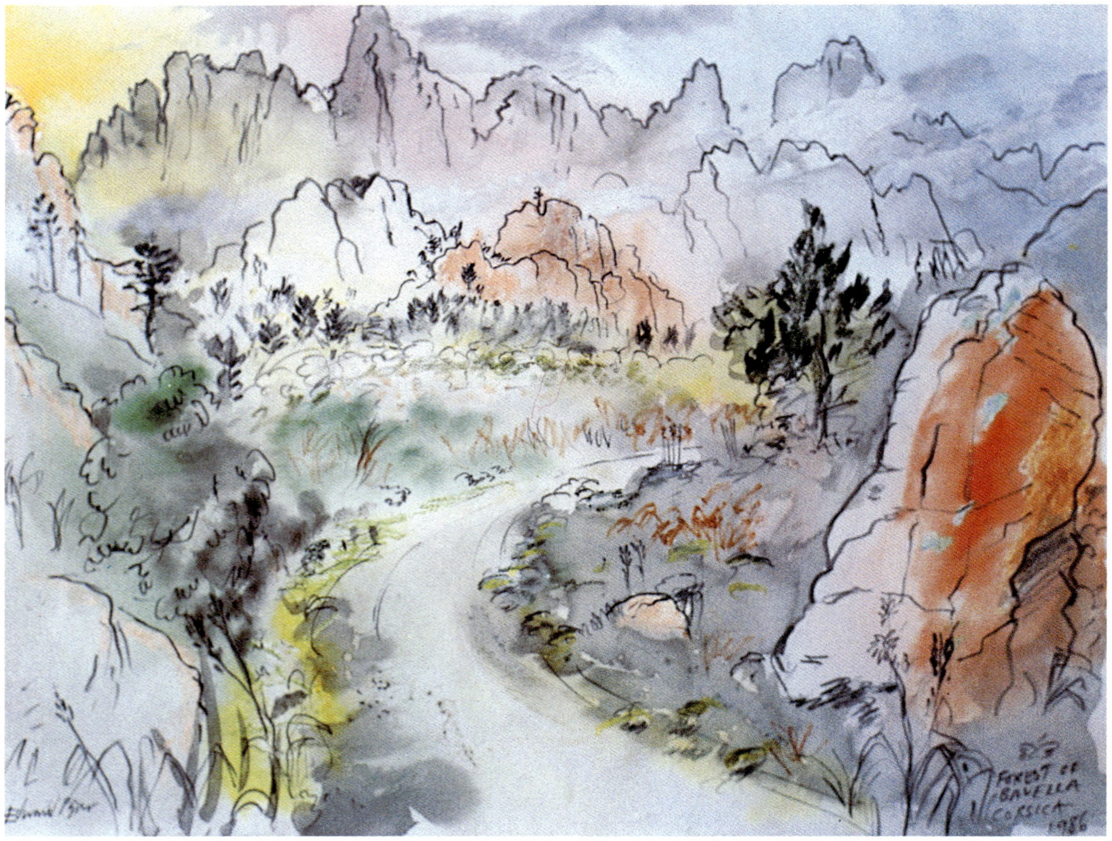

Forest of Bavella, Corsica
Ink and watercolour, 15 × 20ins, 1986

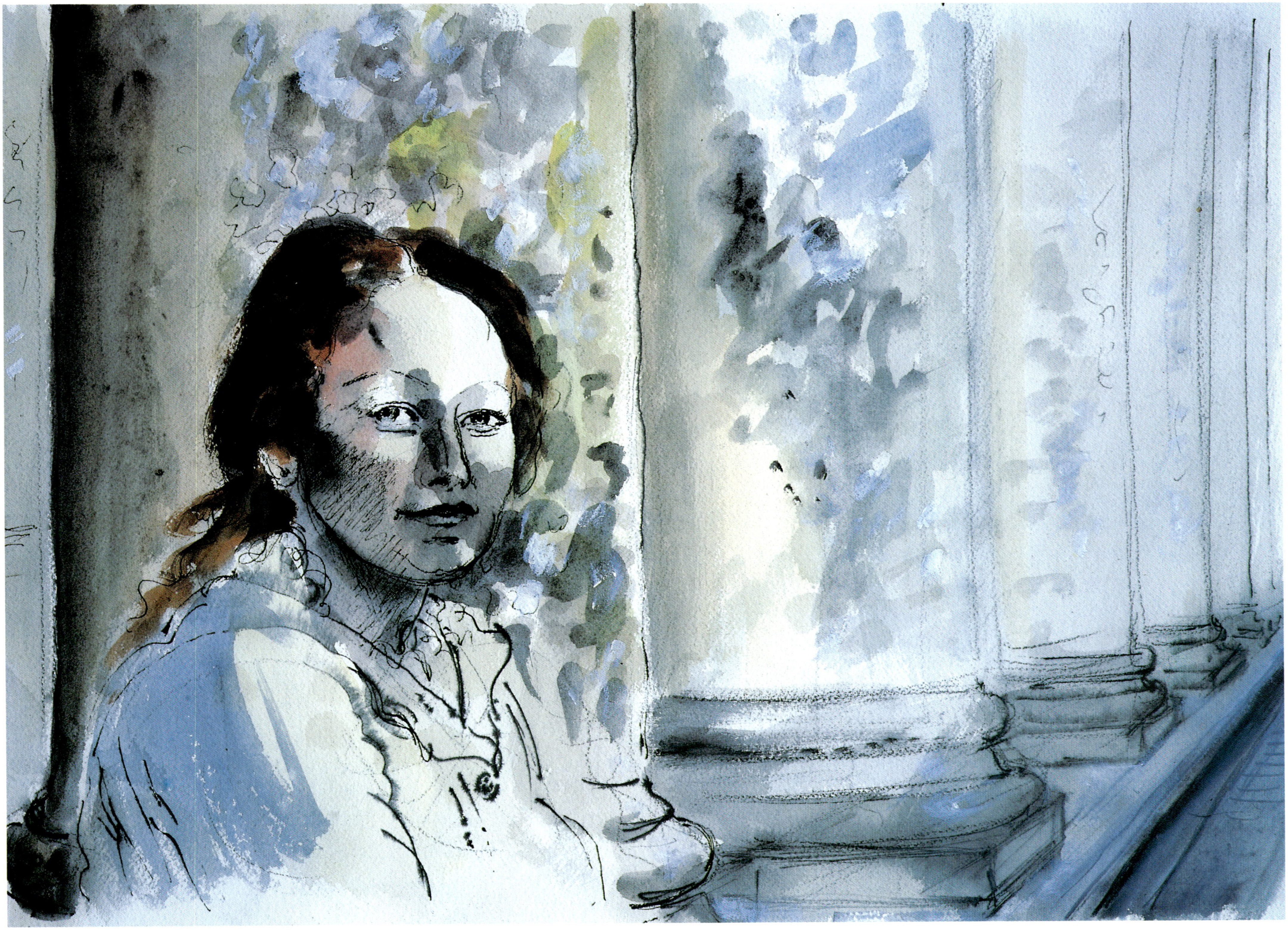

Portrait of a Girl with Pillars
Ink and watercolour, 15 × 20ins, 1986

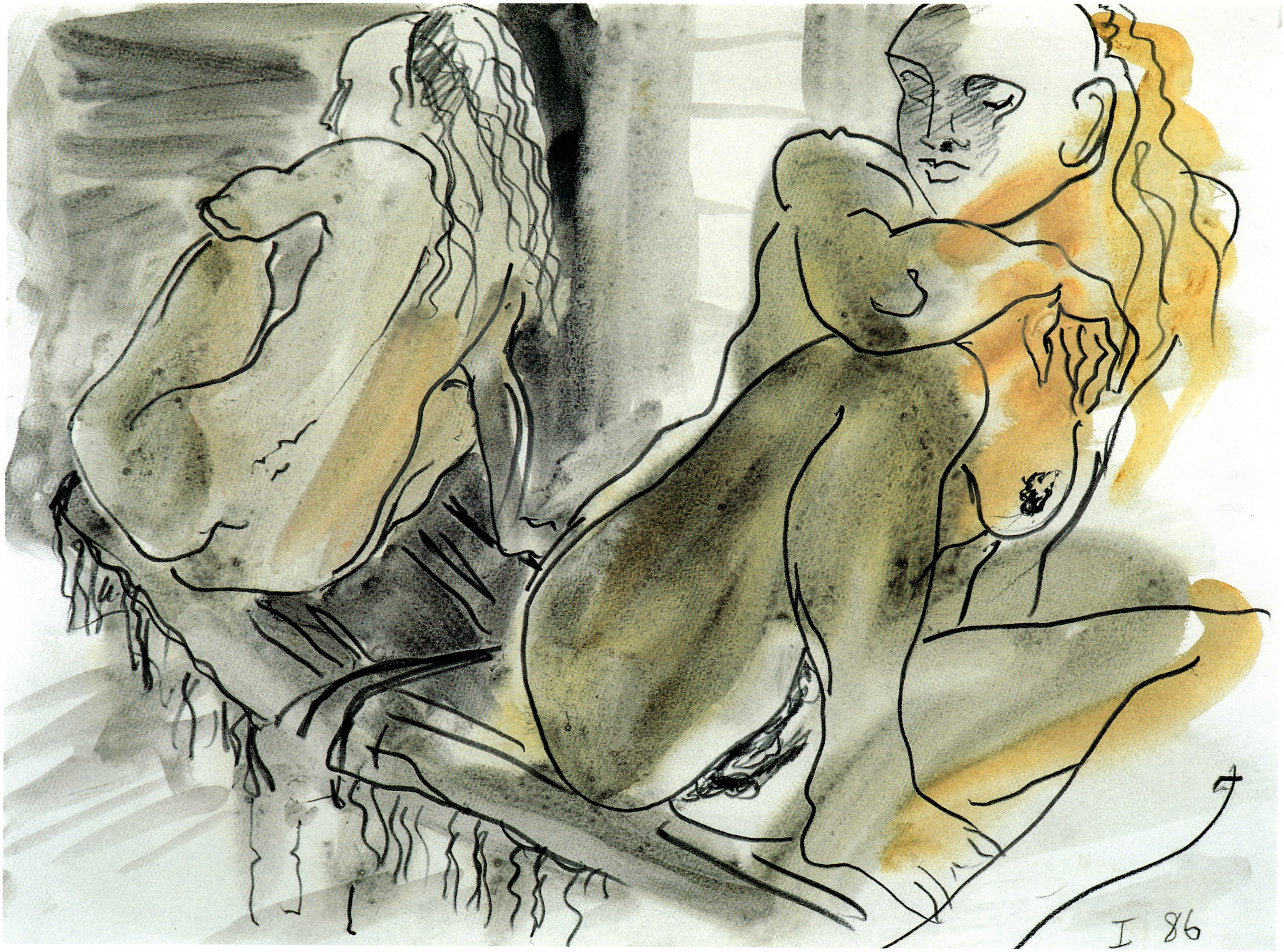

Masked Girl, seated Back to Mirror
Pencil and watercolour, 15 × 20ins, 1986

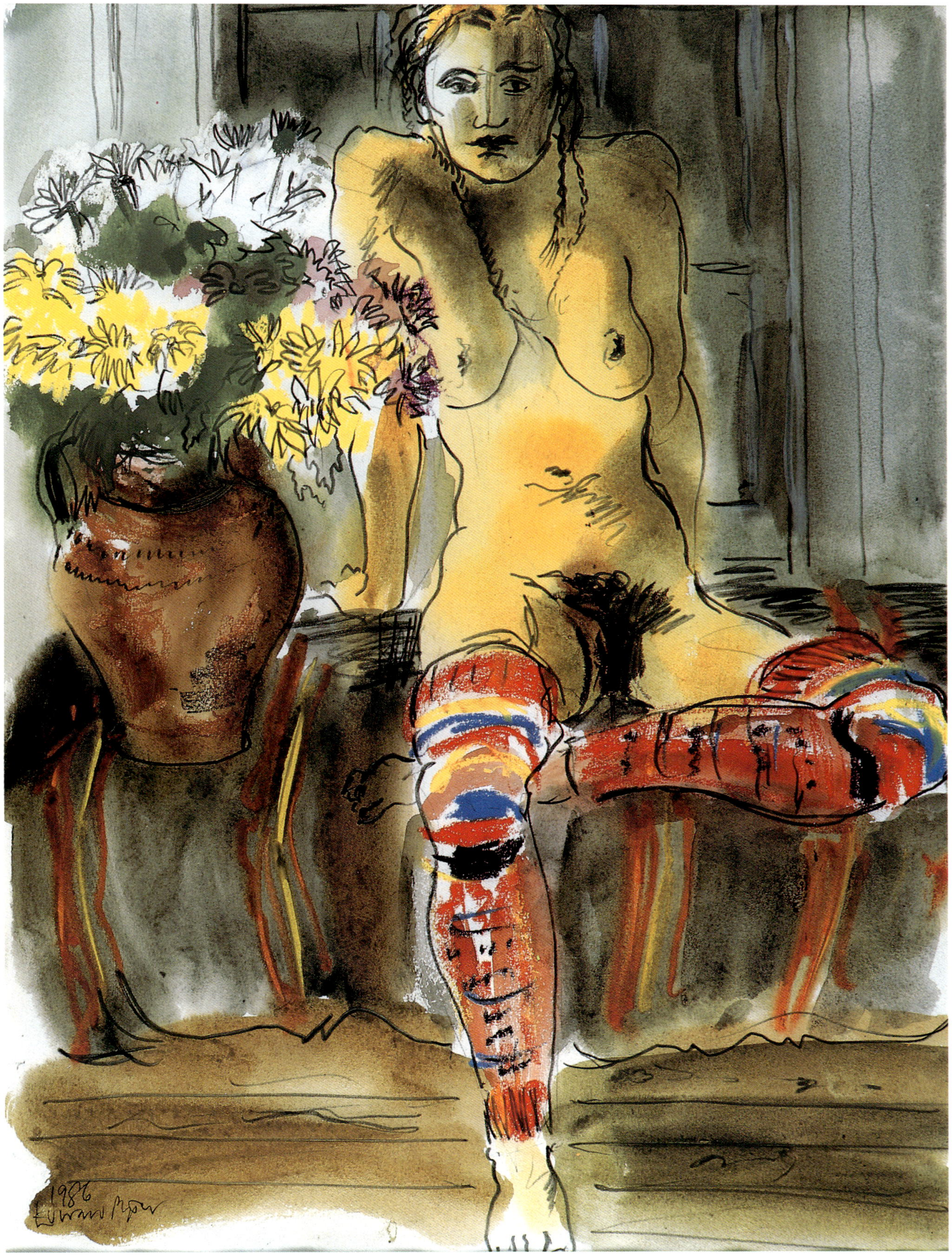

Seated Girl with Leg-Warmers, Chrysanthemums
Pencil, watercolour and chalks, 20 × 15ins, 1986

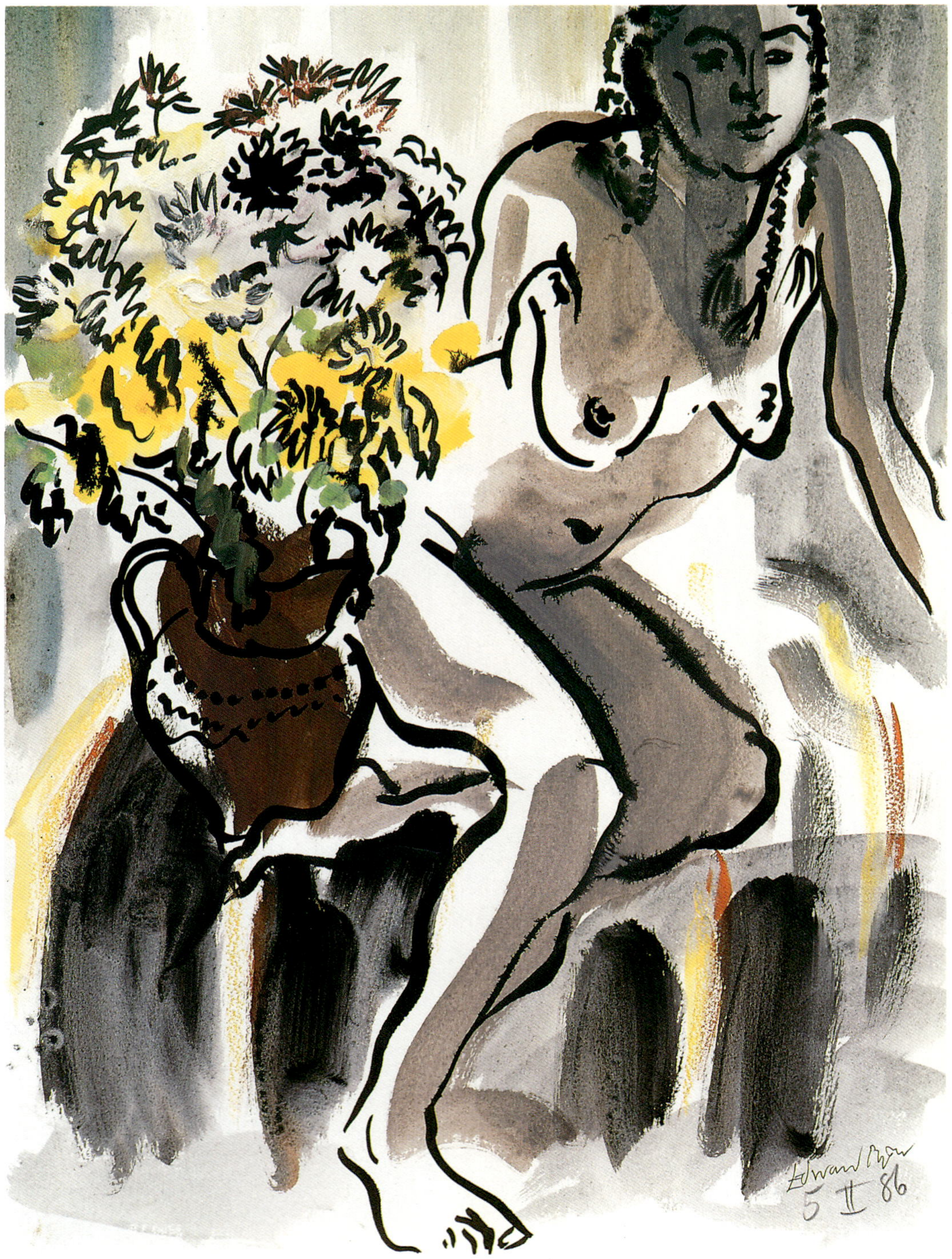

Seated Girl with Plaits, Contre Jour
Ink, watercolour and chalks, 20 × 15ins, 1986

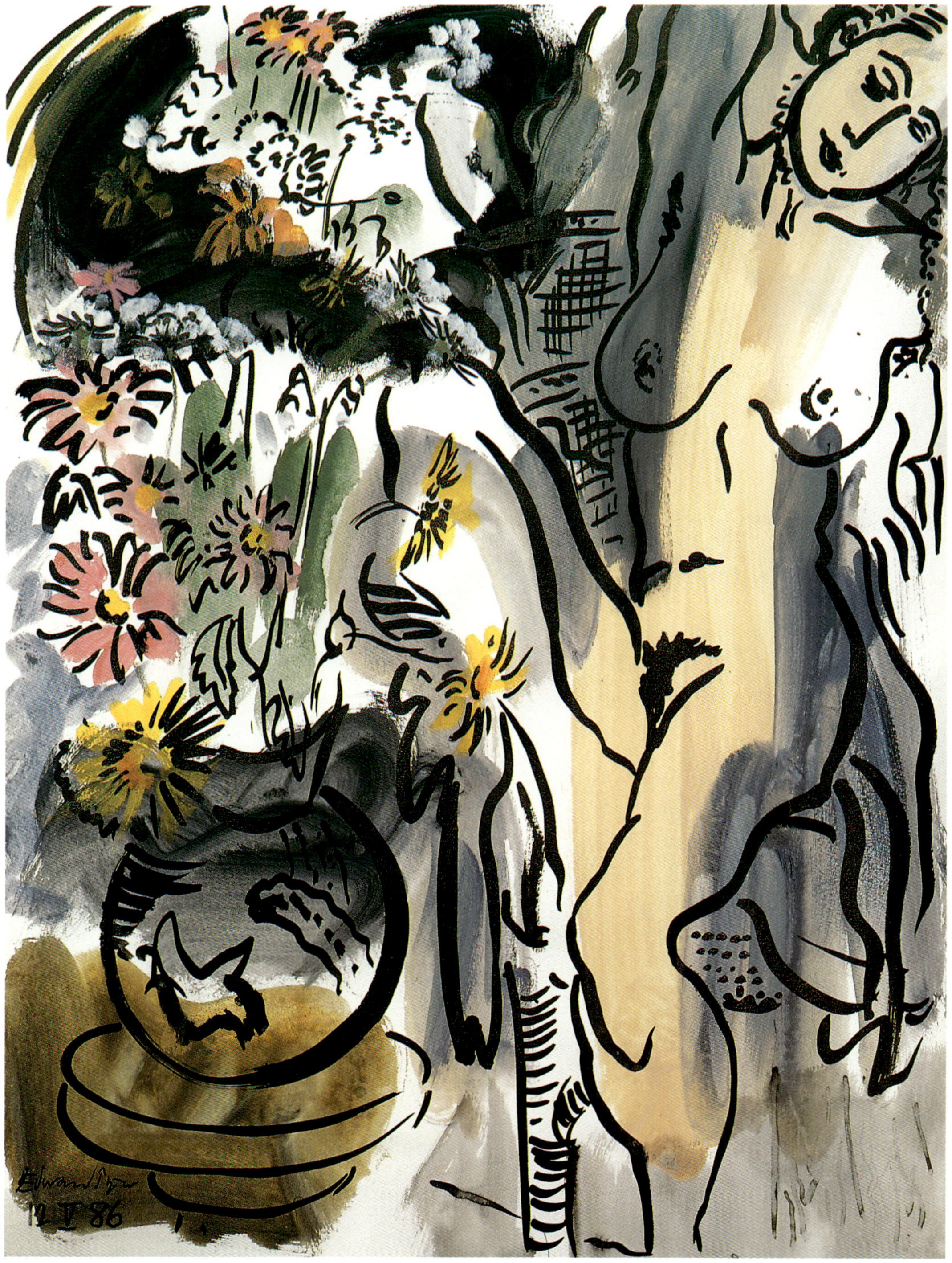

Seated Girl, Right leg and arm up, Flowers in Black Pot
Ink and acrylic, 24 × 18ins, 1986

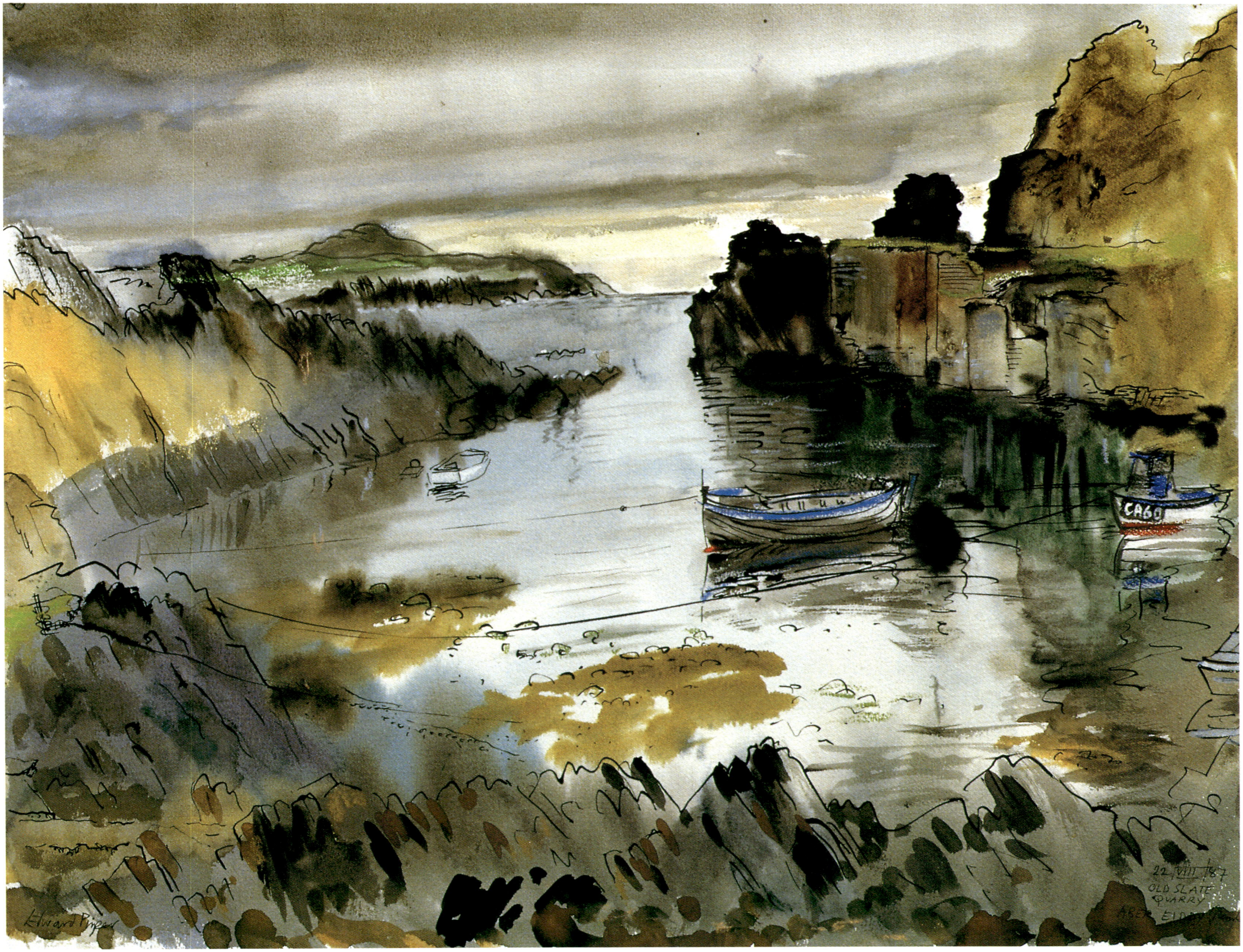

Old Slate Quarry, Abereiddy, Pembrokeshire
Ink, watercolour, chalks, 15 × 20ins, 1987

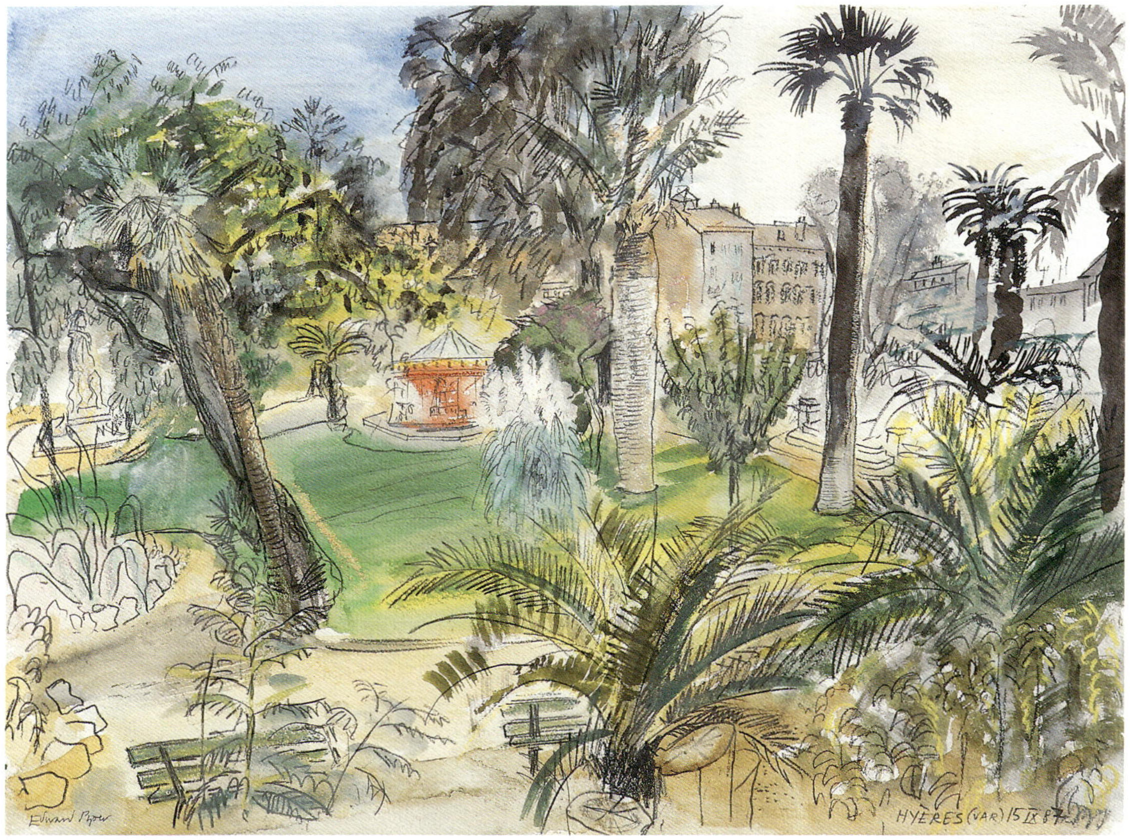

Hyères (Var) Municipal Gardens
Pencil, watercolour, chalks, 18 × 24ins, 1987

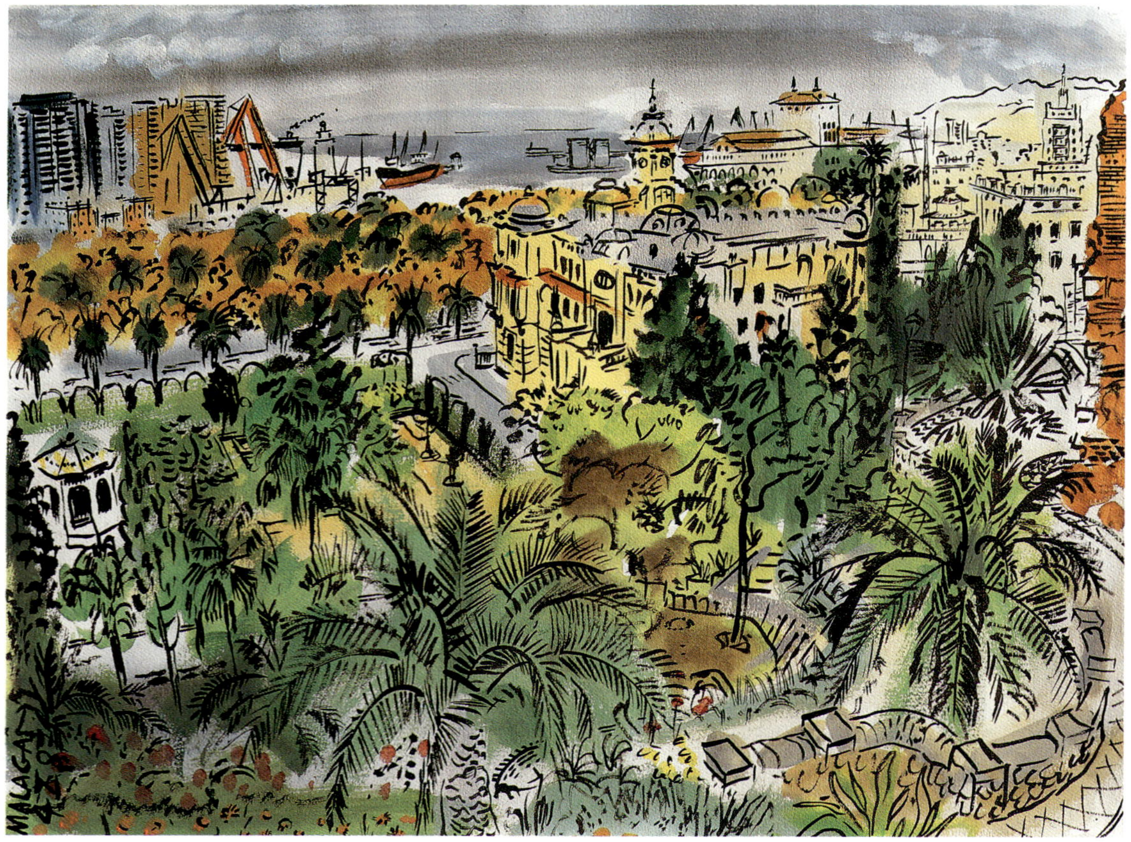

Malaga
Ink, acrylics, 18 × 24ins, 1987

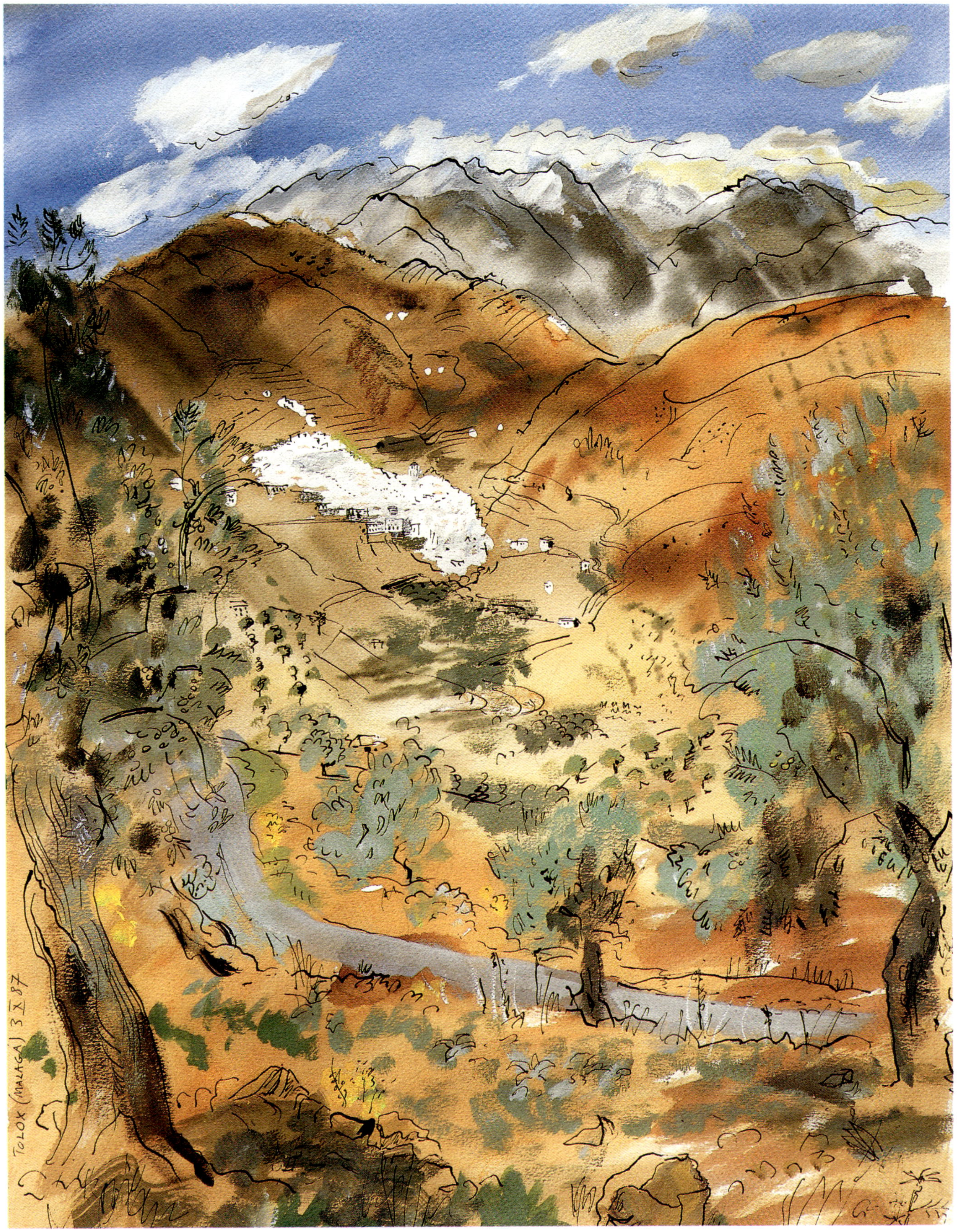

Tolox, Andalucia
Ink, watercolour, chalks, 24 × 18ins, 1987

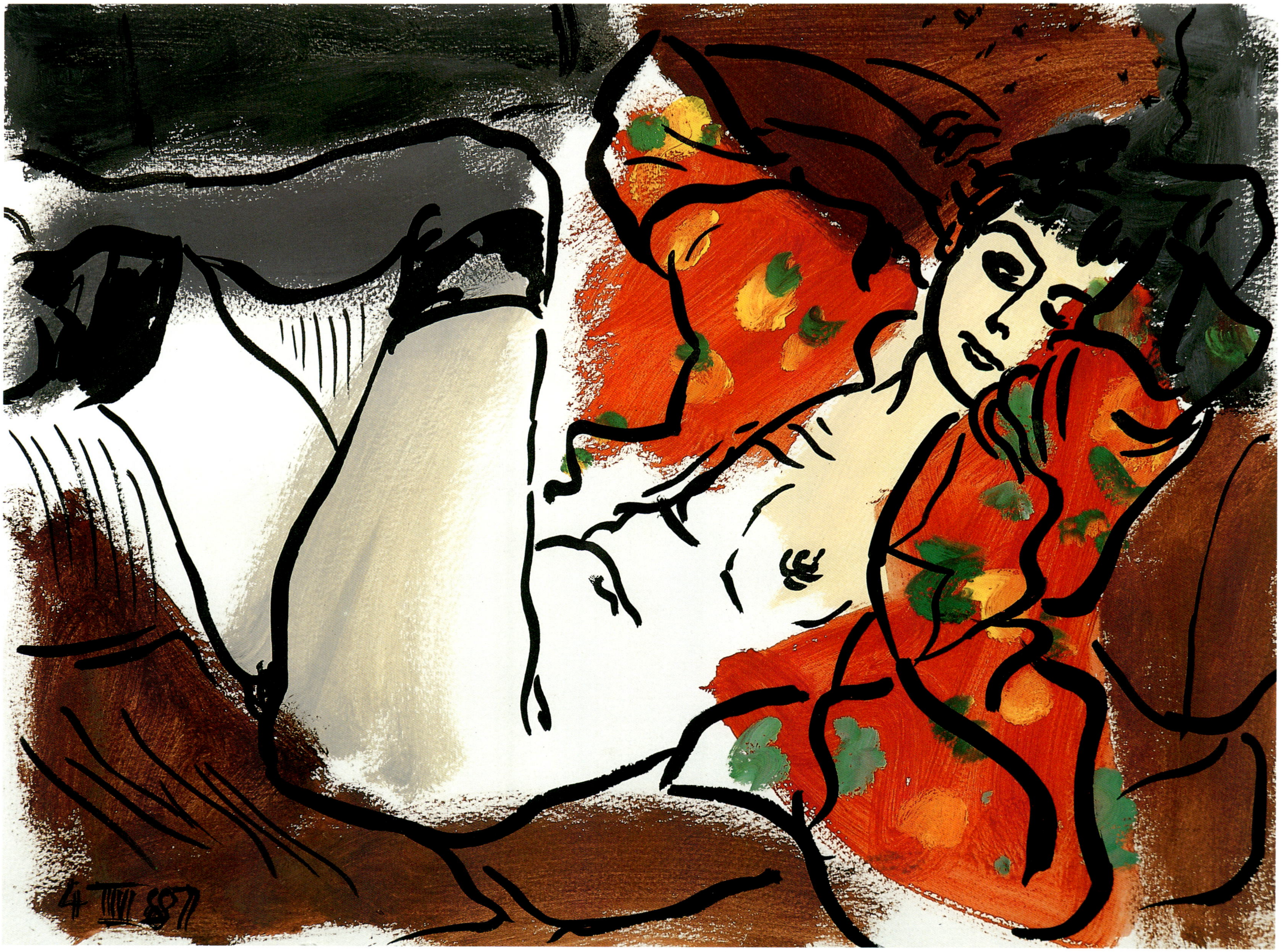

Reclining Girl, Red Jacket
Ink and acrylic, 18 × 24ins, 1987

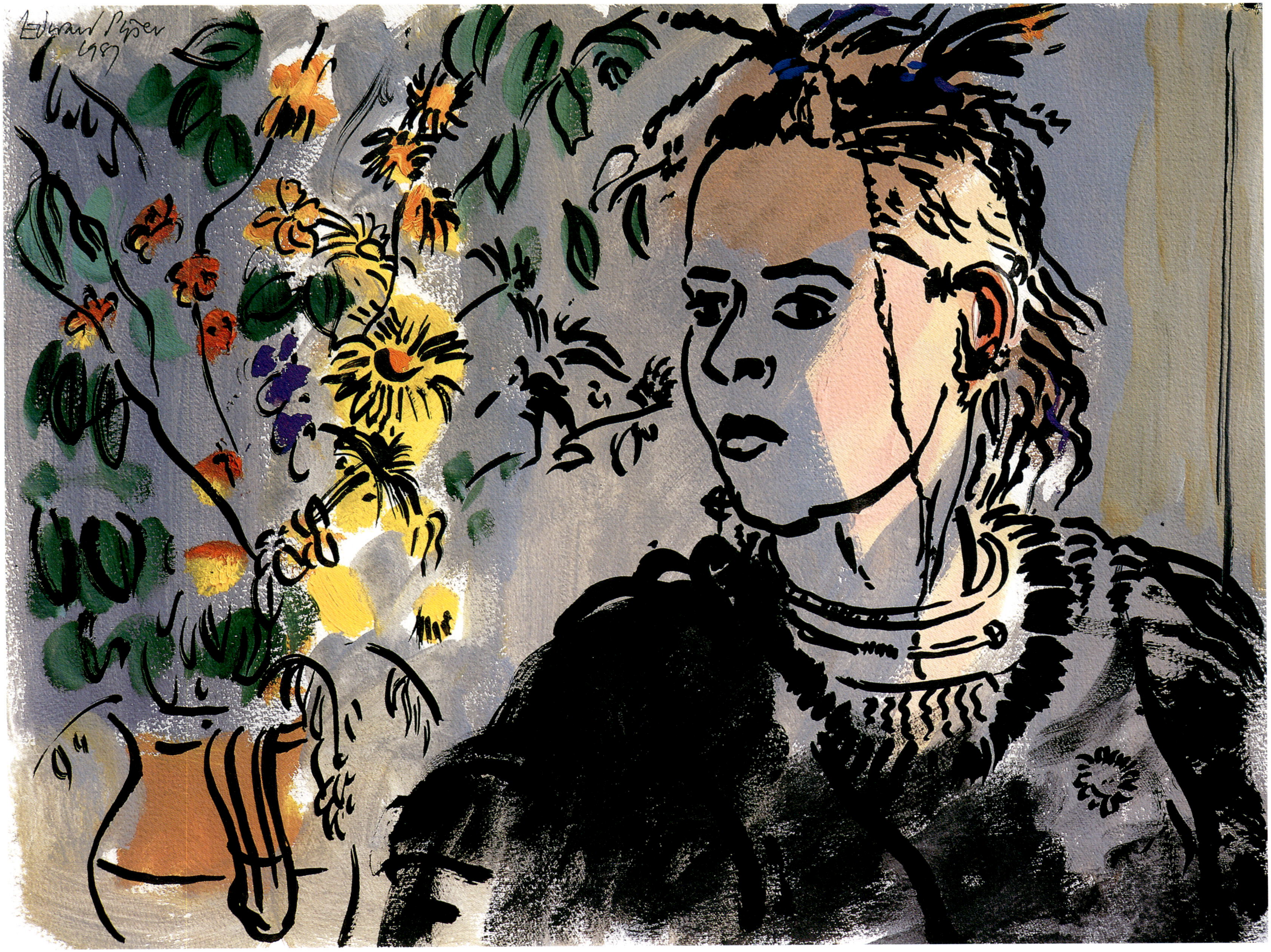

Portrait of a Girl with Punk Hairstyle
Ink and acrylic, 18 × 24ins, 1987

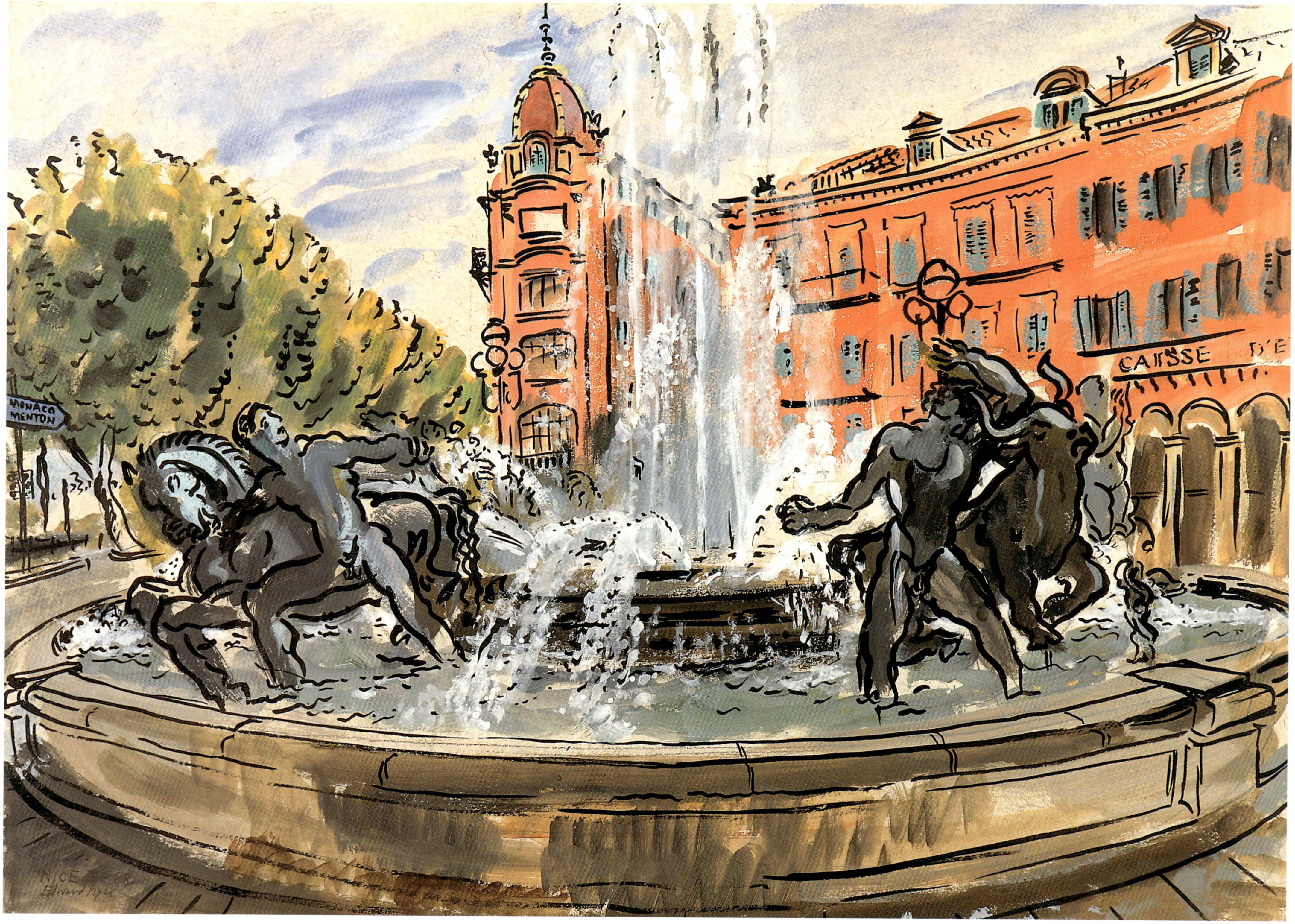

Fountain at Nice
Ink, acrylic, on Indian paper, 22 × 30ins, 1988

Lucca, Pfanner Garden
Acrylic on Indian paper, 22 × 33ins, 1988

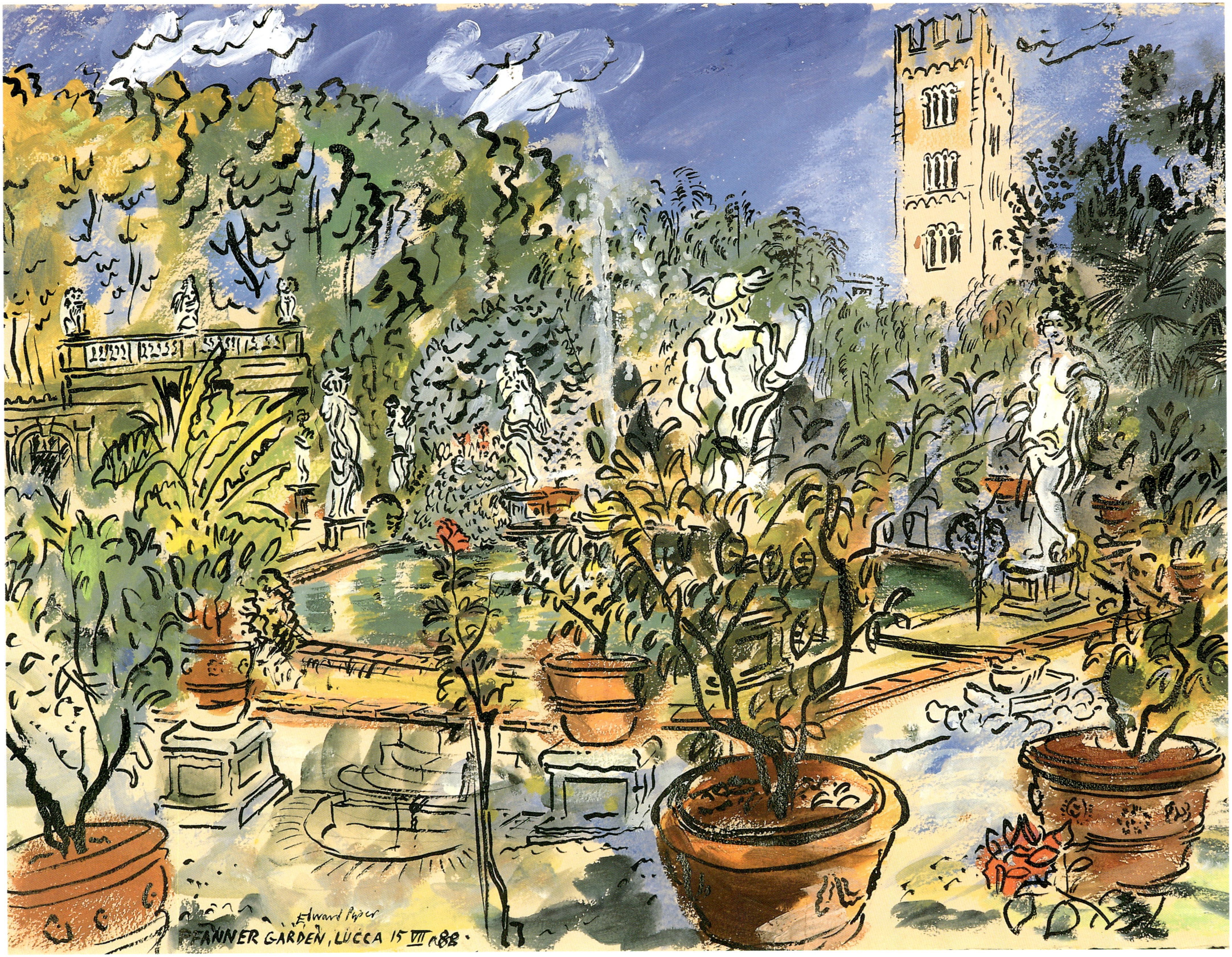
Edward Piper
PFANNER GARDEN, LUCCA 15 VII 88

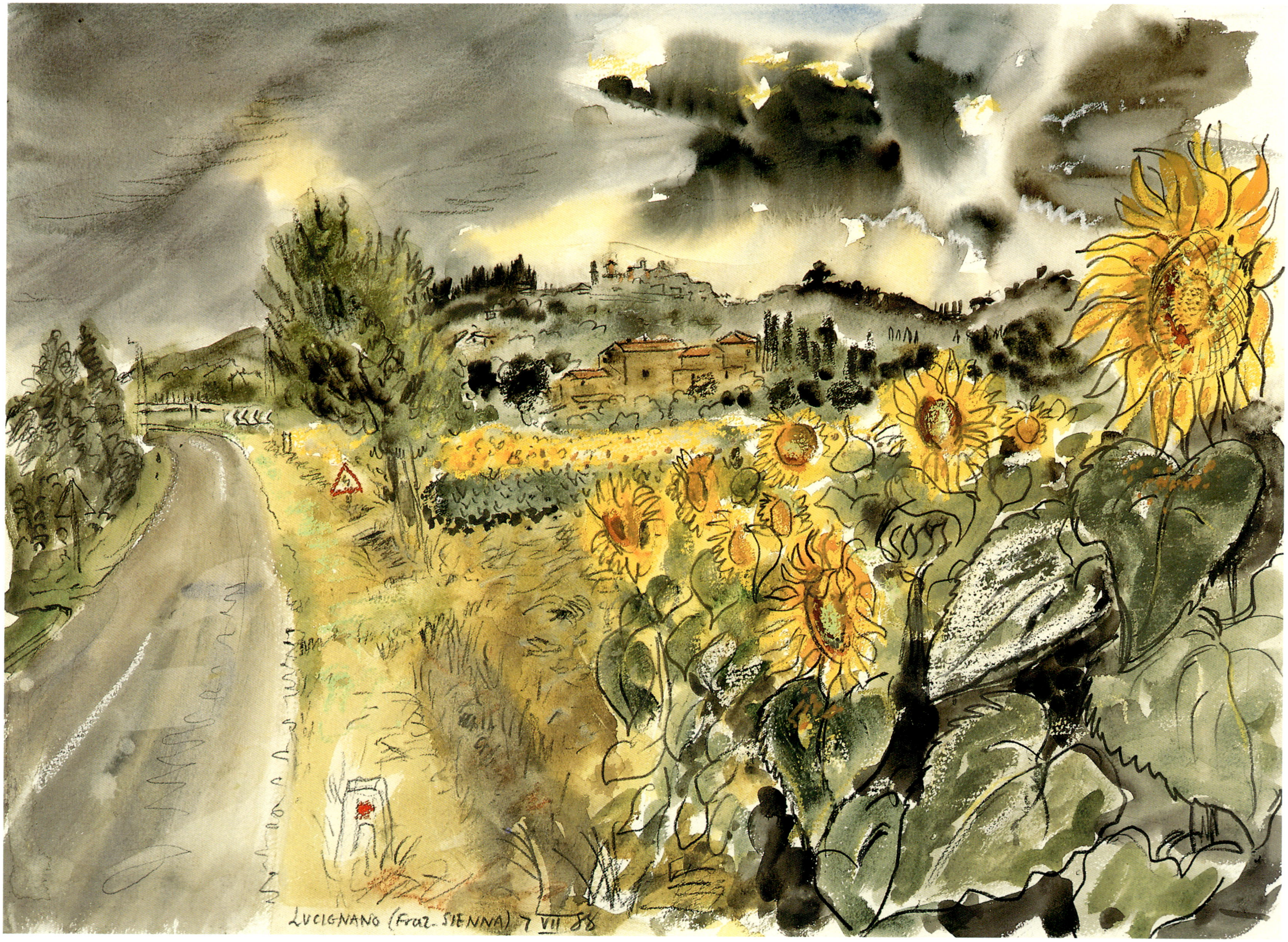

Sunflowers at Lucignano, near Siena
Mixed media, 18 × 24ins, 1988

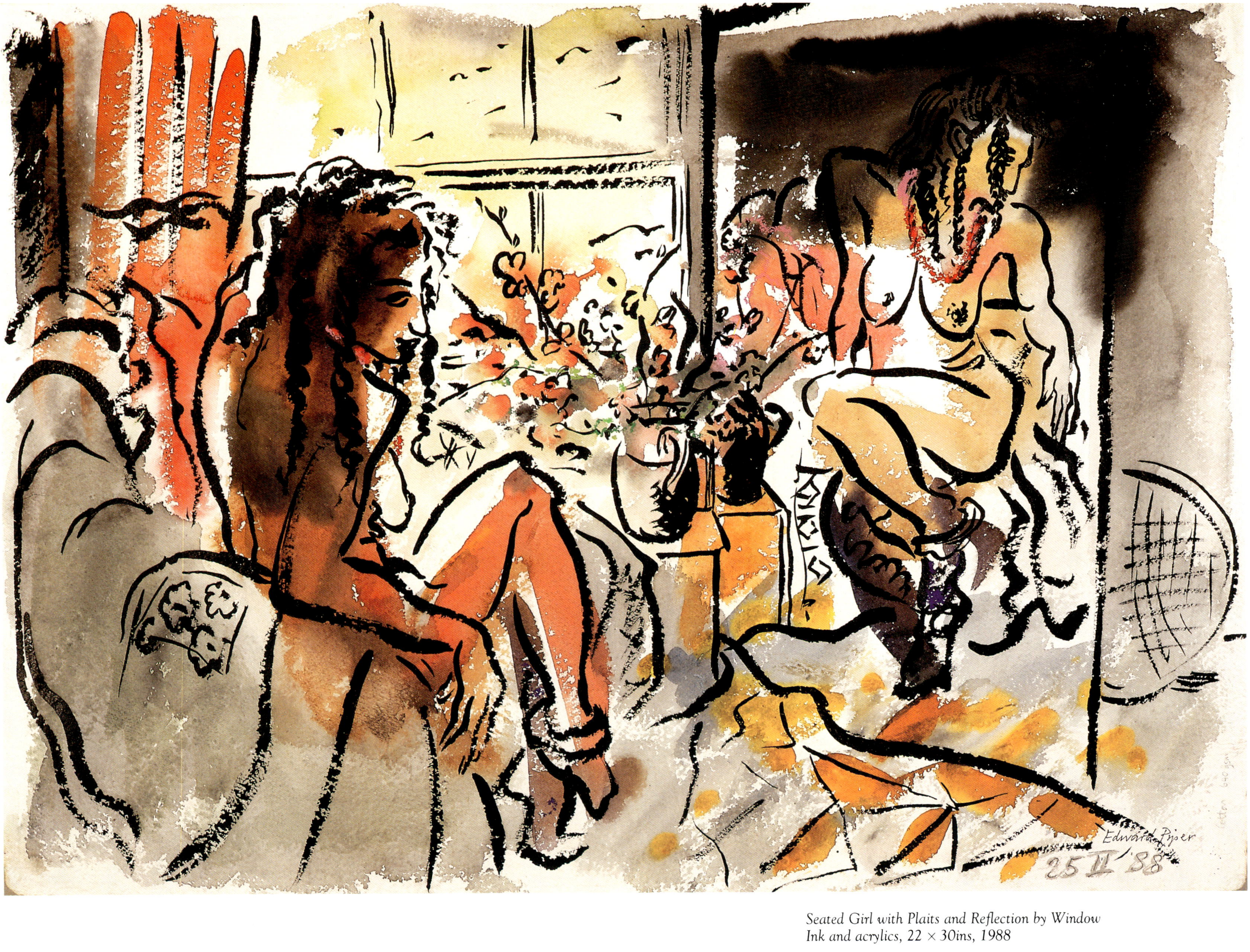

Seated Girl with Plaits and Reflection by Window
Ink and acrylics, 22 × 30ins, 1988

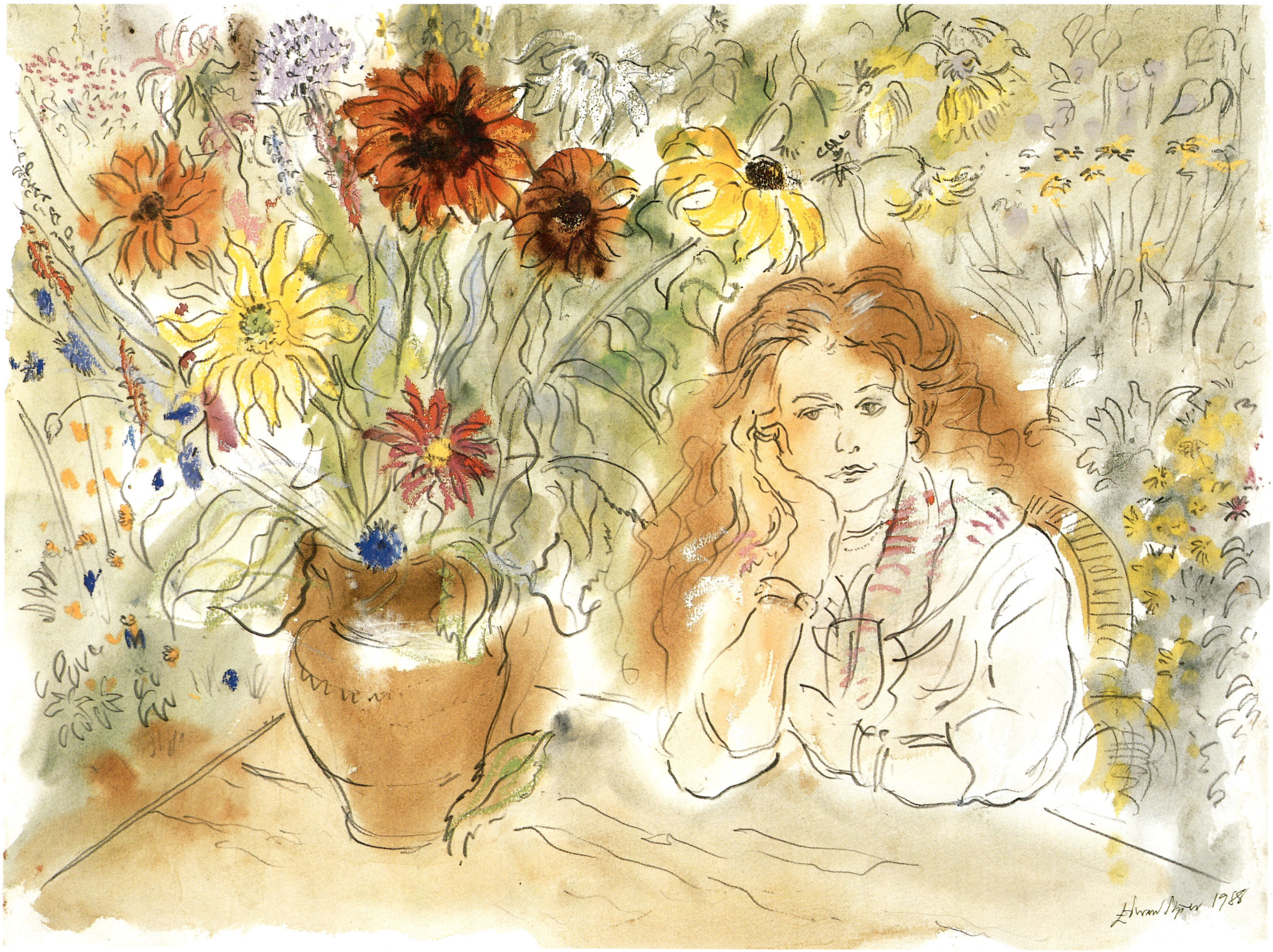

Girl at Garden Table with Jug of Flowers
Pencil and watercolour, 18 × 24ins, 1988

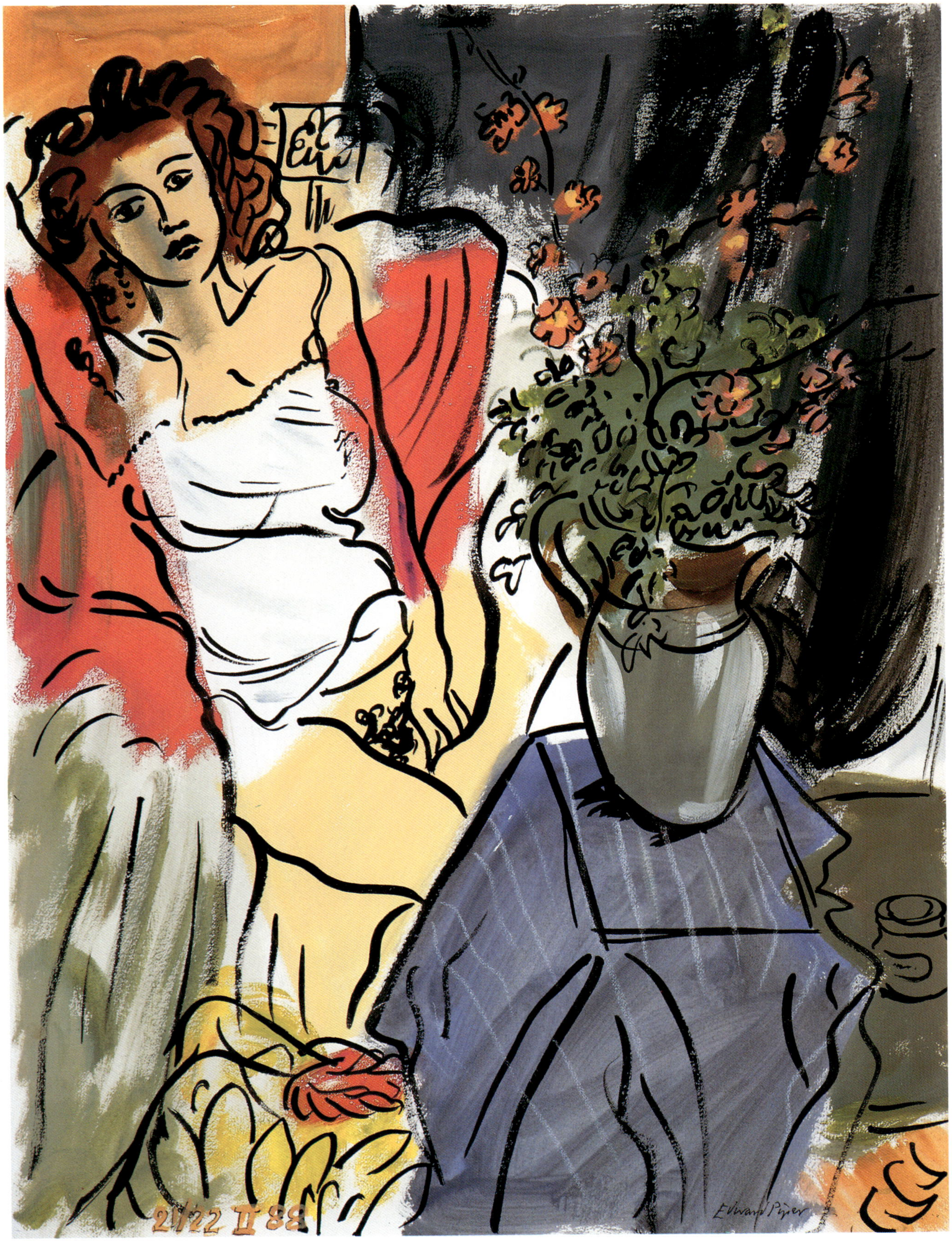

Pregnant Girl Seated, Japonica in Jug
Ink and acrylic, 24 × 18ins, 1988

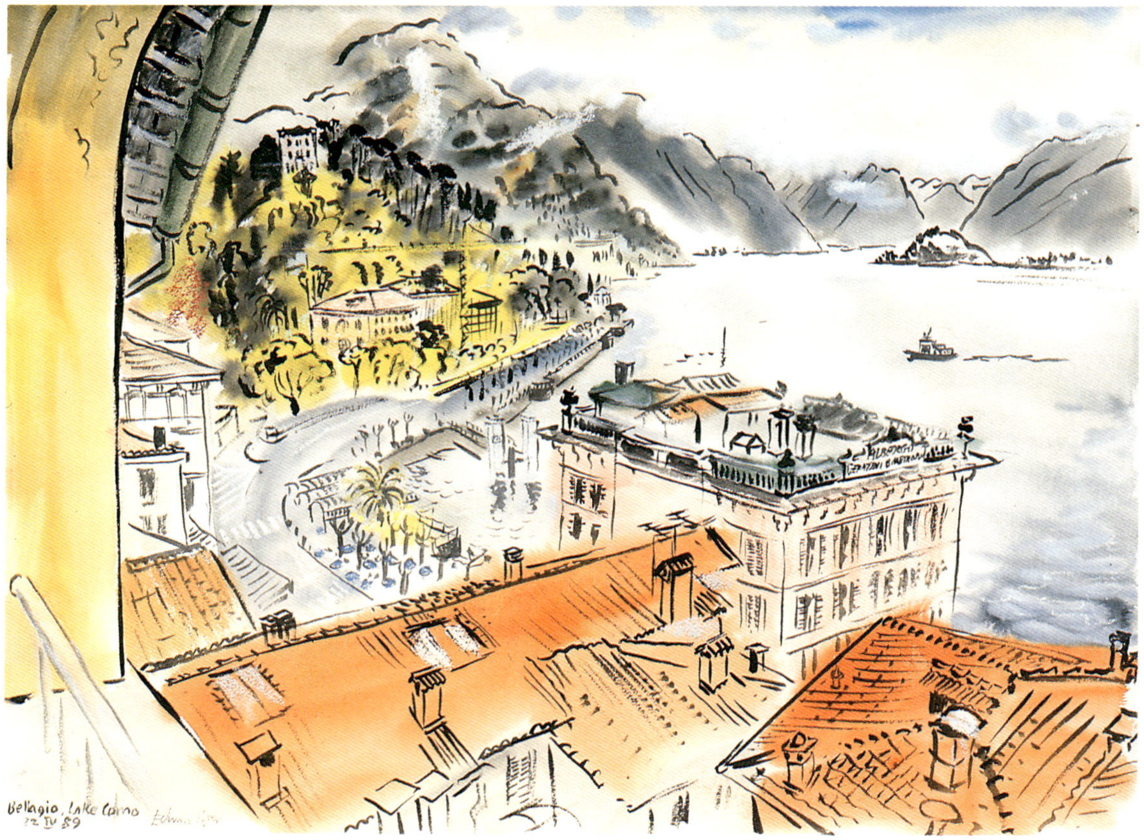

Bellagio, Lake Como
Ink and watercolour, 18 × 24ins, 1989

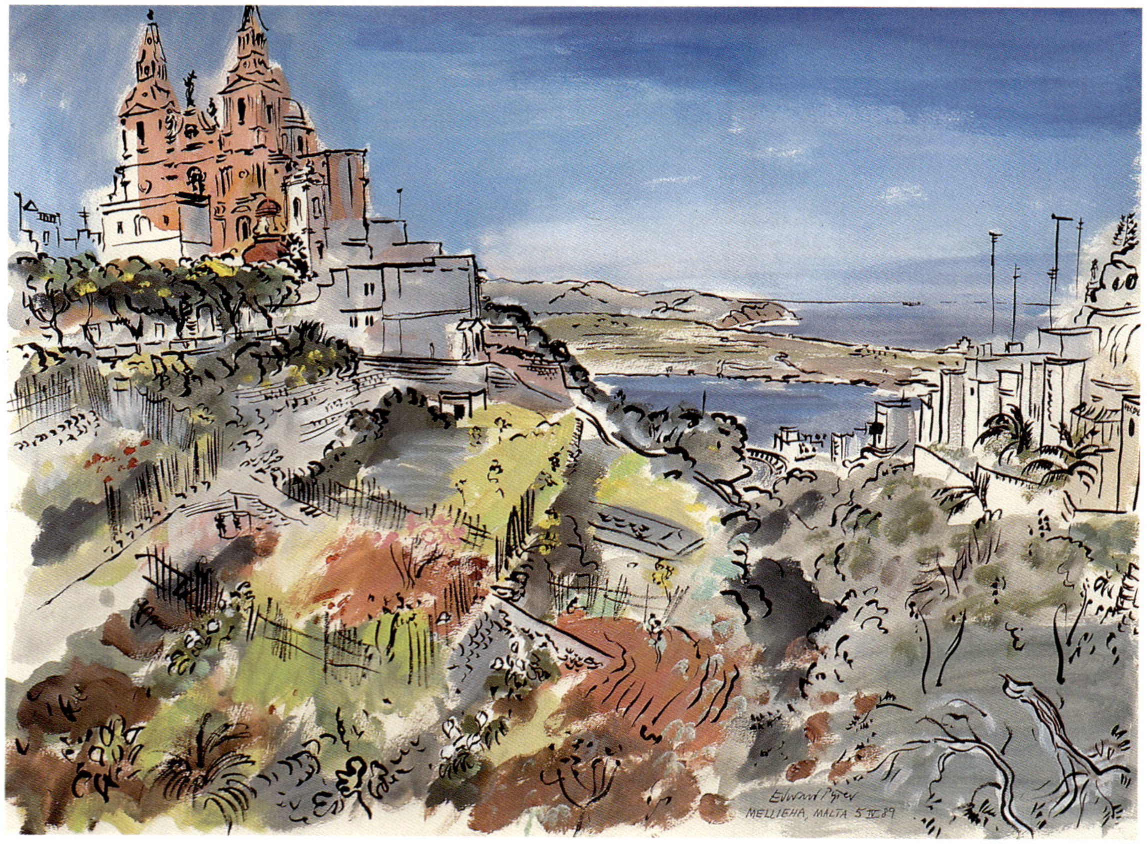

Mellieha, Malta
Watercolour, chalks, 18 × 24ins, 1989

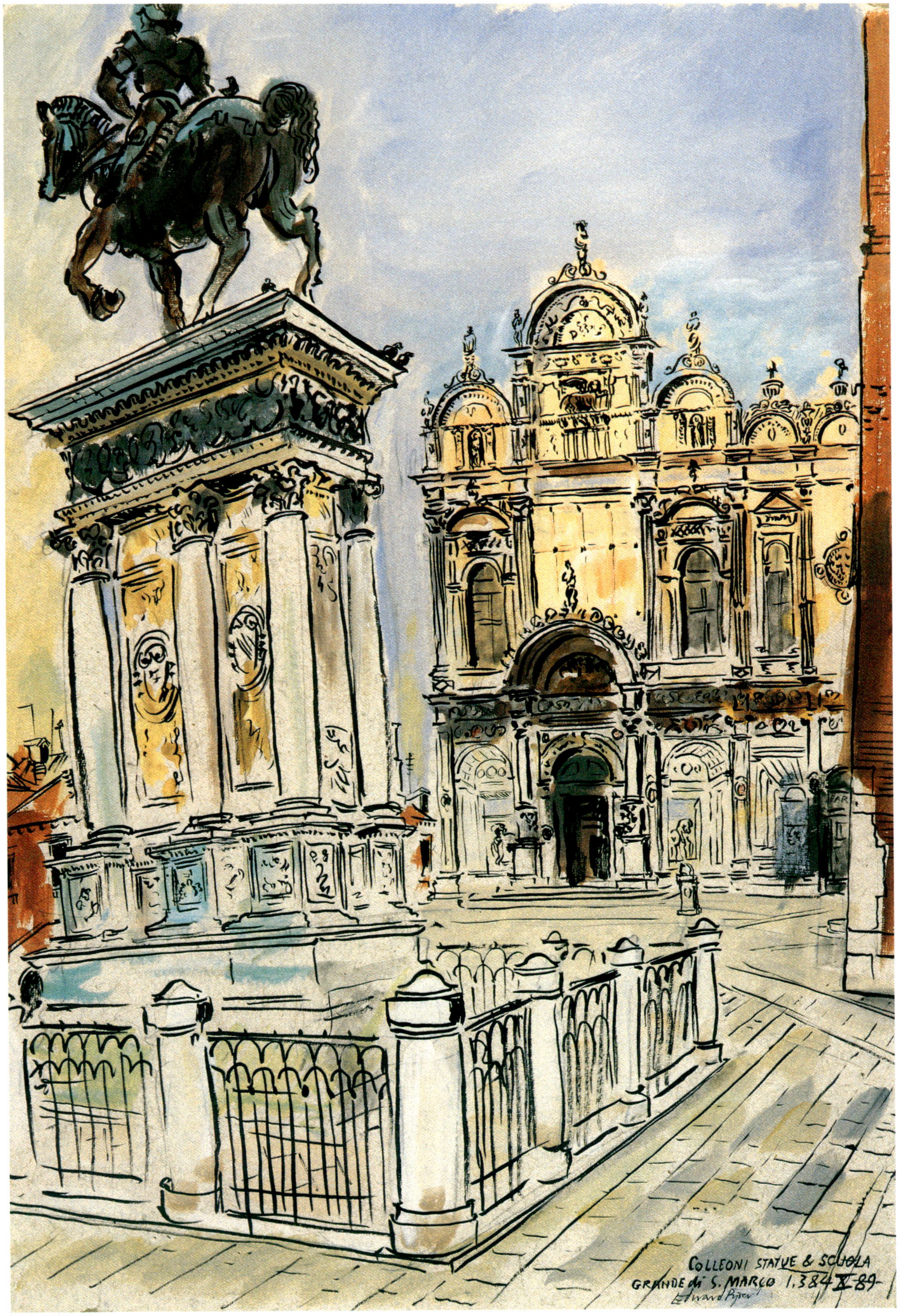

Colleone Statue and Scuola Grande di S. Marco
Ink, watercolour, acrylic on Indian paper, 30 × 22ins, 1989

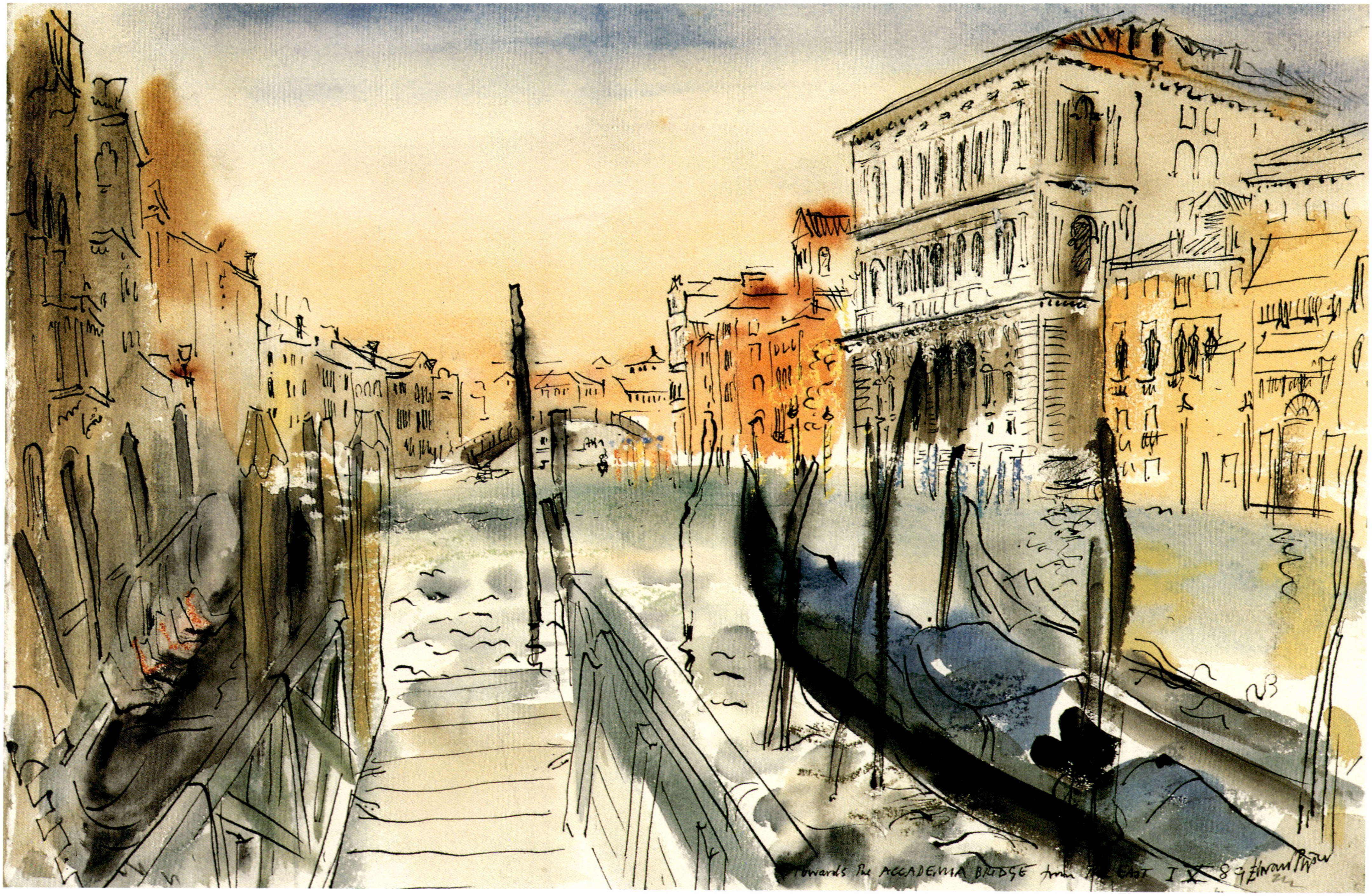

Accademia Bridge from the East
Ink and watercolour, 15 × 20ins, 1989

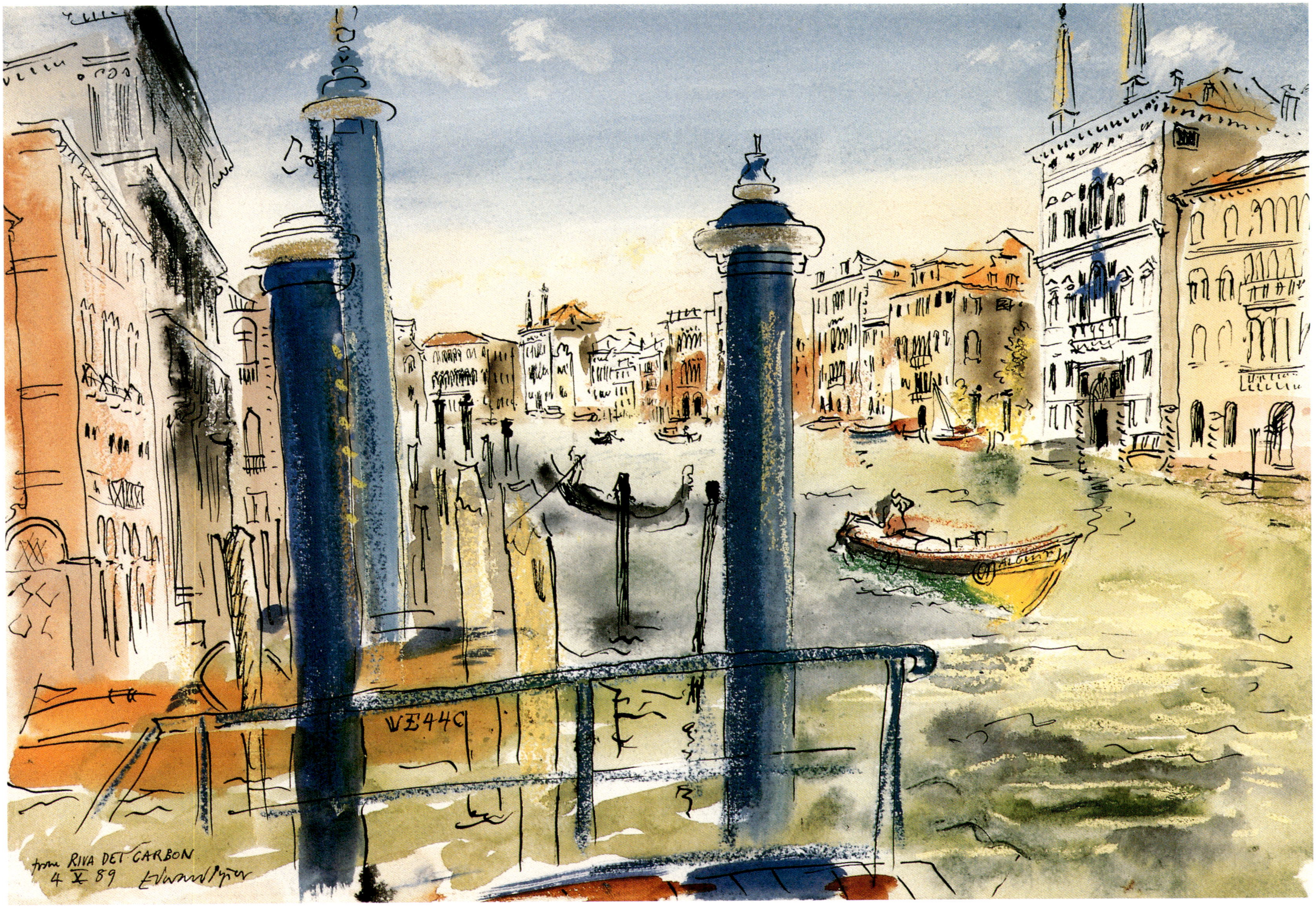

Grand Canal from Riva dei Carbon
Ink and watercolour, 15 × 20ins, 1989

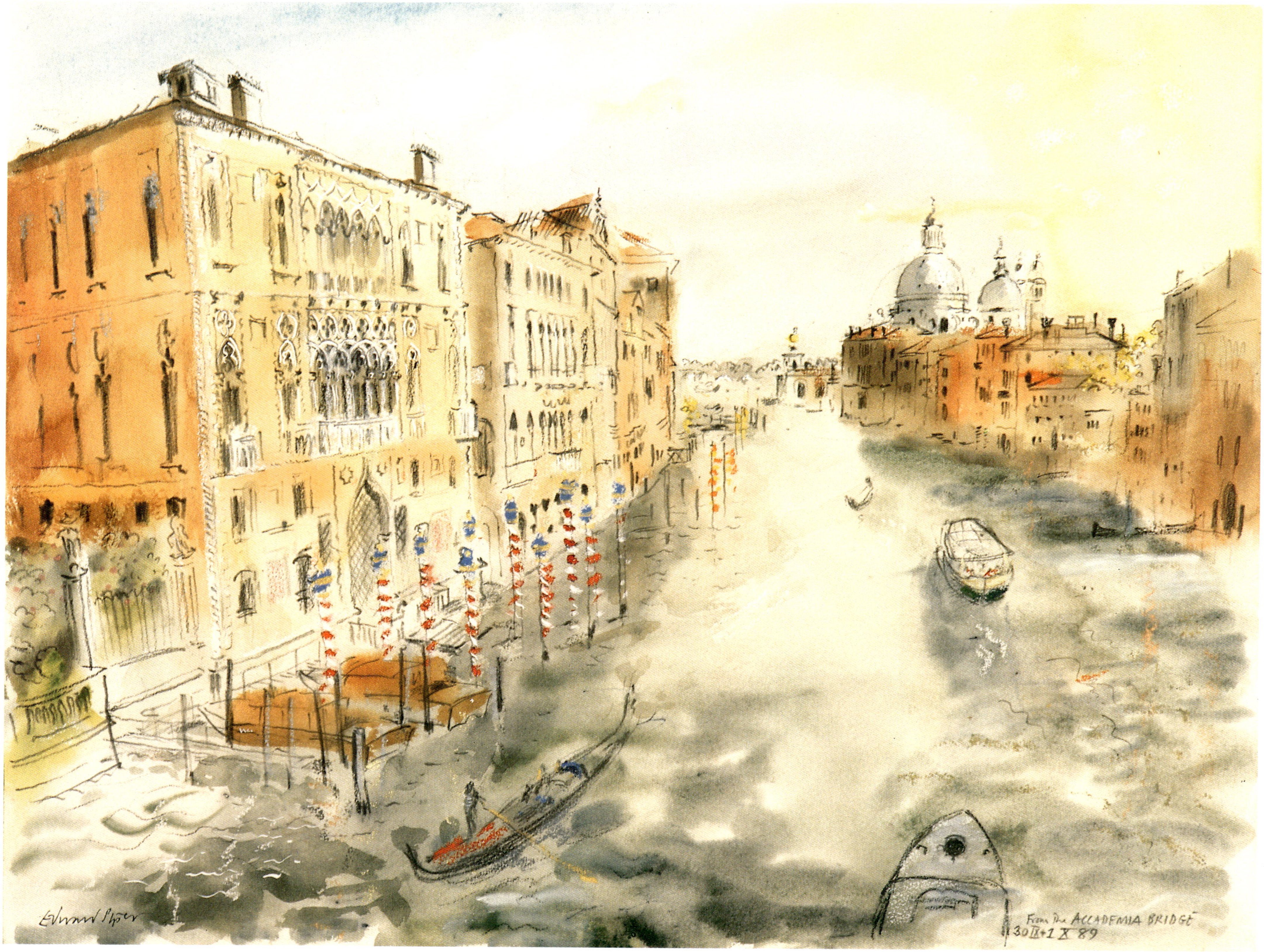

From the Accademia Bridge
Ink, pencil, watercolour and chalk, 18 × 24ins, 1989

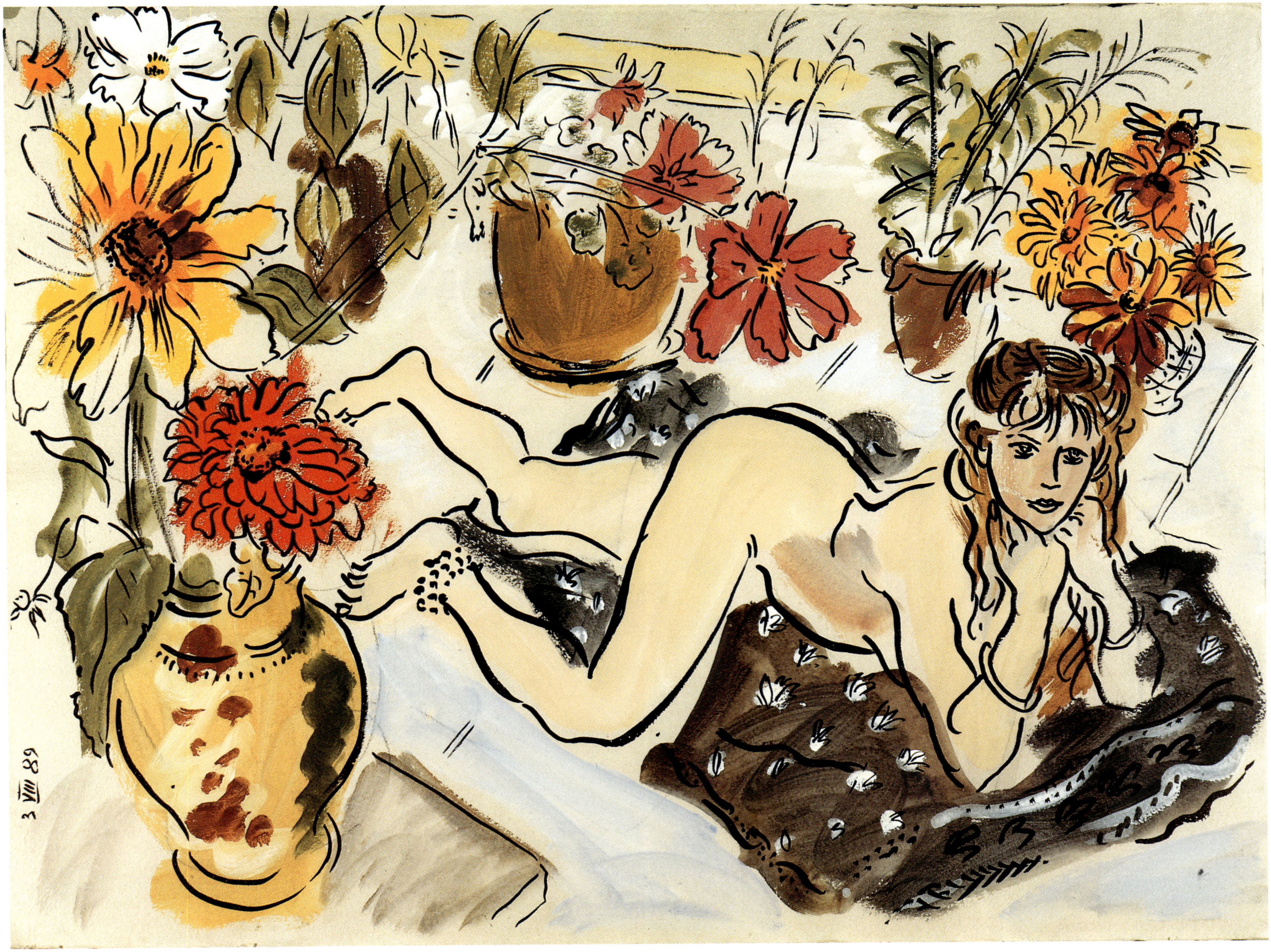

Girl Lying on Arab Print Among Flowers
Ink and acrylic on Indian paper, 22 × 30ins, 1989

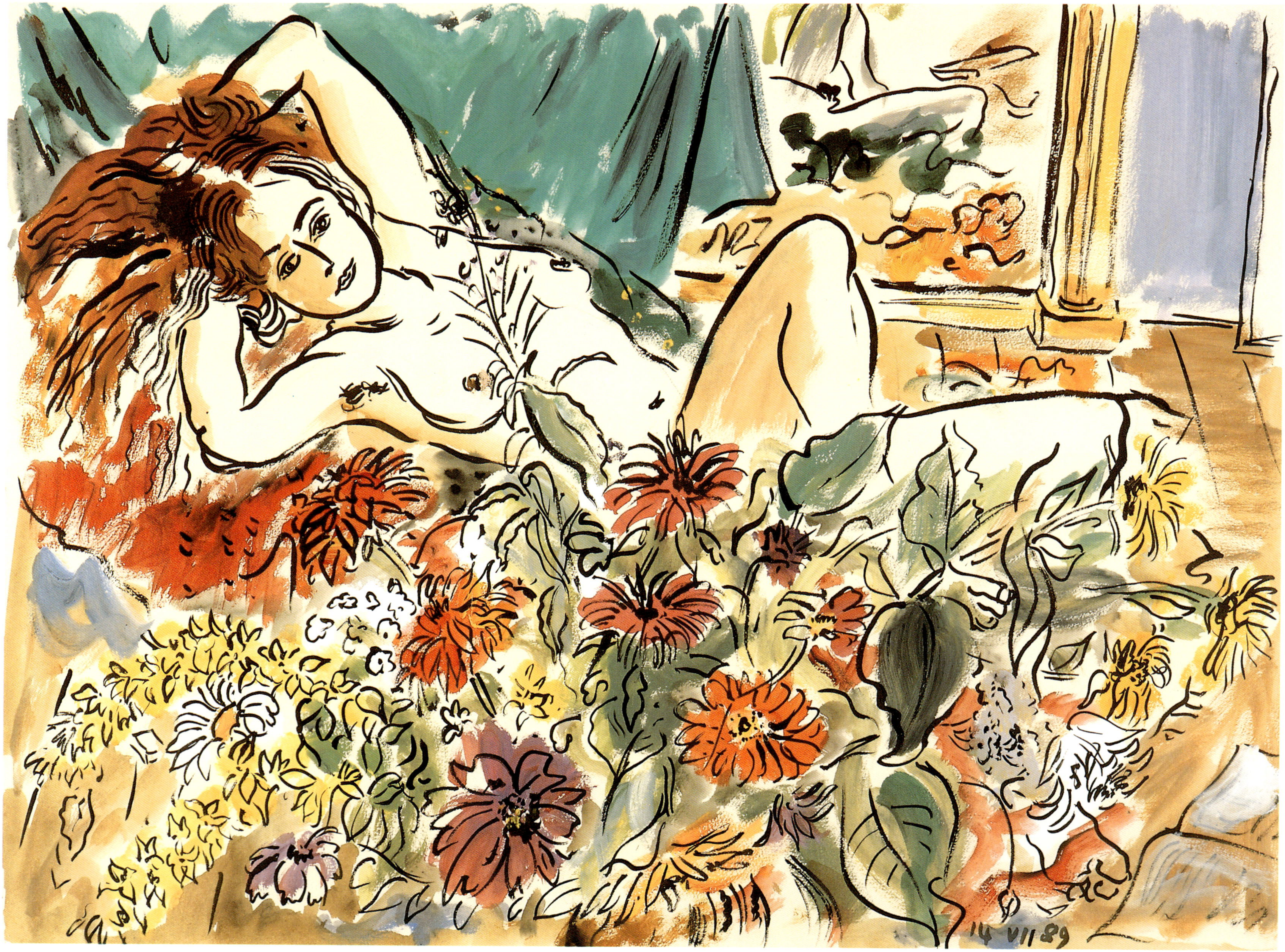

Reclining Girl, Arms up, Flowers in Foreground
Ink and acrylic, 22 × 30ins, 1989

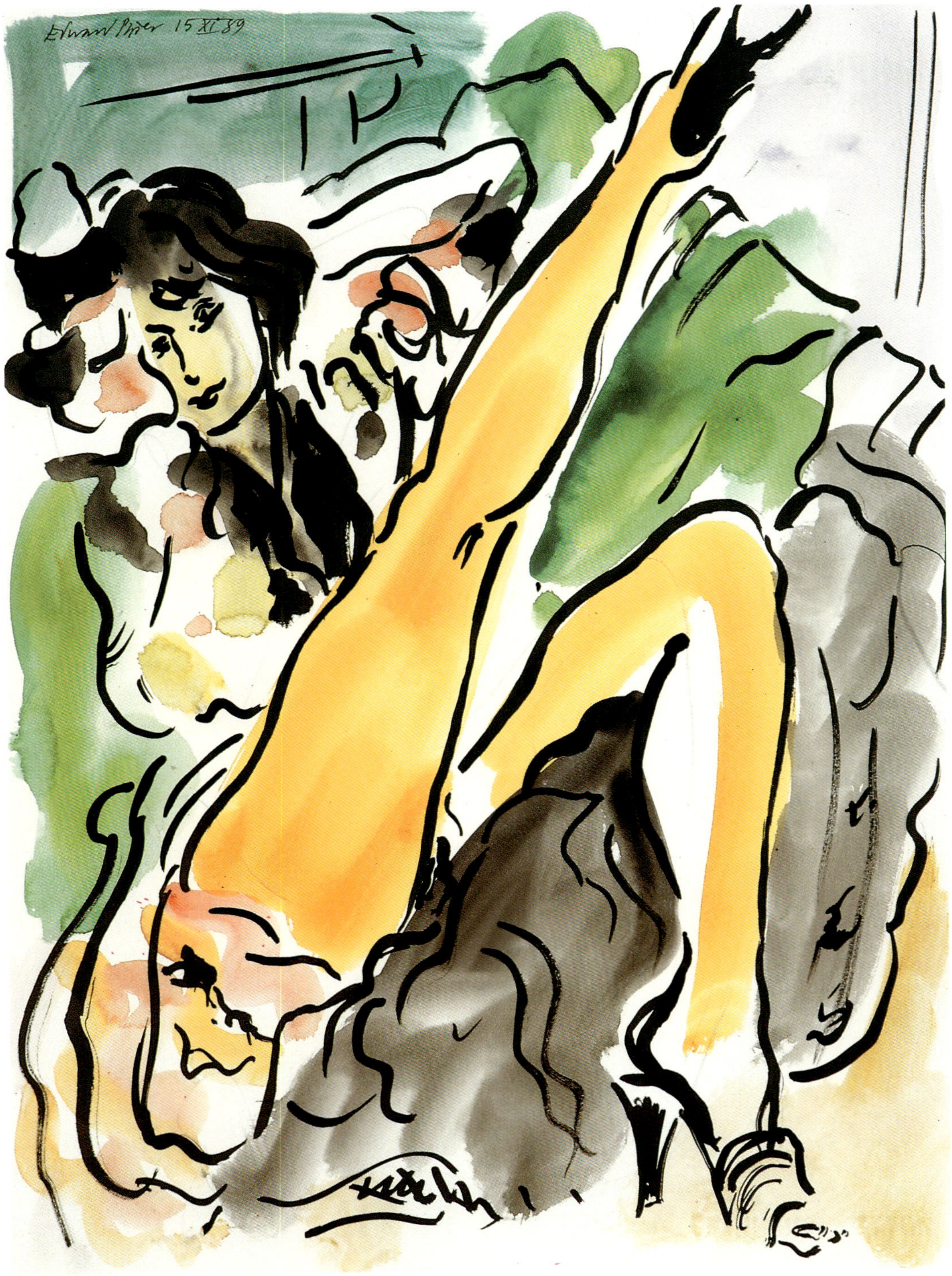

Seated Girl, Orange Stockings, Flowered Kimono
Ink and acrylic, 20 × 15ins, 1989

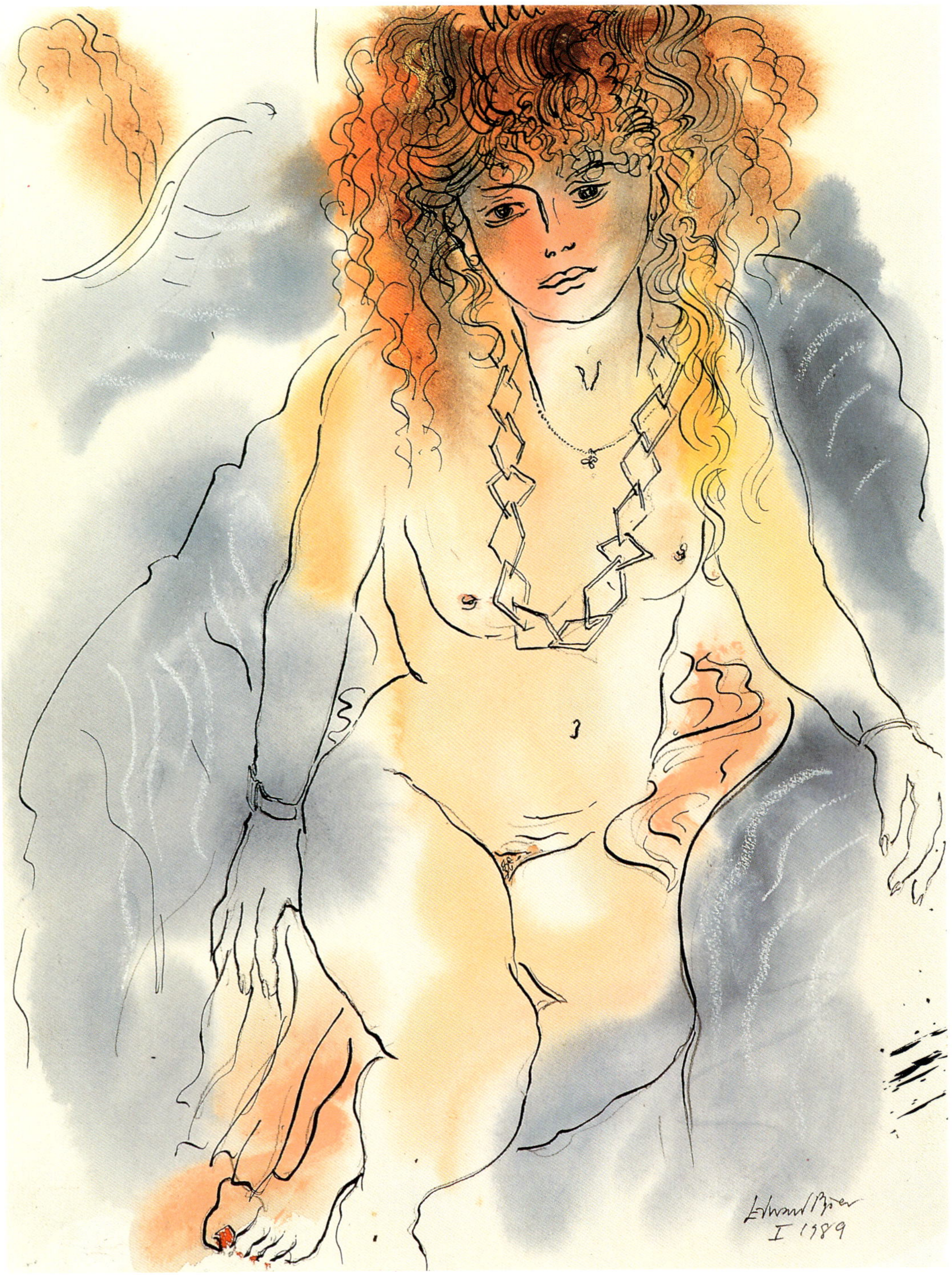

Seated Girl with Metal Necklace
Ink, pencil and watercolour, 20 × 15ins, 1989

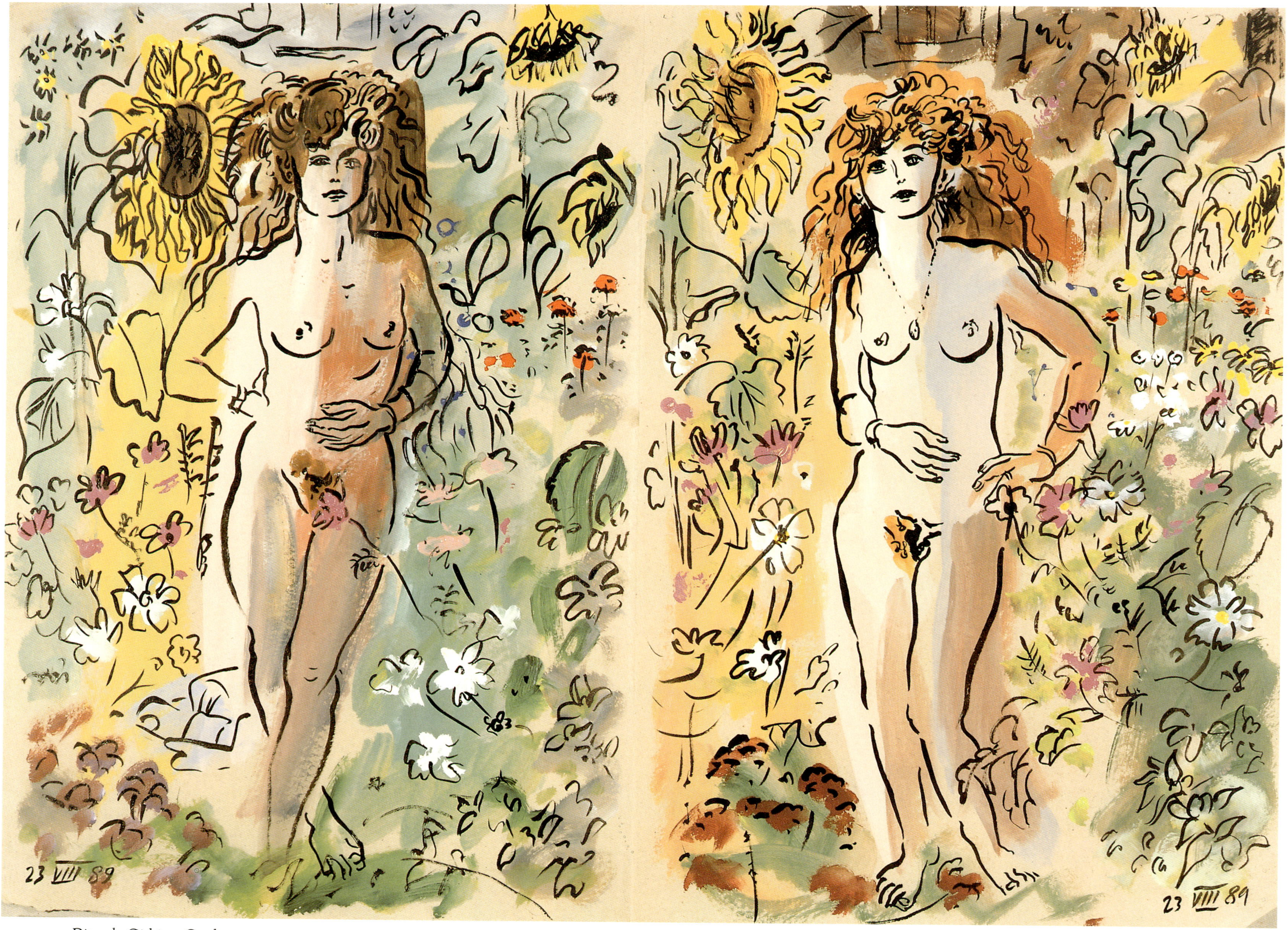

Diptych, Girl in a Garden
Ink and acrylic, 22 × 30ins, 1989

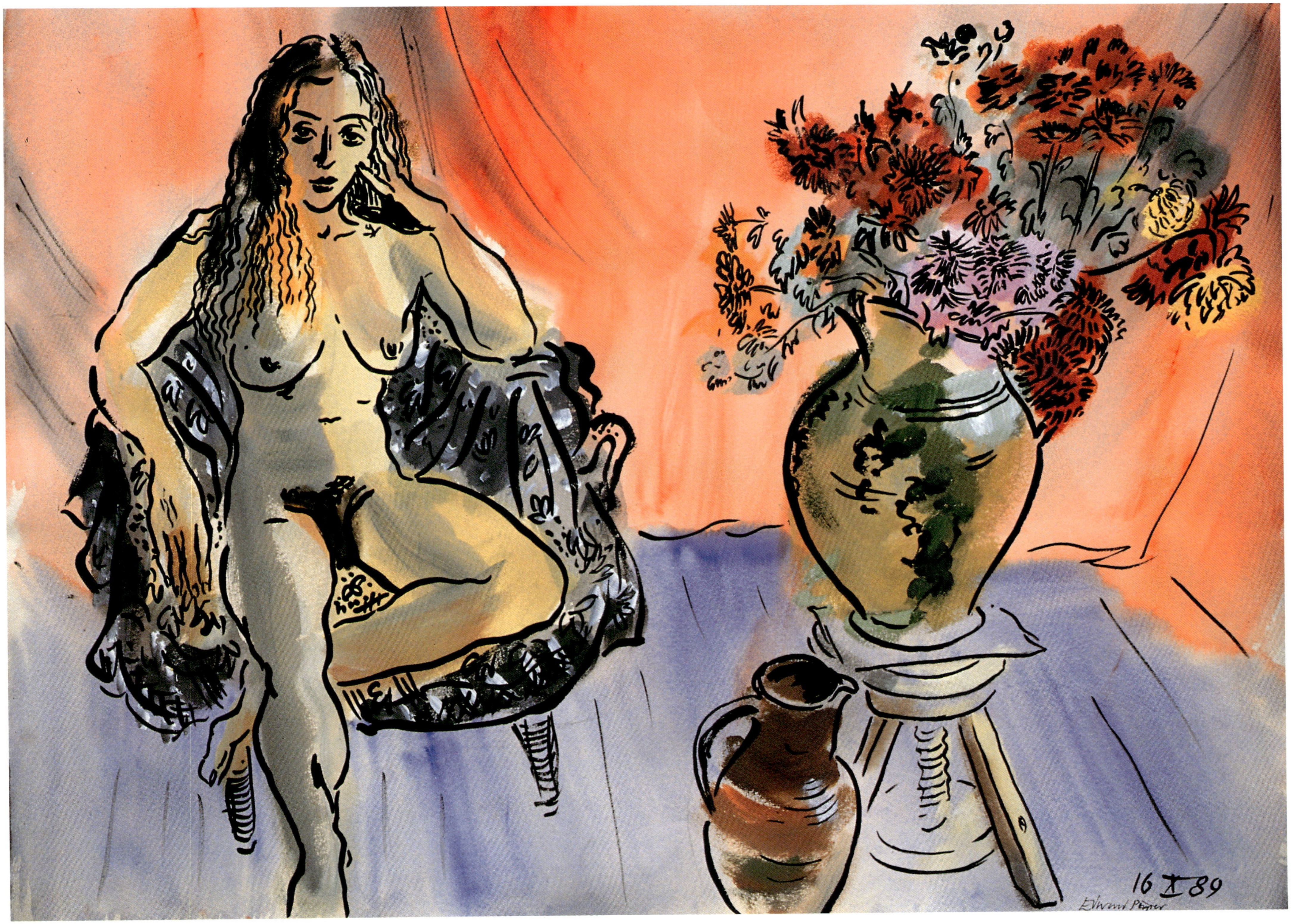

Girl Seated on Arab Print, Flowers on Stool
Ink and acrylic on Indian paper, 22 × 30ins, 1989

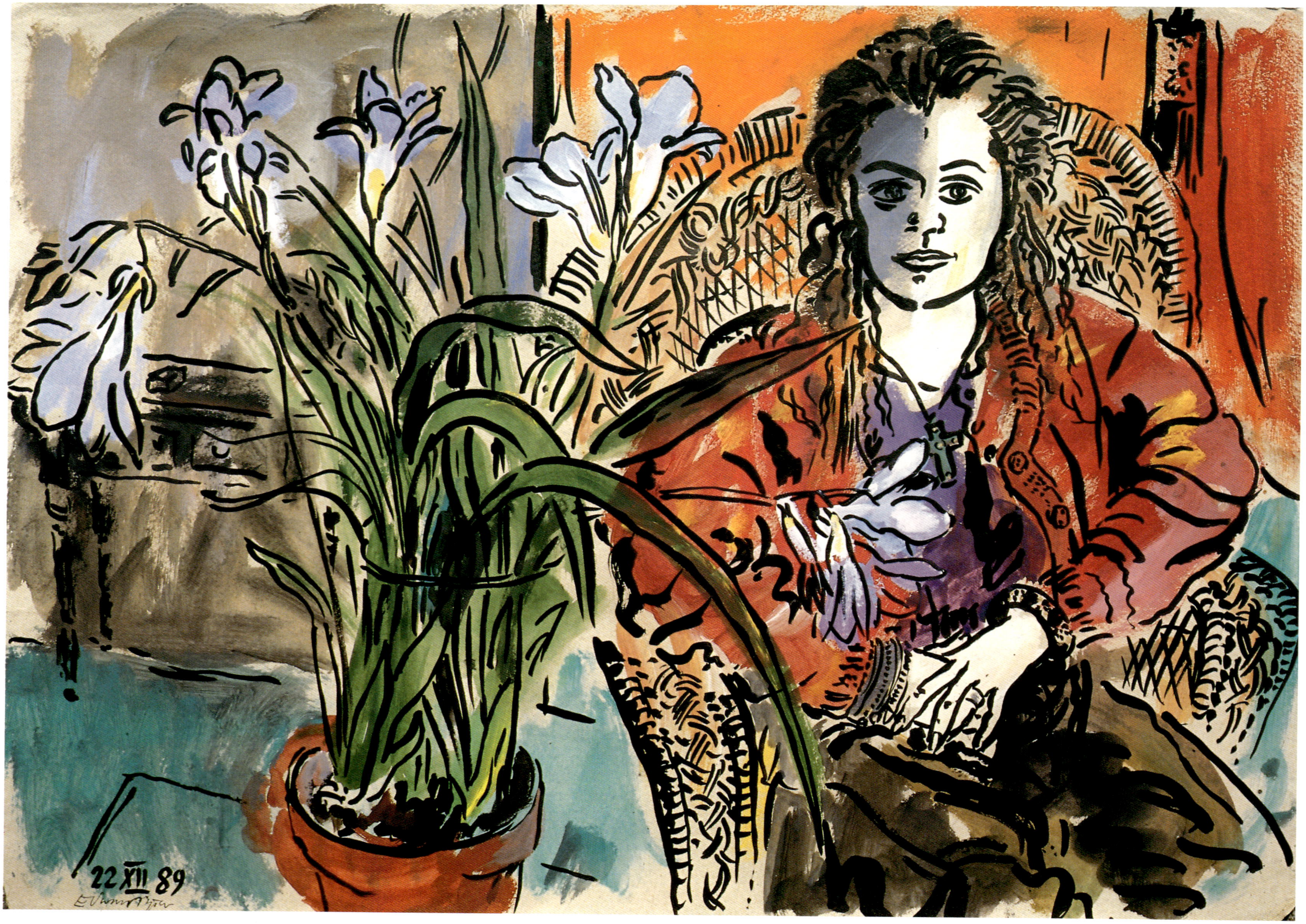

Girl Seated in Cane Chair, Blue Freesias
Ink and acrylic on Indian paper, 22 × 30ins, 1989

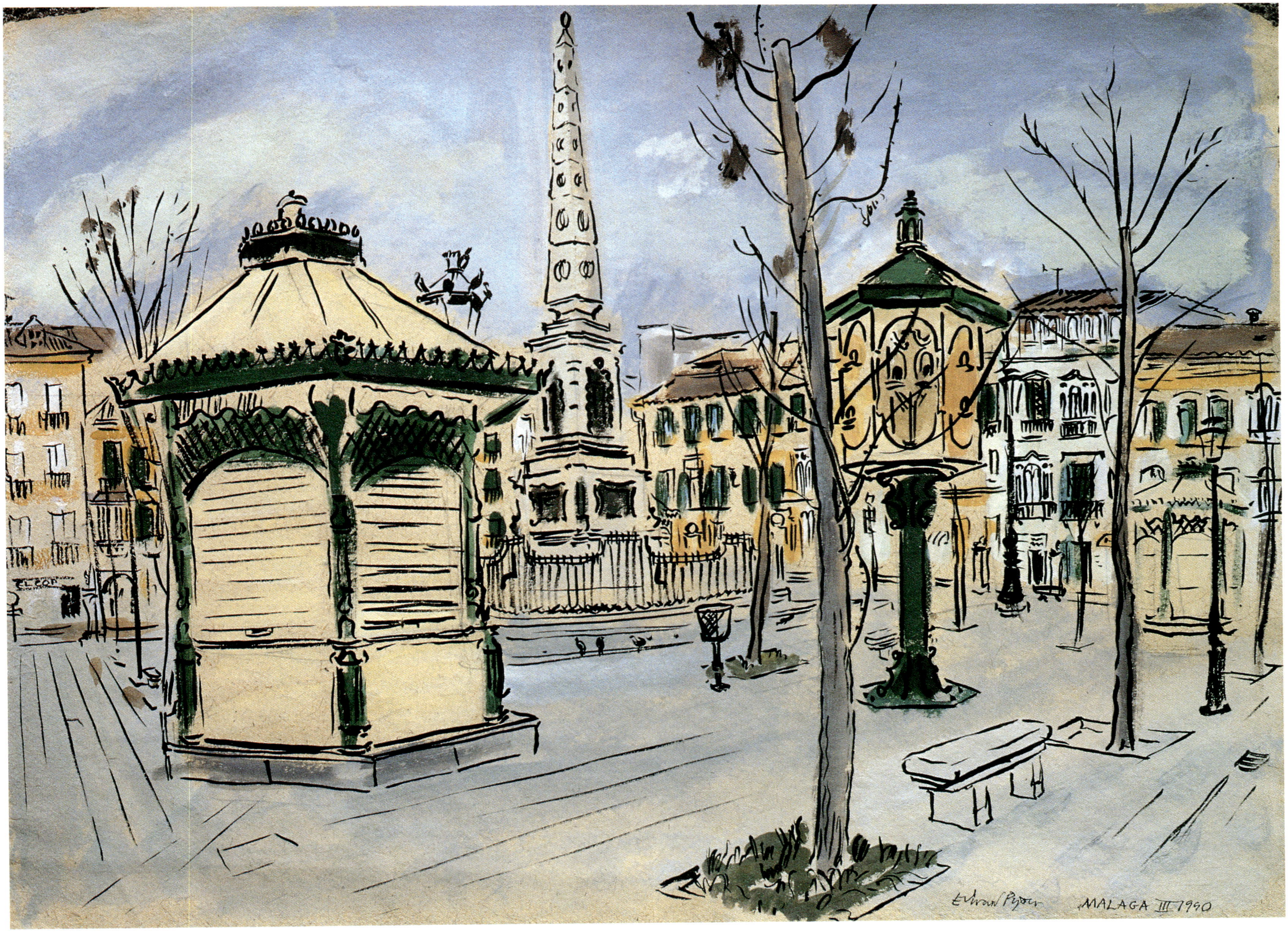

Malaga, Picasso's Birthplace
Ink on Indian paper, 22 × 30ins, 1990

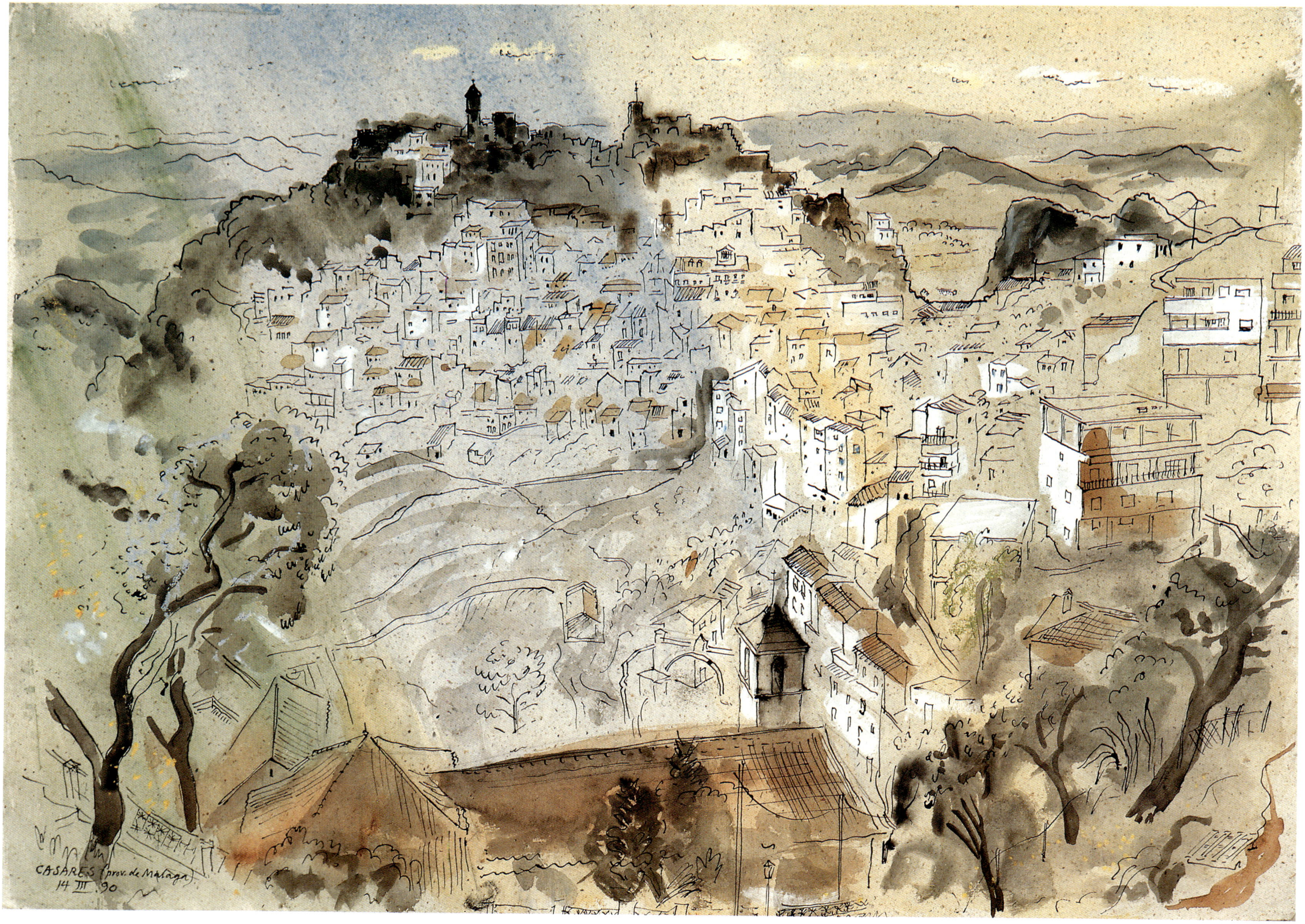

Casares (prov. de Malaga)
Ink and watercolour on Indian paper, 22 × 30 ins, 1990

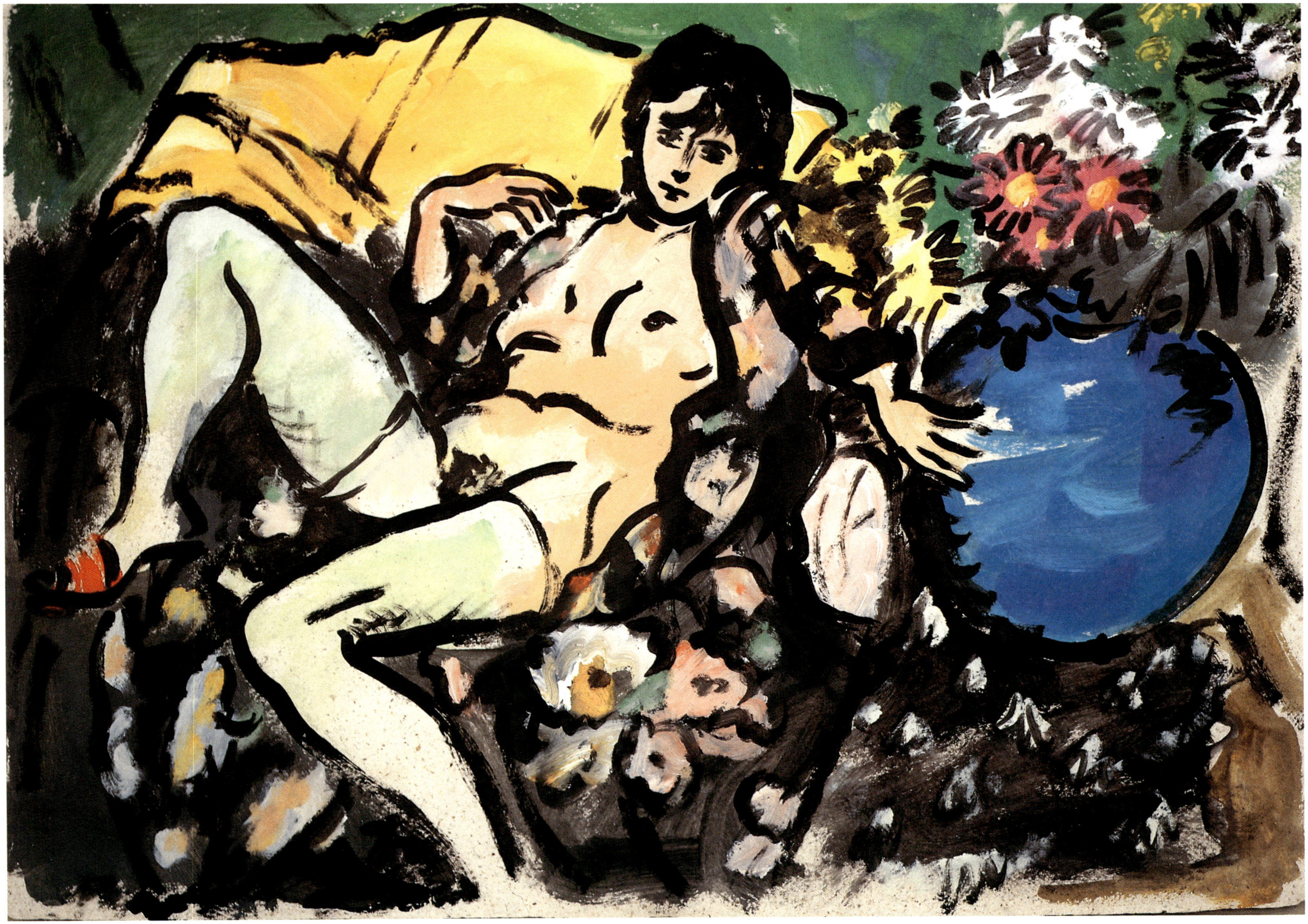

Girl in Green Stockings, Reclining in Chair, Blue Pot with Flowers
Ink and acrylic on Indian paper, 22 × 30ins, 1990

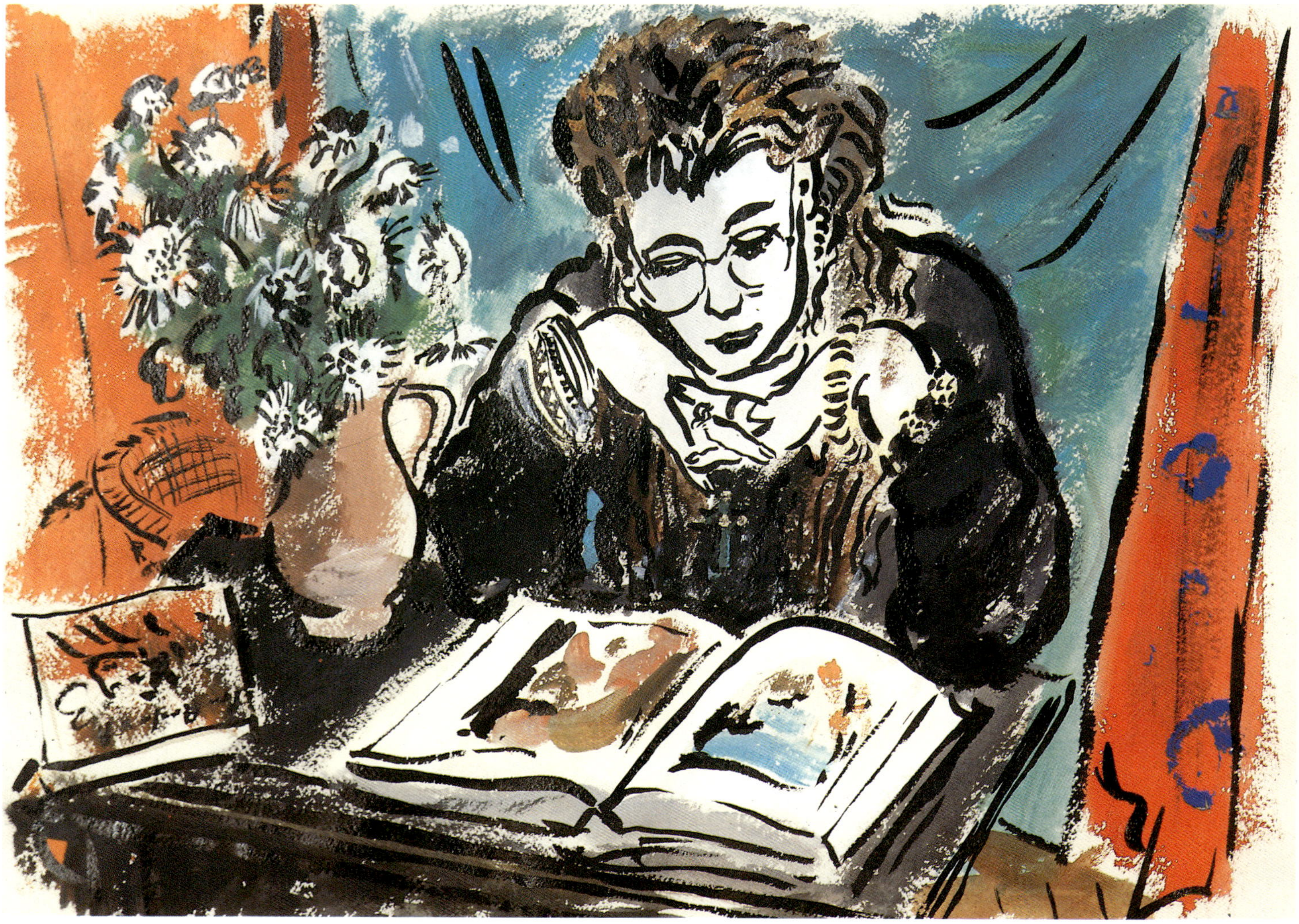

Girl with Glasses, Reading, Jug of White Flowers
Ink and acrylic, 15 × 20ins, 1990

Biography

Born Buckinghamshire, 12 November 1938, eldest child of John and Myfanwy Piper. Educated Lancing College, Sussex, 1951–6, Bath Academy of Art, Corsham, 1956–7, where he was taught drawing by Howard Hodgkin, Slade School of Art, 1957–61. Part-time work for printing firm, 1961–4. Married Prudence Mackillop, 1961. Lived in London 1957–64, Newcastle-upon-Tyne 1964–6, and then in Wiltshire and Somerset. Two sons, Luke (b. 1966) and Henry (b. 1969).
Died Marston Bigot, Friday 11 May 1990.

Paintings Exhibited

1965 'Six Artists', ICA, Dover Street.
1966 'London Under 40', Galeria, Milano.
1967 'Young Britain: the New Scene', Sears Vincent Price, Chicago.
1970 Six silk-screens published by Marlborough Graphics.
1982 'Two Generations', joint exhibition with John Piper, Beaux Arts Gallery, Bath.
1982 New Ashgate, Farnham.
1985 and 1986 Affordable Arts, Bristol.
1985 Solomon Gallery, Bruton Place, W1.
1986 No. 4, Nailsworth, Gloucester.
1985, 1986, 1988 Bath Contemporary Art Fair.
1985 and 1986 International Contemporary Art Fair, Beaux Arts Gallery, Bath.
1987 Grape Lane, York.
1987, 1988 Eye Gallery, Bristol.
1988 CCA Galleries, Theme shows, Kew, 'London Life'.
1988 New Ashgate, Farnham.

One-Man Shows

1975 Marjorie Parr, London. Life drawings.
1979 Maze Gallery, Frome.
1981 Savile Club, London.
1981 Scribes Cellar, London EC4.
1981 Sherborne School, Dorset, with John Piper.
1982 Newbury Spring Festival.
1983 36th Aldeburgh Festival.
1983 Oriel 31, Welshpool, a three-man art show.
1984 Hambledon Gallery, Blandford Forum.
1985 Beaux Arts Gallery, with John Piper.
1986 On-the-Wall Gallery, Chalk Farm, London.
1986 Sirota Gallery, Wells.
1987 Beaux Arts Gallery, Bath.
1987 The 40th Aldeburgh Festival.
1987 Catto Gallery, Hampstead.
1988 Sirota Gallery, Wells.
1988 Grape Lane Gallery, York.
1988 Retrospective Exhibition, Eye Gallery, Bristol.
1989 Catto Gallery Hampstead.
1990 Malvern Festival.
1990 Beaux Arts Gallery, Bath.